If you appreciate this book being made available for near or below our cost, please show your appreciation and support of our years of work by making a tax deductible donation to:

Worldview Weekend Foundation
P.O. Box 1690
Collierville, TN 38027

You can also donate online at wvwfoundation.com

GRAVE
INFLUENCE

21 Radicals and Their Worldviews
that Rule America from the Grave

Brannon Howse

Collierville, Tennessee

GRAVE INFLUENCE
21 RADICALS AND THEIR WORLDVIEWS THAT
RULE AMERICA FROM THE GRAVE
Published by Worldview Weekend Publishing
a division of Worldview Weekend

© 2009 by Brannon Howse
Third Printing July, 2022
All rights reserved.
International Standard Book Number:
0-9785014-7-0

Cover Design by Joe Potter

For Information:
www.worldviewweekend.com

Printed in the United States of America

DEDICATION

*T*his book is dedicated to: My wife, Melissa, who travels with me to city after city, cheerfully helping me fulfill what God has called me to do with our Worldview Weekend conferences.

Dr. David Noebel, who encouraged me to host the first Worldview Weekend in January of 1993. We both spoke for the two-day conference, which was the first of more than 195 conferences sponsored by Worldview Weekend between 1993 and 2009. Dr. Noebel has trained tens of thousands of students through his worldview camps over the past 45 years. Thank you, Doc, for your friendship, encouragement, and example as a Christian statesman; your spiritual legacy will not be fully realized this side of heaven.

Dr. Ron Carlson, whom I first heard speak on the topics of worldviews and apologetics when I was in seventh grade. Little did I know then that Dr. Carlson and his wife, Marge, would become some of the closest friends that Melissa and I and our children would ever know. Ron and Marge have traveled to city after city with us over many years, speaking at our Worldview Weekend conferences. Thank you, Ron, for being such a supportive colleague and friend.

ACKNOWLEDGMENTS

I would like to thank my editor, Greg Webster of The Gregory Group, for his excellent editing and work on this book. This is the seventh book Greg has edited for me. Greg is a true talent, and I am very fortunate to have him as a part of my team.

I would also like to thank Bob Heyer for his excellent work in laying out the pages of this book. This is the sixth book Bob has worked on with me, and I appreciate his late hours of work and gracious spirit when making the last-minute changes.

CONTENTS

PART 5—AND NOW FROM THE GOVERNMENT-CORPORATE COMPLEX

Introduction

Why Our Focus Should Be on
Reclaiming the Church Instead of the Culture

We've lost the culture war.

I wish I could tell you otherwise and go happily along with the many Christians who still think we can recapture America, return to our moral and spiritual roots, and revitalize our wayward institutions. But I can't, and someone needs to tell you— loudly and clearly. My job is not to be optimistic or pessimistic but to be realistic.

When I say we've lost the culture war, what I mean is that we are not going to reclaim the culture in America and return to the days of June and Ward Cleaver. We won't see a majority of the officials in legislative and judicial branches of our government go back to the original intent of America's founding fathers as reflected in the U.S. Constitution and other original documents. We are not going to witness prayer, Bible reading, and posting of the Ten Commandments in public schools again. There will be no drastic decline in divorce, sexually transmitted diseases, abortion, and homosexual "marriage." The United Nations will not be eliminated. The undermining of our national sovereignty and parental authority will not be reversed. And we will not return to unlimited religious freedom.

Please understand I am not advocating that Christians retreat from the culture. I am asking Christians to stand for righteousness by defending the unborn, opposing same-sex marriage, fighting active euthanasia or the attacks on religious and parental authority—even if we know the laws and hearts of Americans resist our Biblical worldview.

We must proclaim Christian values based on Scripture regardless of persecution and despite knowing that America, as I explain in Chapter 2, has passed the point of no return morally. Standing firm is our duty, and the results—whatever they may be—belong to God.

The culture war itself has been merely the symptom of a much more profound conflict—a spiritual battle that most Christians don't understand and are ill-equipped to fight. In fact, our losing the culture war is tied directly to the fact that American Christians, churches, Christian colleges, and seminaries have not done an adequate job in understanding what they believe, why they believe it, and proclaiming it from an uncompromising Biblical standpoint.

Skirmishes will continue, and I expect the spiritual battle will actually intensify. What we must now come to grips with is how to handle the new reality in which we live. The solidly post-Christian culture that Francis Schaeffer warned of more than two decades ago is now here.

Conservative commentator Patrick Buchanan describes what has happened:

> The European-Christian core of the country that once defined us is shrinking, as Christianity fades, the birth rate falls, and Third World immigration surges. Globalism dissolves the economic bonds, while the cacophony of multiculturalism displaces the old American culture.[1]

The spiritual war rages, and the stakes are much higher because the battle is no longer for our culture but for the souls, hearts, and minds of our children and grandchildren. We must disciple them in Biblical truth, or they will be taken spiritual captives.

This worldview war can be won by those who understand the

times and the opposition. First Chronicles 12:32 tells us the tribe of Issachar was called wise because they understood the times and knew what God would have them do. In the New Testament, Jesus criticized the liberal religious leaders of His day for being able to discern the weather but not the times. He chided, "You know how to interpret the appearance of the sky, yet you can't interpret the signs of the times?" (Matthew 16:3). God desires that His people understand what is happening around them and respond with Biblical leadership.

Every Christian must prepare and understand the nature of this spiritual battle because it is coming with an intensity none of us ever imagined—right here, right under the dimming light of our U.S. Constitution. Second Timothy 3:1 tells us that in the last days perilous times will come, and, my friend, they are here.

The spiritual battles revealed in this book will make the culture war look like a cake walk. Ephesians 6:12 tells us that "we wrestle not against flesh and blood, but against principalities, against powers, against the rulers of the darkness of this world, against spiritual wickedness in high places." But, take heart, for Jesus Christ has assured us He is building His Church, and the gates of hell will not prevail (Matthew 16:18). If you are part of the Church—and I pray you are through faith and repentance in Jesus Christ—then you are on the ultimate winning side. But, as in any battle, there will be casualties. Yet we should not fear those that can only destroy the body. Rather, we should fear the One that can destroy our souls, and throw them into hell (Matthew 10:28). As Romans 8:37 declares: "In all these things we are triumphantly victorious due to the one who loved us."

My purpose in writing this book is to help you see the world and all the events taking place as a big picture, not just bits and pieces. I want to inspire, train, and raise up godly leaders of all ages to lead the

Church during this hour—to take over, if necessary, from those who are failing in their present leadership roles. For those godly pastors who *are* leading, I am thankful, but we also need lay people to fulfill God's calling for their lives. Above all, we need parents to train and prepare their children for what lies ahead.

Lies have been cleverly packaged in positive, masking terms, but behind them remains a destructive spiritual agenda. If you're ready for this spiritual battle, you'll stand a better chance of keeping the faith, proclaiming the truth, standing firm for your family and its convictions, and enduring till the end. I'm fairly certain our national future is not bright, but your personal future can be sustained in the light of Jesus Christ. This can also be the greatest hour for the proclamation of the Gospel if we understand the times and prepare our family and friends with a Biblical worldview.

In order for you to be ready, it's important to understand what has overwhelmed us in the culture war and to see that the enemy's next goal is to establish a new order, satanic at its very foundation. Forces attack from every major social direction, and in the pages that follow, I'll detail how it's happened and how it continues so you can earnestly contend for the faith.

Part of my passion for doing this is that I believe the Church can still be God's redemptive vessel in the years to come. And since one arm of attack has been directly through the Church, we can at least remove it from our midst if we act wisely and assertively. The Church *can* be reclaimed—even if our culture can't.

Through the years, I've written extensively (this is my ninth book) on what it means to have a thoroughly Biblical worldview. Detailing the specifics of holding to a truly Christian worldview is beyond the scope of this work, but I encourage you to visit my online bookstore at worldviewweekend.com and acquire for your personal library some of my previous books (for a detailed, verse by verse, Biblical response and rebuttal to the attacks on Christianity, I especially recommend *Put Your Beliefs to the Test*).

Train Up a Church in the Way It Should Go

The worldviews and people discussed in this book are destroying America from their graves. Yet most Americans have never even heard of a number of the individuals discussed. As for the names they do recognize, they know little of their astonishing influence or how their worldviews still undermine America to this very day.

Some of you may recall an exceptional book by David Breese, originally published by Moody Publishers in 1990, called *Seven Men Who Rule the World from the Grave*. I remember a telephone conversation with Dr. Breese when I was in my early twenties and just beginning to write and speak on worldview topics. He strongly encouraged me, and I never forgot how kind and gracious he was. A man of deep Biblical convictions, David Breese went home to be with the Lord in May of 2002. He ran the race and finished well.

This book is not a replay of his work. Rather, I believe it picks up where he left off. Much has happened in America, to America, and in the hearts of Americans in the 20 years since Dr. Breese's book was published. *Grave Influence* is largely an examination of those changes in light of the ideas, values, and worldviews of 21 dead radicals, seven of whom were also covered in the Breese book.

I know Dr. Breese would not be surprised at what's happening to America. After all, he tried to awaken the Church that has now been largely compromised and has become part of the problem. Most of all, I know Dr. Breese would be encouraged, because his life, testimony, commitment, and faithful service to Jesus Christ influenced not only me but countless others. I look forward to seeing David in glory, and I have such respect for his groundbreaking work that I hope I have honorably expanded on his approach and offer even greater insight into the destructive forces that are ruining not just our country, but the Judeo-Christian aspects of Western Civilization that have benefited mankind for nearly two millennia.

Sadly, most Christians are just as clueless as their non-believing fellow citizens as to what is happening. For the most part, the Church has contributed to the loss of the culture war by surrendering—often in ignorance—to the agendas arrayed against it. That's why we're losing many of our churched youth to aberrant philosophies. We're not preparing children to know what they believe, why they believe it, and how to defend their Biblical worldview.

I established Worldview Weekends in January of 1993 to train and equip adults and students to understand how to apply Biblical principles to every area of life. My first goal was specific worldview training. Secondly, I wanted to teach Christian apologetics—to defend essential Biblical doctrines such as how we know the Bible is true, how we know Jesus is God, how we know Christ rose from the dead, and how we know He was God incarnate.

The Church in America has had *billions* of dollars at its disposal in modern times. In theory, this money has been available to fulfill the Great Commission—making disciples of Jesus Christ. Training and equipping adults and students in apologetics and a Biblical worldview is how this is accomplished. Yet, with all of its monetary resources, the Church has largely failed. Untold billions have been spent on buildings and entertainment rather than establishing Christians in the faith.

Worldview Weekend was born to fill the vacuum left by an

ineffective and self-serving Church. We now hold up to 50 *free* conferences every year. By year's end, we will have trained more than 50,000 adults and students in person *in 2009 alone.* This does not include our online training institute, magazines, website, radio program, and DVD resources. Most churches do not care to do this work of creating followers of Jesus Christ. They are too concerned about maintaining and growing a club complete with social activities, entertaining programs, and multi-million dollar buildings.

You may think I'm being too harsh, but in fact, I'm being reserved in my criticism. Yes, some churches are led by godly pastors. But from what I've seen of the congregations in America, these faithful churches represent merely a remnant.

How hard is it to train adults and youth pastors to teach apologetics and a Biblical worldview? Not that hard. You simply have to *want* to train a church staff, Sunday school teachers, parents, and grandparents to do it. The typical evangelical church prefers, rather, to simply provide people with employment, to make those who show up on Sunday morning feel comfortable, and to provide activities for the kids so they stay out of trouble. Most evangelical churches do not have a comprehensive Biblical worldview curriculum for kindergarten through adult. There are no benchmarks, no tests, no building one year of training on the previous year. There is no interest in teaching "line upon line and precept upon precept."

And herein lies one of our greatest areas of surrender. The Church may not be interested in instructing our kids, but many others "out there" salivate over the opportunity. Humanist and educator Charles Francis Potter, in his book *Humanism: A New Religion,* understood the prospects for equipping students to know what they believe and why they believe it:

Education is the most powerful ally of Humanism [atheism], and every American public school is a school of Humanism. What can the theistic Sunday Schools, meeting for an hour once a week, and teaching only a fraction of the children, do to stem the tide of a five-day program of humanistic teaching?[2]

"Ah," you say, "but what about those students that attend a Christian school?" Numerous studies reveal that Christian school students have a worldview almost identical to those in the public school system. Why? Because the average private, Christian school in America is far more "private" than it is "Christian." While there are a few Biblical worldview Christian schools, there aren't many, and it is for essentially the same reason that we don't have many solid Bible-teaching churches. Their goal is not *Christian* education, the leadership often lacks a comprehensive Biblical worldview, and the focus is more about how many people attend, whether or not the bills get paid, and how popular it is in the community. Christian schools put more effort into their sports programs than into their Bible curriculum. I attended a Christian school growing up and have spoken in enough of them to have seen this problem firsthand, over and over again.

Name It and Re-Claim It

Why is it so crucial to accept that the culture war is lost? It's because there's still much to be won if we correctly grasp the job ahead of us. We must articulate the problem in order to solve it. And the only solvable problem left is the Church. To those who spend time, money, and energy still trying to reclaim the culture, I remind them of Founding Father John Adams' words to Thomas Jefferson:

Have you ever found in history, one single example of a Nation

thoroughly corrupted that was afterwards restored to virtue?...
And without virtue, there can be no political liberty....Will
you tell me how to prevent luxury from producing effeminacy,
intoxication, extravagance, vice and folly?[3]

Indeed, the average American male has become a feminized
wimp. Many may still hunt, fish, and watch football, but that's only a
façade of masculinity. "Tough guys" who refuse to lead, to boldly speak
truth, to disciple their children, or to take charge in their churches are
merely white-washed wimps. All too many men today shun leadership
positions that "real men" would grab hold of.

Adams was right. Luxury has made us weak, and a nation so
thoroughly corrupted cannot be restored. Once virtue has been
compromised, liberty is lost. Without virtue and liberty, the culture
is lost.

My friend and Worldview Weekend speaker Ken Ham has
written a troubling yet inspiring book with Britt Beemer and Todd
Hillard entitled *Already Gone: Why Your Kids Will Quit Church and
What You Can Do to Stop It*. Working with a professional pollster, Ham
surveyed those who attend church every week or nearly every week in
conservative congregations. Some highlights from the book will show
the monumental reclamation job ahead of us. The researchers found
that:

> • A mass exodus is underway. Most youth of today will
> not be coming to church tomorrow. Nationwide polls and
> denominational reports are showing that the next generation
> is calling it quits on the traditional Church. And it's not just
> happening on the nominal fringe; it's happening at the core
> of the faith.

• Only 11 percent of those who have left the Church did so during the college years. Almost 90 percent of them were lost in middle school and high school. By the time they got to college they were already gone! About 40 percent are leaving the Church during elementary and middle school years!

• If you look around in your church today, two-thirds of those who are sitting among us have already left in their hearts. It will only take a couple years before their bodies are absent as well.

• The numbers indicate that Sunday school actually didn't do anything to help them develop a Christian worldview. The brutal conclusion is that, on the whole, the Sunday school programs of today are statistical failures.

• Part of the concern is that the mere existence of youth ministry and Sunday school allows parents to shrug off their responsibility as the primary teachers, mentors, and pastors to their families.[4]

What this means is that the Church may be good at teaching Bible stories but not at teaching Biblical principles or applying those principles to all areas of life. How many churches do you know, for instance, that teach the Biblical worldview for law, science, economics, history, family, social issues, religion, and education—the crucial disciplines of all of life and society? At church, does anyone learn about the lies of global warming, radical environmentalism, socialism, evolution, postmodernism, situational ethics, political correctness, or population control? The myth of the separation of Church and State, the Biblical reasons for marriage as one man and one woman, the Biblical role of men and women, and the deceptions of feminism? Every one of these issues can and must be addressed from the Bible, and when we do that, we are not "politicizing religion," we are making disciples who think and live like Christians are meant to.

I've written on every one of these issues, including a 13-week curriculum for teens through adults that addresses these areas with Power Point slides, video clips, a student manual, and student worksheets. Dr. David Noebel of Summit Ministries has developed a worldview curriculum for *kindergarten* through adult. So why don't more churches, Christian schools, and families use resources like these? (This is not just an advertisement!) Because they truly don't care. Their real priorities are demonstrated by what they do emphasize. This "not caring" is how we surrendered the culture war in America.

If we have lost the culture war, then who has won?

The winners are the people I tell you about in this book—and those who wittingly or unwittingly follow them. Alice Bailey, Helen Schucman, Julius Wellhausen, Søren Kierkegaard, Friedrich Nietzsche, John Dewey, The Frankfurt School, Betty Friedan, William James, Alfred Kinsey, Aldous Huxley, Benjamin Bloom, B. F. Skinner, Charles Darwin, Karl Marx, John Maynard Keynes, Christopher Columbus Langdell, Saul Alinsky, Sigmund Freud, Margaret Sanger, and Roger Baldwin. What most disturbs me is that these people had the terms of surrender spelled out before we even knew the war was underway.

Most pastors, church staff, and Sunday school teachers are products of a secular school system that did not warn them about the worldviews of these influential people. Schools, for the most part, promoted many of their ideas. Even pastors who attended seminary did not learn the significance of the competing worldviews represented by such people, and most seminaries did not teach apologetics or a comprehensive Biblical worldview. Even evangelical seminaries often avoid applying a Biblical worldview to many issues like those discussed in this book because they think it violates the separation of Church and State or that such things are not the calling of a pastor but a politician.

How can we win the battle for hearts and minds if we do not understand or even know the foundational worldviews and philosophy of the opposition? The spiritual battle that rages is based on the anti-God, anti-moral, anti-family ideas of the people discussed in this book.

As I said earlier, the war may be over, but the heaviest fighting is yet to come. In the midst of a lost culture, we must stand up for righteousness and oppose abortion, active euthanasia, and the attempt to eliminate our Biblical, parental authority. Your first step is to "see to it that no one enslaves you through philosophy and empty deceit according to human tradition, according to the basic principles of the world, and not according to the Messiah" (Colossians 2:8, ISV). Then we must take action: fight the implementation of hate-crime laws and the efforts to shut down Christian radio, and oppose evil because it goes against God's character and nature. We must accept that we are past the point of restoring our culture and focus on how to preserve our families. We must evangelize, disciple, and raise up those who can lead the remnant. Read on, and let me show you how.

PART 1

THINGS ARE WORSE THAN YOU THOUGHT

1

BRINGING THE WORLDVIEW AND PEOPLE TOGETHER UNDER ONE AGENDA

I f the culture war is lost, exactly how did we lose it? What are the goals and tactics of the spiritual battle that continues? Where are we going, and how should we prepare for whatever comes next? These are the questions I will answer in this book. I'll share answers that I would guess only 1% of Americans, if that, know and understand.

The people and worldviews discussed in this book are neither random, nor unconnected. The ideas, beliefs, convictions, and values of these 21 influencers have, whether you know it or not, affected your faith, family, and freedoms. Their influence is so pervasive that one of my biggest challenges in writing this book has been knowing when to stop writing. The transformation of America is happening so fast that each day brings a new revelation of what government, religious, and educational leaders are doing to accomplish their goal of re-making America in very un-American ways.

Once you've explored the worldviews of these individuals and you understand the nature of the spiritual battle in which we're engaged, you'll want to visit my website, worldviewtimes.com, regularly to keep up with this astounding transformation. The speed at which the world is moving toward a "new order" is bewildering and stands in complete contrast to a Biblical worldview and America's founding documents.

The Four Forces of Evil

God created and ordained certain institutions here on earth that are charged with different but complementary responsibilities. To bring honor and glory to God and to fulfill His commandments and objectives, He established the family (Genesis 1:26-27, Genesis 2:21-25), church government (Acts 20:28, Titus 1:5-16, Ephesians 5:22-27, 1 Timothy 3:1-15), and civil government (Exodus 18:20-25, Romans 13:1-7, 1 Peter 2:13-17).

Mimicking God's approach, Satan is using four human institutions to wage war against God's three. Although I've read the end of the story (Satan loses), for now the battle rages, and many victims will be taken spiritually captive to his lies and deceitful worldview.

Anti-Biblical worldviews have infected virtually every arena of life—law, science, economics, history, family, social issues, education, and religion—and these worldviews consistently connect back to four major forces destroying America from within. The government-corporate complex (Corporate Fascism), which includes the State itself, non-government organizations, trade unions, and the UN; occultism and pagan spirituality; the apostate Church; and the educational establishment have attacked on all fronts, aggressively helping national and international governments accomplish their ultimate goal of global control.

With regard to labor unions: for years Communists have used them to aid the socialist cause. Lenin specifically outlined this strategy in his book, *"Left-Wing" Communism, an Infantile Disorder*. He explains that infiltrating unions is a key to carrying out the communist agenda. Once in place unions can be mobilized to stir up chaos, create discontent with capitalism, and use strikes to bring economic and political pressure to bear on the opposition.

Other groups are in play on behalf of socialism as well. Apollo Alliance is one such group that brings together community organizers, environmental radicals, and unions with the help of government officials and taxpayer funds. The personal history of Jeff Jones, leader of Apollo, reveals much about his worldview and where he wants to take America. Although Jones once spent 11 years running from the law, the September 9, 2009 *New York Post* reveals what he is up to today:

> With Mark Rudd and Bill Ayers, Jones in 1969 co-founded the radical Weathermen, which orchestrated the violent "Days of Rage" riots in Chicago, and later undertook an anti-government bombing campaign. Jones is still proud of his terrorist activities—saying as recently as 2004: "To this day, we still, lots of us, including me, still think it was the right thing to try to do." Now Jones is back to revolutionary organizing—but with taxpayers footing the bill. He's the director of the Apollo Alliance's New York affiliate and a consultant to the national group.[5]

According to the *Post*:

> Senate Majority Leader Harry Reid recently credited Apollo with helping him write the stimulus bill and getting it passed. Yet the stimulus' "green jobs" provisions funnel federal tax dollars to unions, green groups and community organizers—that is, the organizations that make up Apollo.

Besides using labor unions and environmental groups, radicals are partial to community organizers like ACORN to move forward their anti-American, anti-Christian worldview agenda.

But all these strategies eventually converge. The question for humanistic leaders as the world neared the 21st century was how to bring the worldviews, values, and agendas of the 21 people we examine in this book to reality through legislation, international treaties, agreements, and public policy. Their agenda could not be optional but compulsory, and it must be backed up with rewards for those who comply and punishment and reprisal for those who dissent. It must be international, not regional. So, after years of writing papers and holding conferences, the major world players—including America—met for the 1992 United Nations Earth Summit in Brazil. The summit meeting crafted a laudable-sounding term to mask their real intentions. In true Orwellian style, "sustainable development" became the new buzzword.

By design of these agents of change, "sustainable development" is difficult to define. But it involves the promotion of socialism, global governance, planned economies, and the end of individual liberties. From the '92 Earth Summit came two documents: "Agenda 21" and the "Biodiversity Treaty." Tom DeWeese of the American Policy Center has been one of America's leading opponents of the freedom-robbing agenda in these two plans. He summarizes the threat this way:

> Here the ideas were officially presented to world leaders that all government on every level needed to be transformed into top-down control over housing, food production, energy, water, private property, education, population control, gun control, transportation, social welfare, medical care, and literally every aspect of our lives. To get the full picture, add to these the U.N. Convention on the Rights of the Child and the convention on the elimination of all forms of discrimination against women, both of which create UN mandates on abortion, child rearing, and government interference on families.[6]

The leaders in the educational establishment, the apostate Church, occultism/pagan spirituality, or the government-corporate complex want the idea of social and spiritual evolution embraced worldwide in order to bring about their desired "new order" or "new world order." Secular humanist and Fabian Socialist Julian Huxley (brother of Aldous) was the first Director General of the United Nations Educational, Science, and Culture Organization (UNESCO). He explained, "The task is to help the emergence of a single world culture...."[7]

This "task" is even at work in America's political arena. Bill Clinton's mentor and former professor Carrol Quigley made this clear in his book, *Tragedy and Hope*:

> The chief problem of American political life...has been how to make the two Congressional parties more national and international. The argument that the two parties should represent opposed ideals and policies, one, perhaps, of the Right and the other of the Left, is a foolish idea acceptable only to doctrinaire and academic thinkers. Instead, the two parties should be almost identical, so that the American people can "throw the rascals out" at any election without leading to any profound or extensive shifts in policy.[8]

And it's working. While there are some truly conservative Republicans, most embrace the same worldview and agenda of their fellow politicians across the aisle. This is a form of Marx's dialectic process, the true intent of which is revealed by Julian Huxley:

> ...at the moment, two opposing philosophies of life confront each other....You may categorize the two philosophies as super nationalism, or as individualism versus collectivism...

or as capitalism versus communism, or as Christianity verses Marxism. Can these opposites be reconciled, this antithesis be resolved in a higher synthesis? I believe not only that this can happen, but that, through the inexorable dialectic of evolution, it must happen.[9]

Those who buy into Darwinian or neo-Darwinian evolution and apply it to society embrace this concept of social evolution. There are others who apply it not only to the social and cultural arenas but also to the spiritual world. Generally, these are New Age devotees of the New Spirituality. Generally—but not always.

Emerging Trouble

The pastors and authors of one of America's fastest growing spiritual movements, the Emergent Church, sing the praises of socialism. As I'll explain in more detail later, the Emergent Church champions the neo-Marxist call for a utopian society through spiritual evolution where good and evil merge to form a "better" third option. This idea derives from the belief system of philosophers such as Georg Wilhelm Friedrich Hegel and finds its contemporary manifestation in the "Third Way" movement of Bill Clinton and Tony Blair. In the Third Way, capitalism, socialism, and communism merge to form a misanthropic combination of the three. This blending is now represented in the terms "the New World Order" and "the new enlightenment."

The Third Way promotes Communitarianism, a toxic blend of communism, socialism, capitalism, atheism, and Cosmic Human-ism. Communitarians believe in universal health care, government-subsidized housing and education, radical environmentalism, Fabian socialism, and the like.

An article on the website of the Democratic Leadership Council explains how Clinton and Blair have promoted Third Way thinking across the globe:

> Starting with Bill Clinton's Presidential campaign in 1992, Third Way thinking is reshaping progressive politics throughout the world. Inspired by the example of Clinton and the New Democrats, Tony Blair in Britain led a revitalized New Labour party back to power in 1997. The victory of Gerhard Shroeder and the Social Democrats in Germany the next year confirmed the revival of center-left parties which either control or are part of the governing coalition forming throughout the European Union. From Latin America to Australia and New Zealand, Third Way ideas also are taking hold.
>
> On Sunday, April 25, 1999, President Clinton and the DLC hosted a historic roundtable discussion, "The Third Way: Progressive Governance for the 21st Century," with five world leaders including British PM Tony Blair, German Chancellor Gerhard Schroeder, Dutch PM Wim Kok, and Italian PM Massimo D'Alema, the First Lady Hillary Rodham Clinton and DLC President Al From.[10]

Not to be hoodwinked by the window dressing of Third Way advocates, however, Vaclav Klaus, prime minister of the Czech Republic, warns against the real future it offers: "The Third Way is the fastest route to the Third World."[11] But that seems to be where communitarians want to take us.

Dr. Amitai Etzioni, often referred to as the "guru" of the

communitarian movement, founded the *Communitarian Network* in 1990. Etzioni received his Ph.D. in sociology from the University of California, Berkeley, served as professor of sociology at Columbia University, and then went to George Washington University as director of the Institute for Communitarian Policy Studies.

Etzioni characterizes President Obama as a communitarian in a February 4, 2009, *Jerusalem Post* article: "There is no philosophy that better describes Obama's position than Communitarianism," which Etzioni calls a philosophy "that would speak for community and the common good."

Prior to Obama, Dr. Etzioni even observed Communitarianism at work in the Bush administration. In "Needed: Catchword for Bush Ideology; 'Communitarianism' Finds Favor," a February 1, 2001 *Washington Post* article, Etzioni described the inaugural address of President George W. Bush as "a Communitarian Text." The article also revealed that staffers inside the Bush White House were familiar with Communitarianism and the Third Way:

> "This is the ultimate Third Way," said Don Eberly, an adviser in the Bush White House, using a favorite phrase of President Bill Clinton, who also sought, largely unsuccessfully, to redefine the debate with an alternative to the liberal-conservative conflict. "The debate in this town the last eight years was how to forge a compromise on the role of the state and the market. This is a new way to rethink social policy: a major reigniting of interest in the social sector."[12]

Some have pointed to Communist Mikhail Gorbachev's "perestroika"—which sought to merge socialism with capitalism when he was president of the USSR—as an example of the Third Way. Whatever you call it and no matter how it evolves, it is the foundation of tyranny and punishment over those who dissent and reject collectivism. Communitarians have repackaged socialist ideas that are contrary to a Biblical worldview and to the principles declared as the purpose and responsibility of civil government in America's founding documents. Christians must expose and fight all degrees of socialism, communism, and Marxism/ Leninism. Regardless of how it begins or the assurances given, the end will be infringement of parental authority and freedom of religion, the elimination of freedom of speech (such as radio programs that speak out against the government's tyranny), the establishment of hate-crime laws that criminalize Christianity, and much more.

Many within the apostate Church, civil government, the educational establishment, national and international corporations, charities, foundations, and non-government organizations (NGOs) have bought into what is called the sustainable development version of Communitarianism. Henry Lamb explains the danger:

> From the highest rafters of academia comes another enemy of freedom: Communitarianism. This is a belief system that opposes both authoritarianism and individualism, and promotes instead a social organization that is governed by policies designed by civil society to limit individual freedom as required for the benefit the community. Dr. Amitai Etzioni is credited with founding this communitarian movement.

> For more than 200 years, all these questions were addressed by elected representatives of the community. Individual members of the community have always been free to propose

projects to meet unmet community needs. Elected officials who failed to respond to the wishes of the community could always be replaced at the next election.

In the 1980s and 1990s, the environmental movement, joined by "social justice" advocates, grew impatient with the rate of change under this traditional policymaking procedure. That's why the *President's Council on Sustainable Development* declared, "We need a new decision process…." This new decision process is constructed on a communitarian philosophy and employs the consensus process.

Typically, these councils have been initiated and funded by special interest groups or by the federal government—not by the local community. These councils inevitably create a plan that incorporates the recommendations set forth in Agenda 21, the U.N.'s bible on sustainable development. These plans limit individual freedom and impose individual responsibilities in order to create a community that the vision council has determined to be in the best interest of the whole.[13]

Americans in Washington State and Wisconsin are learning the hard way about the freedom-robbing ways of sustainable development:

The King County, Wash., plan, for example, limits the freedom of property owners to use only 35 percent of their land, while imposing the requirement that 65 percent of the land be left in its natural condition. In Houston County,

Wis., the plan limits individual freedom to build no more than one home on a 40-acre parcel. Similar restrictions on individual freedom have been imposed by so-called vision councils all across the country in order to "balance the rights of individuals against the needs of the community"— as determined by a non-elected group of communitarians.

Communitarianism has been called "communism-lite." Others refer to it as "sophisticated socialism." On the ground, it appears to be academic justification for transforming the policymaking process, taking authority away from elected officials and empowering non-elected representatives of special interest groups. [14]

As I document in this book, many of today's educators, government bureaucrats, and corporate leaders are committed to a radical environmentalism stemming from their mysticism and pantheistic pagan spirituality that requires the worship of nature. For another view of the interconnection of the government, corporation, education, and pagan spirituality I'll be talking so much about in this book, I recommend "Business, Government, Academic Leaders Convene on Sustainable Real Estate Development,"[15] an article by Melissa Anderson on the website of the University of Wisconsin-Madison.

You'll recall that the counter-cultural revolution of the 1960s was largely about the promotion of mysticism, pagan spirituality, and socialism. Many 60s radicals grew up to become educators, reporters, elected officials, corporate officers, and leaders in the radical foundations now implementing sustainable development policies. To drastically understate the case: It's a big problem.

The end game of sustainable development is global governance. If you doubt my claim, then consider the words of the Commission on Global Governance, an organization allied with the United Nations:

> The environment, perhaps more than any other issue, has helped to crystallize the notion that humanity has a common future. *The concept of sustainable development is now widely used and accepted as a framework within which all countries, rich and poor, should operate.* The aspect that particularly concerns us is the global governance implications.[16] [emphasis mine]

After the Brazil Earth Summit, President Bill Clinton created the President's Council on Sustainable Development. As DeWeese explains, the Clinton Administration side-stepped Congress to approve the sustainable development agenda and implement its policies in America:

> All cabinet officials had to do was change some wording of existing programs and reroute already-approved funding to begin to implement the agenda—without Congress and without debate. Former Commerce Secretary Ron Brown told a meeting of the President's Council that he could implement 67% of the Sustainable Development agenda in his agency with no new legislation. Other agencies like Interior, EPA, HUD and more did the same thing. To help it all along, Clinton issued a blizzard of Executive Orders.[17]

Some of the groups pushing the sustainable development agenda include Planned Parenthood, the Sierra Club, the National Education Association, and a host of government bureaucrats serving both Republican and Democrat administrations.

As this book is published—October 2009—Americans are watching the destruction of free-market capitalism under our most socialistic, left-wing administration ever. Yet, in my second book, published in 1995, I warned of this and quoted Maurice Strong, who was head of the 1992 Earth Summit in Rio. I'll repeat his words to point out that what is happening in America is a long-planned transformation of America into a socialist nation: "Isn't the only hope for the planet that the industrialized civilizations collapse? Isn't it our responsibility to bring that about?"[18]

He also extolled the need to destroy the concept of individual sovereign nations:

> It is simply not feasible for sovereignty to be exercised unilaterally by individual nation-states, however powerful. It is a principle which will yield only slowly and reluctantly to the imperatives of global environmental cooperation.[19]

In a corollary to Strong's position, Helen Caldicott of the Union of Concerned Scientists has declared the "horrors" of free-market capitalism:

> Free enterprise really means rich people get richer. They have the freedom to exploit and psychologically rape their fellow human beings in the process....Capitalism is destroying the earth.[20]

It is not only free-market capitalism they seek to destroy but Christianity itself, since the Protestant Reformation is what gave birth to free-market capitalism. Bible-minded Christians are further enemies of these globalist goals because Christians do not believe in the worship of nature as does the pantheistic, pagan spiritualism behind the movement.

The Worldview War Is a Spiritual Battle

I hear people say that we are all God's children, but that's only wishful thinking. In John 8:42, Jesus says, "If God were your Father, you would love Me, for I proceeded forth and came from God." In verse 44 He continues, "You are of your father the devil, and the desires of your father you want to do. He was a murderer from the beginning, and does not stand in the truth, because there is no truth in him. When he speaks a lie, he speaks from his own resources, for he is a liar and the father of it." Then in verse 47: "He who is of God hears God's words; therefore you do not hear, because you are not of God."

So when and how can one come to be called a child of God? John tells us in John 1:12-13: "But as many as received Him, to them He gave the right to become children of God, to those who believe in His name: who were born, not of blood, nor of the will of the flesh, nor of the will of man, but of God."

Jesus Christ, fully God and fully Man, declared in John 14:6 that He is truth, and thus truth is that which is consistent with the character and nature of God. The Bible reflects God's character and nature, and so it is true. Jesus prayed this in John 17:17 when He said, "Sanctify them by Your truth. Your word is truth."

But the Bible makes it clear we are in a spiritual, worldview war, and the leader of the opposition is Satan himself. Man serves either God or Satan, and thus every issue is theological and spiritual. The Apostle Paul calls Satan "the god of this world" in 2 Corinthians 4:4, and John states in 1 John 5:19 that "the whole world lies under the sway of the wicked one." First Peter 5:8 warns, "Be sober, be vigilant; because your adversary the devil walks about like a roaring lion, seeking whom he may devour."

Satan is committed to everything contrary to the character and nature of God. He is an enemy of truth and the father of lies. I believe Satan desires the demise of America for two reasons. First, it was founded as a Christian nation, and many of its founders saw America as a place from which to propagate the Gospel of Jesus Christ. With the printing of the Bible and the establishment of seminaries, Christian Sunday school associations and mission agencies, Americans have spent billions upon billions discipling nations of the world. Satan hates America for this. Secondly, he hates America for our defense of Israel and the Jewish people. America stepped into World War II and ended Satan's attempt to destroy the Jewish people through a demonically influenced Adolf Hitler. And, until recently, America has been a friend and defender of Israel. As a result, Satan is quite pleased by the work of those who further the lies that contribute to the destruction of our once great city on a hill.[21]

To review what I often tell my listeners, there are six main worldviews: Biblical Christianity, Secular Humanism, Cosmic Humanism (New Age), Islam, Postmodernism, and Marxism/Leninism. Yet only one of these is built on truth. The other five have brought destruction, despair, mass murder, and chaos. Among the many proponents of these views, a small group of seminal thinkers has done more than any others to assure that these aberrant philosophies still influence and undermine America long after the philosophers have exited this life. Their values and ideas are driving America itself to an early grave.

Romans 1:25 tells us that one of the signs a nation has rejected the God of the Bible is that its people begin to worship creation rather than the Creator God. By destroying the influence of Biblical Christianity within a culture, globalists remove their main obstacle to socialism, radical environmentalism, active euthanasia through socialized medicine, compulsory abortion, the end of parental authority, the elimination of an armed populace, private property, homosexuality (homosexuals are favored because they do not reproduce and add to world population), and the indoctrination of our children with their worldview. Peter Singer, who teaches ethics at Princeton University, makes this clear: "Christianity is our foe.... We must destroy the Judeo Christian religious tradition."[22]

In *The Historical Roots of Our Ecologic Crisis*, Lynn White, Jr., accuses Christianity of being the root of the world's major crises:

> What we do about ecology depends on our ideas of the man-nature relationship. More science and more technology are not going to get us out of the present ecological crisis until we find a new religion, or rethink our old one...as we now recognize, somewhat over a century ago science and technology...joined to give mankind powers which... are out of control. If so, Christianity bears a huge burden of guilt....Our science and technology have grown out of Christian attitudes towards man's relation to nature....No new set of basic values has been accepted in our society to displace those of Christianity. Hence we shall continue to have a worsening ecological crisis until we reject the Christian axiom that nature has no reason for existence save to serve man. By destroying pagan animism, Christianity made it possible to exploit nature in a mood of indifference to the feelings of natural objects....The spirits in natural objects, which formerly had protected nature from man, evaporated.[23]

Throughout this book we are going to see that the educational establishment is one of four key fronts in the battle to implement globalism and undermine the Christian worldview. The editors of *Empowerment for Sustainable Development: Toward Operational Strategies* acknowledge the vital role education plays in indoctrinating students with their radical worldview:

> Education has been advanced as significant in bringing about changes in attitudes, behavior, beliefs, and values....In order to redirect behavior and values towards institutional change for sustainable development, there is a need to investigate strategic options in relations to educational philosophies, scope for propagation and adoption, and groups most likely susceptible to change.[24]

Mikhail Gorbachev has played a major role in the sustainable development agenda. Through his foundation to promote globalism and pagan spirituality, Gorbachev speaks of the need for a new world religion:

> First of all, we must return to the well-known human values that are embodied in the ideals of the world religions and also in the socialist ideas that inherited much more from those values. Further, we need to search for a new paradigm of development that is based on those values and that is capable of leading us all toward a genuinely humanistic or, more precisely, humanistic-ecological culture of living.[25]

I have predicted for years that this new world religion will include pantheism, occultism, and Darwinian evolution, all of which fit perfectly with the values of socialism, world government, the worship of Mother Earth, and the hatred of Biblical Christianity.

A large component of the global agenda is population control. The late Dr. Jacques Cousteau declared, "In order to stabilize world population, we must eliminate 350,000 people per day."[26]

Professor Eric R. Pianka of the University of Texas (Austin) goes even further. He advocates using airborne Ebola to eliminate 90% of the earth's population. Even more chilling is the recognition Dr. Pianka has received. At its 109th annual meeting at Lamar University, the Texas Academy of Science named Dr. Pianka the 2006 Distinguished Texas Scientist.[27]

Others come at the same conclusion from different directions. For instance, David Brower, the first executive director of the radical environmentalist organization The Sierra Club, declared:

> Childbearing [should be] a punishable crime against society, unless the parents hold a government license....All potential parents [should be] required to use contraceptive chemicals, the government issuing antidotes to citizens chosen for childbearing.[28]

Similarly, Paul Ehrlich, in his alarmist book *Population Bomb,* further explained this strategy:

> The first task is population control at home. How do we go about it? Many of my colleagues feel that some sort of compulsory birth regulation would be necessary to achieve such control. One plan often mentioned involves the addition of temporary sterilants to water supplies or staple food. Doses of the antidote would be carefully rationed by the government to produce the desired population size.[29]

In 1977, Ehrlich and his wife wrote the book *Ecoscience* with John Holdren. Years later, in 2009, Holdren became President Obama's "science czar." *Ecoscience* made clear what Holdren is now in position to implement: "The neo-Malthusian view proposes…population limitation and redistribution of wealth." They concluded, "On these points, we find ourselves firmly in the neo-Malthusian camp."

The philosophy on which the Ehrlichs and Holdren base their thinking, of course, is that of economist Thomas Malthus. In his paper "An Essay on the Principle of Population," Malthus declared, "All the children who are born beyond what would be required to keep up the population to a desired level, must necessarily perish, unless room be made for them by the death of grown persons."[30]

In agreement with Malthus, Holdren and the Ehrlichs share their vision for population control:

> It has been concluded that compulsory population-control laws, even including laws requiring compulsory abortion, could be sustained under the existing constitution if the population crisis becomes sufficiently severe to endanger society….If some individuals contribute to general social deterioration by overproducing children, and if the need is compelling, they can be required by law to exercise reproductive responsibility. [31]

This is serious, folks! President Obama's science czar buys into sustainable development! Sustainable development includes provision for a world authority that controls all resources and every aspect of how humans live—whether they are allowed to be born, how and when they die, and the way they are educated. Holdren calls for a "Planetary Regime" to bring this about:

Such a comprehensive Planetary Regime could control the development, administration, conservation, and distribution of all natural resources, renewable or nonrenewable...not only in the atmosphere and oceans, but in such freshwater bodies as rivers and lakes....The Regime might also be a logical central agency for regulating all international trade....The Planetary Regime might be given responsibility for determining the optimum population for the world and for each region and for arbitrating various countries' shares within their regional limits...the Regime would have some power to enforce the agreed limits.[32]

Holdren also encourages "...a more powerful United Nations,"[33] and like the rest of the globalists, he blames Biblical Christianity for the world's problems:

The Christian concept of life in this world, as voiced by Saint Paul, that "here we have no abiding city," for example, conceivably could help explain why some people show rather little concern for the long-term future of the global environment or for the well-being of future generations.[34]

In support of ever more radical approaches to population control, Peter Singer lays the groundwork for rationalizing the destruction of unwanted children. Singer, who from his platform at Princeton University has influenced many educators, students, and law-makers, asserts in *Rethinking Life and Death*:

Human babies are not born self-aware or capable of grasping their lives over time. They are not persons. Hence their lives would seem to be no more worthy of protection than the life of a fetus.[35]

Notice how Singer takes advantage of the already accepted dehumanization of fetuses. He also uses Down Syndrome babies as an example of how his plans would work:

> We may not want a child to start on life's uncertain voyage if the prospects are clouded. When this can be known at a very early stage in the voyage, we may still have a chance to make a fresh start. This means detaching ourselves from the infant who has been born, cutting ourselves free before the ties that have already begun to bind us to our child have become irresistible. Instead of going forward and putting all our effort into making the best of the situation, we can still say no, and start again from the beginning.[36]

The influence of Charles Darwin (Chapter 16) on Singer's thought is clear:

> When we reject belief in God we must give up the idea that life on this planet has some preordained meaning. Life as a whole has no meaning. Life began, as the best available theories tell us, in a chance combination of gasses; it then evolved through random mutation and natural selection. All this just happened; it did not happen to any overall purpose. Now that it has resulted in the existence of beings who prefer some states of affairs to others, however, it may be possible for particular lives to be meaningful. In this sense some atheists can find meaning in life.[37]

In a 1995 article in the London *Spectator* entitled "Killing Babies Isn't Always Wrong," Singer pontificates that, "...when Copernicus proved that the earth is not at the center of the universe. It is ridiculous to pretend that the old ethics make sense when plainly they do not. The notion that human life is sacred just because it's human is medieval."[38]

"Sustainable development" masks all manner of tyranny, oppression, murder, socialism, and global governance. It has become the umbrella under which all the ideas and values of the 21 influencers in this book have converged. And it is what has brought us to the point of no return in our national relationship with the Lord of all nations (Psalm 2).

Before looking in more depth at our "point of no return," allow me to recap some key points you'll want to keep in mind as you continue reading:

- God created three institutions: family government, civil government, and church government. And these three institutions were originally designed to work in harmony one with the other for the creation of a stable and peaceful society in which the God-ordained responsibilities of each institution could be carried out for the ultimate furtherance of the Gospel of Jesus Christ and the building of His Kingdom.

- Satan is using four institutions in an attempt to destroy Christianity and build his kingdom, or "New Order." These four institutions are occultism/pagan spirituality, the apostate Church, the educational establishment, and the government-corporate complex.

- The true Church is made up of faithful followers of Jesus Christ. The false-dominant church will persecute God's bride, but as we have seen throughout history, an unwavering commitment to the Lord Jesus Christ—even in the face of intense persecution—will be a powerful testimony to the unbelieving world and will cause many to come to Christ through faith and repentance.

• The culture war is lost, but the spiritual war continues, and in the end we win. For those of us who fight the good fight, our sufferings will not compare to the glory that shall be revealed in us (Romans 8:18). God's kingdom is made up of His faithful followers, and God will destroy Satan's kingdom. Of God's kingdom there will be no end (Revelation 19-21, Daniel 2:44). Those of us alive today are watching the fulfillment of Biblical prophecy, which continues to reveal the supernatural nature of God's Word.

• Our objective now is not the restoration of the culture but the redemption of the unsaved and the perseverance of the saints.

• Our goal must not be to reclaim the Congress but to reclaim the Church.

• Our commitment should not be to the liberal, Christ-less social gospel but to the Gospel of Jesus Christ.

• Our objective should not be to entertain but to train. Only if we equip our children and grandchildren with a Biblical worldview and the desire and ability to defend essential Christian doctrines will they be prepared to withstand the lies of the adversary that have been so cleverly packaged in political correctness.

2

AMERICA'S TIPPING POINT WITH GOD

Malcolm Gladwell's brilliant study of social trends defined the nature of cultural sea changes in his landmark 2002 book, *The Tipping Point*. According to Gladwell, "The Tipping Point is that dramatic moment when little causes drive the unexpected to become expected."

While Gladwell's work focused on overarching social and market trends, I believe his concept applies to the perilous tipping point America faces with respect to God's judgment on us as a nation. Countless causes have accumulated to bring us to the brink of something few people expect: God's divine wrath. And I believe we are in the final stages of bringing on the Lord's anger for two reasons, both of which fall neatly under the sustainable development umbrella.

Forsaking Israel

The first is America's withering support for the nation of Israel. For many years, our nation attempted to weaken Israel by pressuring her to give up Covenant land. This increased under George H. W. Bush, Bill Clinton, and George W. Bush and has advanced exponentially under President Obama. In early June 2009, the president traveled to Egypt to address the Muslim world. Numerous times in his speech, President Obama cited what he referred to as "the holy Koran"—the very book that calls for Muslims to murder Jews as well as Christians.

Days before his trip, Obama declared that Iran has the right to a nuclear facility for energy. But we all know that what they really want is a nuclear bomb. Obama has clearly thrown Israel under the bus by weakening Israel's national security and making them vulnerable to a nuclear strike by Iran. In addition, he has increased Iran's threat to America's national security.

Since 1998, Iran has been practicing shooting missiles off of cargo ships. Think about the implications of that not-so-benign act. If even just one missile armed with a nuclear warhead were launched from international waters near the United States and detonated a few dozen miles above the Kansas plains, an electromagnetic pulse would, in nanoseconds, destroy the functioning of all but the barest remnant of America's technological resources—electric power grid, computers, airplanes in flight and on the ground, healthcare equipment, cars, and trucks, to name the most obvious—sending us back to a lifestyle of the mid-1800s *with little or no hope of recovery in the next few years*. Destruction of vital electrical devices would bring about the deaths of millions in the ensuing and prolonged chaos.

Lest you think I exaggerate the threat: Military experts and scientists have testified before the U.S. Congress that the only way our enemies can bring us down militarily is through an EMP bomb—a realistic capability even for those whose nuclear launch technology includes only short-range missiles.

In Genesis 12:3, God says He will curse those that curse Israel and bless those that bless Israel. I believe one of the main reasons God's wrath has been delayed is that we have supported Israel in the past. Yet now America has almost completely withdrawn this backing, and it puts us at great risk for being cursed by God.

From Rejection to Plotting Evil

The second reason for our tipping point is found in the book of Nahum. Nahum showed up in Nineveh about 150 years after Jonah to prophesy that God would not give Nineveh the chance to repent and forestall God's wrath this time around. Why? Because in Nahum 1:11 we read that the people had begun to "plot evil against the Lord." Rejecting God is one thing; plotting evil against Him is the tipping point for national judgment. In fact in Nahum 3:19 we see that their national "injury has no healing, your wound is severe." One translation says, "Your wound is incurable."

Americans have been all too willing to follow the blasphemous worldviews of Charles Darwin, Friedrich Nietzsche, John Dewey, Karl Marx, John Maynard Keynes, Roger Baldwin, and the others discussed in this book—all of whom eagerly plotted evil against the Lord.

When God finally brings His judgment on America, it will be a waste of time even to pray for mercy. No need for a national day of prayer. In Jeremiah 7:16, God specifically tells Jeremiah not to pray for Judah: "Therefore do not pray for this people, nor lift up a cry or a prayer for them, nor make intercession to Me: for I will not hear you." In Jeremiah 15:1, the Lord picks up the theme again: "Even if Moses and Samuel stood before Me, My mind would not be favorable toward this people." And to the prophet Ezekiel, God says that when a nation sins against God in persistent unfaithfulness He will stretch out His hand against it: "Even if these three men, Noah, Daniel, and Job were in it, they would deliver only themselves" (Ezekiel 14:14).

Misinformed individuals have claimed that God would not judge a nation today in the same way because the God of the Old Testament was a God of wrath, but the God of the New Testament is a God of grace. What they don't understand is that the Bible explains in

Hebrews 13:8 that God's character and nature do not change. He is the same yesterday, today, and forever—and His grace is extended only to those who repent.

Add to these two pivotal issues a host of other national sins. In June 2009, Obama signed a proclamation that declared that month as "Lesbian, Gay, Bisexual, and Transgender Pride Month, 2009." And consider these other grievances God could raise against our nation:

- We've murdered nearly 50 million unborn children through abortion;
- States are rushing toward accepting homosexual marriage;
- God is outlawed in our nation's public schools;
- The criminalization of Christianity is increasing daily;
- Only 1% of adults now hold to a genuinely Christian worldview;
- False teachings and pagan spirituality have become mainstream.

Haunting Words from the Past

Abraham Lincoln said, "I know that the Lord is always on the side of the right. But it is my constant anxiety and prayer that I and this nation should be on the Lord's side." In 2 Corinthians 3:17, the Apostle Paul writes: "Where the Spirit of the Lord is, there is freedom."

The deadly serious questions confronting America are: Have we rejected the things of the Lord and thus His Divine providence and protection? Are will still on His side? Does His Spirit remain with us?

Founding Father Dr. Jedidiah Morse warned: "Whenever the pillars of Christianity shall be overthrown, our present republican forms of government, and all the blessings which flow from them, must fall with them." And engraved on the Jefferson Memorial in Washington, D.C., is this sobering admonition from Thomas Jefferson, author of the Declaration of Independence and our third president:

> God who gave us life gave us liberty. And can the liberties of a nation be thought secure when we have removed their only firm basis, a conviction in the minds of the people that these liberties are the gift of God? That they are not violated but with His wrath? Indeed, I tremble for my country when I reflect that God is just; that His justice cannot sleep forever.

George Washington proclaimed: "We ought to be no less persuaded that the propitious smiles of Heaven can never be expected on a nation that disregards the eternal rules of order and right which Heaven itself have ordained."

George Mason, father of the Bill of Rights, speaking at the Constitutional Convention declared: "As nations cannot be rewarded or punished in the next world, so they must be in this. By an inevitable chain of causes and effects, Providence punishes national sins by national calamities."

I believe God uses the same template to judge all nations, and that template can be understood by studying what God said would happen to Israel if that nation disobeyed God and rejected His precepts and principles. God always warns nations before He judges them, and in doing so He gives them the chance to repent. However, if the nation does not repent, God's judgment becomes more severe. Note some of His warnings to Israel if they continued in their rebellion, and consider the self-evident comparisons to America today.

(1) *Deuteronomy 28*. For disobeying God, Israel would be denied

prosperity and abundance, both in regards to their economics as well as in their agriculture.

- Verse 24 describes drought—Many states in America are dealing with severe drought.

- 28 describes confusion of heart—Americans are spiritually confused, mixing Christianity with pagan spirituality.

- 29 tells that the nation shall not prosper in her ways— Look at the state of America's economy, educational and legal systems.

- 30 loss of homes—Starting in 2008 Americas began experiencing historic levels of home foreclosures.

- 38 "You shall carry much seed out to the field but gather little in"—Recently I watched a Fox News reporter standing on the side of a tractor as the farmer tilled his perfect crop of tomatoes back into the ground because it would cost him more to bring the crop to market than what he could sell it for. As a result, he was saving money by plowing under the crop. Watch and see if America's farmers experience poor yields or crops damaged through drought or storms.

- 43 speaks of an invasion of illegal aliens—One study reveals that illegal aliens cost Americans $346 billion per year.

(2) Leviticus 26.

- Verse 16 "I will even appoint terror over you"—America lives under the threat and fear of terrorism.

• 19 "I will break the pride of your power"—America's superpower status faces unprecedented challenges as our military is stretched thin around the world, and overwhelming national debt sabotages our financial stability and dependability, prompting nations to call for a new reserve currency to replace the American dollar.

• 20 and 26 speak of famine—Hard to imagine in America, but possible.

• 22 extreme economic distress—America is certifiably bankrupt. When you combine all our off-record debt and unfunded liabilities like Medicare and Social Security, we are over 99 trillion dollars in debt. The federal government could tax Americans 100% of their total incomes and not cover the federal deficit.

• 31 invasion by enemies and destruction of cities— Intelligence officials and experts admit that terrorist sleeper cells are here in America and are simply waiting for orders to carry out acts of terrorism upon our cities as did those that carried out the attacks on September 11, 2001.

For a nation in our condition, the New Testament is no more encouraging. Romans 1:21-32 clearly states that a nation that rejects God over and over will suffer five specific consequences, and America is experiencing all of these now.

(1) A nation of fools.

• 21-22—Those who reject God over and over become vain, useless, futile or foolish in their thinking. Despite claiming to be "so smart," people become so foolish in their thinking that they succumb to spiritual deception and accept spiritual lies and false teaching.

(2) The nation accepts pagan spirituality.

• 25—*The Denver Post* in June 2008 reported that pagan spirituality is doubling in America every 18 months. Pagan spirituality is the worship of nature, the belief in pantheism, which proclaims that god is all and all is god. Whether you call it Cosmic Humanism, the New Age Movement, the New Spirituality or pagan spirituality, this is becoming the dominant worldview in America with the help of people like Oprah Winfrey and leaders of the Emergent Church.

(3) The nation accepts homosexuality.

• 26-27—States have approved homosexual marriage. The curriculum in many of America's public schools teaches the homosexual agenda. The non-judgmentalism of a postmodern generation dominates our thinking. New laws give special rights to homosexuals, and homosexuality becomes an ever more acceptable lifestyle to an ever increasing percentage of Americans.

(4) The nation becomes violent and debased.

• 28—Since the 1962 and 1963 U.S. Supreme Court rulings outlawing prayer and Bible reading in America's public schools, our nation has seen a spike in the rates of murder, rape, child abuse, unwed pregnancies, and violent crimes.

(5) The nation's leaders are corrupt and immoral.

• 32—Declares that when a nation continually rejects God, they will have leaders that are not only immoral and corrupt in their personal lives but who also approve of and encourage immoral behavior in the people. Whether at the state or federal level, leaders in our legislative, judicial, and executive branches of government are continually passing laws, handing down legal rulings, signing executive orders, and sponsoring legislation against the righteous judgments of God.

Finally, a quick look at Isaiah 5 deepens the sense of monumental consequences that await the unrepentant and the continual sins for which God will bring judgment on a nation. God warned Israel for these sins, and America should also consider itself warned.

• 8-10—Materialism. Money is not the root of all evil, but the *love* of money is. Love of money lies at the heart of materialism. Materialism is a form of idolatry, the devotion to money that also includes knowingly disobeying God's principles and standards in order to obtain money.

• 11-12—Hedonism. Hedonism says that the purpose of life is not to seek God but to seek pleasure. It rejects the absolute truth of right and wrong based on the character and nature of God and instead proclaims "if it feels good do it," "you only live once," or "eat, drink, and be merry for tomorrow we die."

• 12—Apathy and Foolishness. Ideas have consequences,

and bad ideas have bad consequences. Apathy has led Americans to take their freedoms for granted, to become intellectually lazy, to reject reason, logic, and context. The Bible speaks repeatedly about the need to acquire knowledge, wisdom, and understanding, yet Americans have done the exact opposite and rejected knowledge. Knowledge is the acquisition of truth, and wisdom is the application of truth. According to the Bible, Jesus Christ is truth, His Word is truth, and yet Americans have developed apathy toward God that has now turned into disdain toward His character and nature.

• 20—Moral Relativism. Since the late sixties, millions of American public school children have been educated with values clarification courses that proclaim moral relativism, the notion that all values and beliefs are equal because there is no absolute truth or standard of right and wrong.

• 21—Arrogance leading to spiritual deception. People become so arrogant and foolish in their thinking that they accept lies such as pagan spirituality.

• 21-23—Corrupt leadership and rulers drunk with power and enriching themselves with bribes and ill-gotten gains. Examples of this are everywhere. Americans are realizing that the majority of our local, state, and federal leaders are interested only in power and in using their positions to enrich themselves and their special interest groups so as to receive kickbacks, under-the-table payments, and political contributions for re-election. A judge recently made

national news because he had taken hundreds of thousands
of dollars in bribes to sentence minors simply to keep a
private juvenile detention center in business.

What's a Christian to Do?

Christians must occupy till the Lord returns. Sadly, as America goes
under, Christians who were committed only to the reconstruction of
America or building a Christian America will retreat from the culture.
This is not how Christians should respond. If indeed God is judging
America (I believe He is) and if His judgment is going to greatly
increase (I believe it will), then we need to use His judgment as an
opportunity to preach the Gospel to the unsaved.

God's national judgment can allow us to speak in the natural
realm and then shift to the spiritual. Explain to the unbeliever what sin
is, why God must judge sin, and that the judgment nations experience
in this life is nothing compared to the eternal judgment unrepentant
individuals will receive in the next world. We can share with them that
grace and mercy are only extended to those who repent, that Jesus
Christ has provided the way for us to pass from judgment into life.

American Christians should not rate our success on whether or
not we return our culture to its Christian roots. On the contrary, we
may very well see serious persecution of Christians in America. We are
not exempt even from the kind of treatment our brothers and sisters
have endured in China, Cuba, and many other parts of the world.
Faithful fulfillment of the Great Commission must be our standard
for success, not our popularity in the culture, the balance of our bank
accounts, the houses we live in, or the cars we drive.

Peter Marshall put it this way: "It is better to fail in a cause that
will ultimately succeed, than to succeed in a cause that will ultimately

fail."[39] And Dr. Erwin Lutzer applies this thinking directly to the Church: "Better to fail within the church than to be successful outside of it...God wins even when the church appears to lose."[40]

With this ultimate triumph in mind, let's now begin our look at the individuals who are destroying America from the grave. Examine with me how they are connected, how we must respond to protect ourselves and our children and grandchildren from being taken captive by their unbiblical worldviews, and how we can rescue those who have already been taken captive.

PART 2

BROUGHT TO YOU BY THE OCCULT AND PAGAN SPIRITUALITY

3

ALICE BAILEY
(1880-1949)

Lucifer Publishing Company. Cheesy as it sounds, the name is not the front for some nemesis in an old Batman comic. I wish. No, it is the very real and very caustic organization founded by one of the most wide-ranging influencers in this book.

Alice Bailey started her publishing company and its sister New Age organization, Lucis Trust, in 1922. From that locus have spread countless iterations of occultic and pagan spirituality. One of the leading founders of what we now call the New Age Movement, Bailey's worldview and goals have shaped the thinking of many individuals we examine in this book. To fully grasp the worldview war raging among us, we must understand the philosophies of Alice Bailey.

Bailey wrote 24 books totaling thousands of pages. She claimed to have written them under the direction of a spirit guide called Djwhal Khul or the Tibetan. But to be clear: I believe Bailey was communicating with a demon, a practice strictly forbidden in God's Word.

Bailey also wrote about a group of Ascended Masters (more demons) she said were highly evolved individuals, thanks to the wonders of reincarnation. She was the first of many New Agers to teach that Ascended Masters achieve their positions by living lives in which their good karma (deeds) outweigh their bad.

According to Bailey, Ascended Masters "each have a special contribution to make towards human progress in one of the seven major fields of world work: political, religious, educational, scientific, philosophical, psychological or economic."[41] Bailey, through her demonic occultism, has influenced most, if not all, of these disciplines. Many of America's rich and powerful—including high-ranking government officials—have been members of Bailey's Lucis Trust, and for many years the organization's headquarters were located at the United Nations Plaza.

Disappointing as it may seem, the young Alice Bailey worked with a bona fide Christian organization. She reached a turning point, though, upon reading Helena Petrovna Blavatsky's *The Secret Doctrine*. It replaced her reading of the Bible, and so began her travels down the path of demonic influence and occultism:

> My mind woke up as I struggled with the presented ideas and sought to fit my own beliefs and the new concepts together....I sat up in bed reading *The Secret Doctrine* at night and began to neglect my Bible, which I had been in the habit of doing....I discovered, first of all, that there is a great and divine Plan....I found that race after race of human beings had appeared and disappeared upon our planet and that each civilization and culture had seen humanity step forward a little further upon the path of return to God. I discovered, for the second thing, that there are Those who are responsible for the working out of that Plan and down the centuries. I made the amazing discovery, amazing to me because I knew so little, that the teaching about this Path or this Plan was uniform, whether it was presented in the Occident or in the Orient, or whether it had emerged when I, in my orthodox days, talked about the Christ and His Church I was really speaking of Christ and the planetary Hierarchy.[42]

Today, the New Age Movement is often referred to as the New

Spirituality. Let me make this very clear: When Bailey speaks of the Christ, she is not talking about the Jesus Christ of the Bible but a redefined New Age Jesus. New Agers claim He was just like you and me but through reincarnation had become one of the Ascended Masters. The New Spirituality teaches that every person can become an Ascended Master.

The Public Face of Bailey's Private God

Bailey proclaimed that the world needs to prepare the way for the "the Christ" by tapping into our unconscious minds and collectively understanding our own "personal deity." The demonic entity, Djwhal Khul, gave Alice Bailey the following "Great Invocation" that has been reprinted by the Lucis Trust in national publications, including *Reader's Digest*:

> From the point of Light within the Mind of God
> Let light stream forth into the minds of men.
> Let Light descend on Earth
> From the point of Love within the Heart of God
> Let love stream forth into the hearts of men.
> May Christ return to Earth.
> From the centre where the Will of God is known
> Let purpose guide the little wills of men—
> The purpose which the Masters know and serve.
> From the centre which we call the race of men
> Let the Plan of Love and Light work out
> And may it seal the door where evil dwells.
> Let Light and Love and Power restore the Plan on
> Earth.[43]

Satan and his army of demons have used Alice Bailey to foster their spiritual lies and lay the foundation for the acceptance of one-world government, one-world religion, and one-world economy to be led by Satan's one-world leader, the Antichrist. In the following excerpts from Bailey's writing, she and her demon bemoan Christianity, the cross, the exclusivity of Jesus Christ, the Jewish people, and nation of Israel (keep in mind that the Hierarchy is an organization of demons posing as more highly evolved humans):

> The Hierarchy is deeply concerned over world events.... The New Age is upon us and we are witnessing the birth of the new culture and the new civilization. This is now in progress. That which is old and undesirable must go and of these undesirable things, hatred and the spirit of separation must be the first to go.[44]

> The Hierarchy is struggling hard with the so-called "forces of evil," and the New Group of World Servers is the instrument....These forces of evil...the entrenched ancient ideals...which must now disappear if the New Age is to be ushered in as desired. The old established rhythms, inherent in the old forms of religion, of politics and of the social order, must give place to newer ideals, to the synthetic understanding, and to the new order. The laws and modes of procedure which are characteristic of the New Age must supersede the old, and these will, in time, institute the new social order and the more inclusive regime. [45]

Those who help political, religious, economic and educational leaders bring about the "new order'" are the "New Group of World Servers." How often do you now hear world leaders using the language of the New Age Movement or New Spirituality as they call for a "New World Order" that includes a one-world economic structure, a merging of all the world's religions and political authority, and a stronger United Nations. Satan is using men and women throughout the world to change every discipline of life toward occultism—an anti-God, anti-Biblical worldview. Bailey asserts:

> Through the medium of certain great and outstanding personalities who were peculiarly sensitive to the will-to-power and the will-to-change and who...have altered the character of their national life, and emphasized increasingly the wider human values. The men who inspired the initiating French revolution; the great conqueror, Napoleon; Bismarck, the creator of a nation; Mussolini, the regenerator of his people; Hitler, who lifted a distressed people upon his shoulders; Lenin, the idealist; Stalin and Franco are all expressions of the Shamballa force [demonic forces] and of certain little understood energies.[46]

Bailey and her demon regard "will-to-power and the will-to-change" as personality traits to be admired in individuals like Hitler, Mussolini, Lenin, and Stalin. Some role models! This quotation should make it very obvious that the Communist, Marxist, socialist, and Fascist regimes of years gone by have been doing the work of Satan as he attempts to destroy Christianity, the freedom of the pulpit, the freemarkets that have funded the spread of the Gospel of Jesus Christ, and the God-ordained institution of the family.

The Tibetan makes it clear to Bailey that some of the world's most notorious dictators, tyrants, mass murders, and enemies of Christianity have been agents of Satan himself:

> These have wrought significant changes in their day and generation....They are being used to engineer great and

needed changes and to alter the face of civilization....They are the agents of destiny, the creators of the new order and the initiators of the new civilization; they are destroyers of what must be destroyed before humanity can go forward along the Lighted Way.[47]

This obsession to destroy Christianity should make it clear that what is happening in America and the world is a spiritual battle. Adolf Hitler, one of the Bailey's "agents of destiny," was seeking to bring about a demonic kingdom of globalism. At its root, globalism is based on occultism, and Hitler was an agent of Satan.

Dr. Erwin Lutzer in his award-winning book, *Hitler's Cross*, documents Hitler's satanic worldview:

• Even those who knew Hitler from his early days were well aware of his occult powers. August Kubizek, a friend, said, "It was as if another being spoke out of his body....It was not a case of a speaker carried away by his own words.... I felt as though he himself listened with astonishment and emotion to what broke forth from him."[48]

• Hitler's closest advisors were into occultism and pagan spirituality such as Rudolf Hess, Dietrich Eckart, Karl Haushofer, Joseph Goebbels, Alfred Rosenberg and others.

• Hitler confided to those who were closest to him that he was under orders from a higher being in his unique mission. "I will tell you a secret," he told Rausching, "I am founding an order...the Man-God, that splendid being will be an object of worship....But there are other stages about which I am not permitted to speak."[49]

- After reading his friend Alfred Rosenberg's blasphemous book entitled *The Myth of the Twentieth Century*, Hitler declared, "Creation is not yet at an end. Man is becoming God....Man is God in the making."[50]

- Allan Bullock, who wrote an extensive biography of Hitler, dutifully listed what Hitler studied in his youth: yoga, hypnotism, astrology, and various other forms of Eastern occultism...[51]

Hitler and the German people stand as a lesson for our own culture. The people and nation who follow leaders who follow Satan are traveling a road of individual and national spiritual suicide.

The Age of Collectivism

The Tibetan made a number of provocative claims about the future. It will be about socialism—collectivism, or group-thinking—not individualism or dissent:

> This coming age will be as predominantly the age of group interplay, group idealism and group consciousness...for the will of the individual will voluntarily be blended into group will.[52]

The future and new order will be about pluralism (the belief all religions are equal) and universalism (the belief all roads lead to God):

> I refer to that period which will surely come in which an *Enlightened People* will rule; these people will not tolerate authoritarianism in any church...they will not accept or permit the rule of any body of men who undertake to tell them what they must believe in order to be saved...[53]

The educational establishment would be a key to bringing about the new order through politically correct courses that teach tolerance and pluralism:

> World unity will be a fact when the children of the world are taught that religious differences are largely a matter of birth....He will learn that religious differences are largely the result of manmade quarrels over human interpretations of truth. Thus gradually, our quarrels and differences will be offset and the idea of One Humanity will take their place.[54]

The exclusivity of Jesus Christ and the cross will be seen as foolishness to the more enlightened followers of the New Age:

> Up till now the mark of the Saviour has been the Cross, and the quality of the salvation offered has been freedom from substance or the lure of matter and from its hold—a freedom only to be achieved at a great cost. The future holds within its silence other modes of the Cross are well-nigh finished.[55]

In recent years, a new voice for the Tibetan has arisen and captivated one of the largest television followings in history. Oprah Winfrey and her New Age guests promote the Bailey lies:

> There is, as you well know, no angry God, no hell, and no vicarious atonement...and the only hell is the earth itself, where we learn to work out our own salvation....This teaching about hell is a remainder of the sadistic turn which was given to the thinking of the Christian Church in the Middle Ages and to the erroneous teaching to be found in the Old Testament agent Jehovah, the tribal God of the Jews.

Jehovah is *not* God....As these erroneous ideas die out, the concept of hell will fade from man's recollection and its place will be taken by an understanding of the law which makes each man work out his own salvation...which leads him to right the wrongs which he may have perpetrated in his lives on Earth, and which enable him eventually to "clean his own slate."[56]

"Lives on Earth" is an obvious reference to reincarnation, one of her many re-directions of the truth. Bailey didn't hide the fact that her worldview was founded in occultism and predicted that future churches—even those that once rejected her worldview—would eagerly accept it in order to attract the masses. If that sounds very "seeker sensitive," it is. Within a generation, countless American churches have wandered from defending a Biblical worldview to teaching that the Word of God is subjective, that all roads lead to God, and that mysticism and pagan spirituality should be embraced to further one's religious experiences. It's all part of the quest for a spiritual salve to quench the dull ache of the human soul. Bailey saw it coming (perhaps because her demonic guides had it planned all along?):

It can be expected that the orthodox Christian will at first reject the theories about the Christ which occultism presents; at the same time, this same orthodox Christian will find it increasingly difficult to induce the intelligent masses of people to accept the impossible Deity and the feeble Christ which historical Christianity has endorsed.

The New Age Jesus came to earth to teach people how to live during the age of the Pisces or the Christ consciousness, the force or energy each individual must tap into in order to understand his or her own deity. References to the coming Christ or Maytria speak of a world leader that enlightened people desire to lead them through this Age of Aquarius. I believe Satan and his demons are using this "Christ" to prepare the world for the acceptance of the anti-Christ. Bailey didn't mince words. She explained clearly that her demon was not referring to Jesus of Nazareth, the Christ of the Bible:

> The Tibetan [Djwhal Khul] has asked me [Alice Bailey] to make clear that when he is speaking of the Christ he is referring to His official name as head of the Hierarchy. The Christ works for all men, irrespective of their faith; He does not belong to the Christian world any more than to the Buddhist, the Mohammedan or any other faith. There is no need for any man to join the Christian Church in order to be affiliated with Christ. The requirements are to love your fellowman, lead a disciplined life, recognize the divinity in all faiths and all beings, and rule your daily life with love.

Robert Muller and the United Nations

Not surprisingly, Bailey supported the United Nations which, in turn, greatly advanced her worldview. She understood the opportunity offered by the UN:

> The new world religion must be based upon those truths which have stood the test of the ages...they are steadily taking shape in human thinking, and for them the United Nations fights.[57]

And what will this world religion be based on? Pagan spirituality or occultism:

The spiritual Hierarchy [demons] of the planet, the ability of mankind to contact its Members and to work in cooperation with Them, and the existence of the greater Hierarchy of spiritual energies of which our tiny planetary sphere is a part—these are the three truths upon which the coming world religion may be based. [58]

This worldview found a devoted adherent in Robert Muller who, in 1948, entered and won an essay contest on "how to govern the world." The prize was an internship at the newly created United Nations.[59] Muller spent more than 40 years at the United Nations and eventually became the assistant secretary-general. He was one of the organization's most powerful insiders, responsible for setting up 11 different UN agencies.[60] Among Muller's numerous books were *The Birth of Global Civilization, My Testament to the UN,* and *New Genesis: Shaping a Global Spirituality*, and he helped create the UN-endorsed global education program known as *The World Core Curriculum* which America and numerous other countries have incorporated into their educational systems. His education agenda won for Muller the designation "Father of Global Education."

Muller also established a school in Arlington, Texas, based on the teachings of Alice Bailey. Though often referred to as the Robert Muller School, the preface of *The World Core Curriculum* clarifies that the Robert Muller School is founded on the ideas of Alice Bailey and the Tibetan:

The underlying philosophy upon which the Robert Muller School is based will be found in the teachings set forth in the books of Alice A. Bailey by the Tibetan teacher, Djwhal Khul (published by Lucis Publishing Company).[61]

Are you grasping the magnitude of all this? Muller developed a global education curriculum, in which many American schools are participating, based on the pagan spirituality and globalism of Alice Bailey. Muller's pronouncement to a group of Canadian school children reflects the influence Alice Bailey has had on his thinking:

> You are not children of Canada, you are really living units of the cosmos because the Earth is a cosmic phenomena...we are all cosmic units. This is why religions tell you, you are divine. We are divine energy...it is in your hands whether evolution on this planet continues or not.[62]

Further, in an obvious acknowledgment of their New Spirituality devotion, Muller and his companion, Barbara Gaughen, refer to themselves as "The Cosmic Couple."[63] As I have pointed out on my radio program many times, the road to globalism has been paved by two tracks, a political one and a spiritual one. Now, these two tracks have merged to become one with help of people like Robert Muller.

The two tracks merge elsewhere as well. Days before Barack Obama was sworn into office as president of the United States, Nobel Peace Prize winner and former Secretary of State Henry Kissinger, gave an interview on CNBC. Speaking of President-Elect Obama, Kissinger said:

> His task will be to develop an overall strategy for America in this period when, really, a new world order can be created. It's a great opportunity; it isn't just a crisis.[64]

Does thinking of the crisis as "a great opportunity" sound familiar? Obama's White House chief of staff, Rahm Emanuel, told business leaders in a November 2008 meeting that the financial crisis was "an opportunity to do things you could not do before." This, of course, is the same Rahm Emanuel who said, "You never want a serious crisis to go to waste."

Kissinger, Obama, and Emanuel are singing from the same song sheet. But especially troubling is the other voices in the same chorus. Mikhail Gorbachev, the last leader of the Soviet Union, is president of the International Foundation for Socio-Economic and Political Studies in Moscow, and he has been pushing a one-world religion and one-world government for years. He has even conducted much of his work right here in America from an office in San Francisco.

On January 1, 2009, Gorbachev wrote a column for the *International Herald Tribune*. He also seemed gleeful over the financial crisis and the great opportunity for using it to further the globalist agenda:

> The G-20 summit meeting in Washington foreshadowed a new format of global leadership, bringing together the countries responsible for the future of the world economy. And more than just the economy is at stake….The economic and political balance in the world has changed. It is now a given that a world with a single power center, in any shape or guise, is no longer possible. The global challenge of a financial and economic tsunami can only be met by working together.[65]

Working together for what purpose? Gorbachev explains:

> A new concept is emerging for addressing the crisis at the national and international levels….If current ideas for reforming the world's financial and economic institutions are consistently implemented, that would suggest we are finally beginning to understand the importance of global governance.[66]

A week later, an AP article by Emma Vandore recounted a two-day meeting hosted by French President Nicolas Sarkozy. Former British Prime Minister Tony Blair, who has been extolling a one-world interfaith dialog for years, is also calling for a new financial order based on "values other than the maximum short-term profits."

Sarkozy, who I believe sees himself as a likely potential one-world supreme leader, proclaimed:

> In the 21st century, there is no longer a single nation who can say what we should do or what we should think....We cannot accept the status quo....In the capitalism of the 21st century, there is room for the state. [67]

When the State moves in, the system ceases to be capitalism, no matter what someone tries to call it. The end of capitalism is the fulfillment of the dream of humanists and socialists. Globalistic philosophy has always been tied to occultism, so don't be surprised when you see more and more evidence that those calling for globalism practice pagan spirituality. I, and a few others, have predicted for years that a global crisis of some kind would be used to implement the freedom-robbing tyranny of global governance.

One World Spirituality—Three Worldviews Merge

As you might guess, I'm a news and worldview junkie, and eagerly study cultural trends, global strategies, public policy, and religious worldviews in order to better understand the times in which we live. In 2007, I began to notice a striking trend. I recognized politicians, religious leaders, actors, and many people in general cherry-picking three different philosophies to form a "new" worldview. While there is "nothing new under the sun" (the lies of Satan are continually being repackaged), almost no one—including even Christian leaders and authors—is recognizing this insidious worldview merger.

Finally, in the spring of 2008, I called one of my favorite worldview speakers and authors and shared with him what I was seeing and proposed the idea that these three worldviews were merging into a dominant new worldview embraced on a global scale. He didn't see it and tried to convince me that the worldviews cannot rightly be merged into one. So I called another worldview expert and author, Dr. Ron Carlson, and found a fellow researcher that not only confirmed my theory but engaged me in a lengthy conversation about his research.

Dr. Carlson and I agree that the worldviews of evolutionary humanism, Hindu pantheism, and occultism have merged to create a worldview I call One-World Spirituality. The theology of this worldview is pantheism; the philosophy is pagan spirituality; the biology is Darwinian evolution; the economic system is socialism; the politics is globalism, and the activism of this worldview is centered on radical environmentalism and political correctness (cultural Marxism). The goals of this One-World Spirituality are just what we've outlined before: a one-world government, one-world religion, and one-world economic system.

Evolutionary humanism denies the Creator God. So, since we are all just an accident of nature, there is no absolute truth and no ultimate judge. "Might makes right." Therefore, a dominant global government that oppresses dissenters is justified.

A few weeks after my revealing conversation with Dr. Carlson, while researching another article, I stumbled onto an alarming fact: Adolf Hitler adhered to this same blending of worldviews. To wit, the swastika was adapted from Hinduism and tweaked to become the symbol of the Nazi Party.

Hindu monism and pantheism teach "All is One, and All is God, and God is Impersonal." The purpose of yoga—which means "yoke or union with God" in Sanskrit—is to help the practitioner become one with the Impersonal All. One-World Spirituality says no one can be better than anyone else, that all religions must be equal, and that no one can be in heaven while someone else is in hell. Theologically speaking, this all-roads-lead-to-God approach is universalism. And the beneficial-sounding, intellectually popular, politically correct, contemporary term for this concept is pluralism.

A belief and commitment to the exclusivity of Jesus Christ in a world of religions is now politically incorrect and does not conform to the mandates of pluralism. The Associated Press reported on June 23, 2008, that a report released by the Pew Forum on Religion and Public Life found:

> 57% of evangelical church attendees said they believe many religions can lead to eternal life. In all, 70 percent of Americans with a religious affiliation shared that view, and 68 percent said there is more than one true way to interpret the teachings of their own religion.

Of course, anyone that believes this is not really an evangelical Christian. This report reveals that Biblical Christianity is now a minority worldview in America.

The social implications of pagan spirituality are stunning. If we are all one, no individual or nation should be better or worse off than anyone else, and thus the only acceptable economic worldview is socialism, the attempt to equalize the distribution of wealth.

Then there is occultism. Occultism encourages practices and experiences that purport to help a person discover his or her version of Christ-consciousness—personal divinity—and, thus, ultimate salvation. It promotes talking to spirit or master guides, as encouraged by Alice Bailey.

Whether consciously or not, many leaders in business, government, and organized religion embrace One-World Spirituality. Within the Emergent Church, some engage in pagan spirituality, promote pantheism and globalism, and praise the economic worldview of Karl Marx.

One of the most visible American politicians living out this One-World Spirituality is former Vice President Al Gore. An ex-Southern Baptist turned New Ager, Gore has embraced pantheism, pagan spirituality, socialism, and globalism and uses radical environmentalism to propagate his worldview throughout America and the world.

I am certain that the president of at least one country understands the Marxist agenda of the One-World Spiritualists—although I'm not sure if he understands these three worldviews have merged to form this new worldview—and he understands that the "crisis" being manufactured to implement it is radical environmentalism. Vaclav Klaus, president of the Czech Republic, survived communism and now warns the world about these people's ultimate goal, the elimination of freedom.

President Klaus authored *Blue Planet in Green Shackles* in which he argues that radical environmentalism masks socialism, communism, and fascism. Cliff Kincaid of Accuracy in Media cites Klaus: "But while communism was an atheistic system, Klaus notes, modern environmentalism has assumed a religious dimension and has become a 'green religion'."

Kincaid ties in other significant players:

> Bush and Senator John McCain…have fallen into the camp, which includes Barack Obama, Hillary Clinton, and most of the Democratic Party, which wants to further erode

individual freedom in the name of saving the environment. It is the modern version of Marxism; "from each according to his ability, to each according to his need," except the needs of the environment are now being placed above those of people.

And Klaus explains that the ultimate goal is "completely about power, and about the hegemony of the 'chosen ones' (as they see themselves) over the rest of us, about the imposition of the only correct worldview (their own), about the remodeling of the world."

He warns that radical environmentalists intend to completely destroy private property rights and the free enterprise system through limiting the "carbon footprint" of individuals and companies, growing the size of government, and ushering in socialism. Klaus told the *Washington Times*, "I understand that global warming is a religion conceived to suppress human freedom."[68]

So why should you care about the merging of three worldviews that come together in Alice Bailey's legacy? In 1 Chronicles 12, Issachar, one of the tribes in Israel, was praised for being wise since they understood the times and knew what God would have them do. Now more than ever, God is calling believers to expose false teaching, false religions, and the lies of Satan. The need is critical now that millions are converting to the One-World Spirituality. The end result will be the destruction of their very souls—and likely most of *our* personal freedoms.

4

HELEN SCHUCMAN
(1909-1981)

January 1, 2008 launched a banner year for promoters of the New Spirituality. The ubiquitous TV mouthpiece for the New Age we mentioned earlier used her XM satellite radio program "Oprah & Friends" to host a year-long series of teachings from *A Course in Miracles* by Oprah and her featured guru, Marianne Williamson. Oprah and Marianne covered all 365 lessons from this seminal work of Helen Schucman.

Schucman began writing *A Course in Miracles* in 1965 while associate professor of medical psychology at Columbia University in New York. Her book was based largely on her experiences channeling "a New Age Jesus" whom she believed would teach mankind how to live in these difficult times. Her Jesus gave her a "new gospel," and she dictated the contents of the course over a seven-year period. Schucman took shorthand as the voice spoke and then read the messages to William Thetford, a colleague at Columbia University, who typed the daily notes from Schucman. As in the case of Alice Bailey, I contend that Schucman was hearing from a demon (or demons) as she transcribed what he told her to write. The book was released for sale in 1976. Her 600-plus-page transcription of these teachings is described by some as the "Bible" of the New Age Movement.

Some telling quotes from the book and workbook include:
- "God is in everything I see."
- A "slain Christ has no meaning."
- "The recognition of God is the recognition of yourself."

- "Jesus is a man, who is like all other men."
- "The Atonement is the final lesson he [man] need learn, for it teaches him that, never having sinned, he has no need of salvation."
- "There is no sin; it has no consequence."
- "Sin is defined as 'lack of Love'."
- "...sin is not real."
- "There is no difference between your will and God's."
- "Do not make the pathetic error of 'clinging to the old rugged cross'."
- "My salvation comes from me."

Kenneth Wapnick assisted Schucman in editing *A Course in Miracles* and believed Jesus was "a symbol of God's love and not the historical Jesus of Nazareth."[69]

Oprah's Non-Doctrine Doctrine

Using the talk on her talk show to hammer her congregation of millions with the messages of New Spirituality, Oprah has variously preached that:

- One of the mistakes human beings make is believing there is only one way to live;
- There are many paths to what you call God;
- There are millions and millions of ways to God; there could not possibly be just one;
- God is a feeling experience, not a believing experience;
- If God for you is still about a belief, then it is not truly God;
- God is in all things.

And in case anyone missed the message on TV, Oprah recently

ratcheted up the level of instruction by teaching an online course with best-selling New Age author Eckhart Tolle. An estimated 2 million people joined Winfrey and Tolle for their virtual course in New Spirituality. In Tolle's book *A New Earth* (a primary resource for the online class), he quotes the Bible exhaustively, yet in such a *new* fashion that Oprah extols his thinking this way: "I love this quote that Eckhart has. This is one of my favorite quotes in chapter one where he says, 'Man made God in his own image'."

She probably feels this way because she's done such a good job of making up her own image of God—starting when she was about 27 years old. That's when, as she tells the story, she rejected the doctrine of her Baptist church because she didn't like it when her pastor claimed God is a jealous God. The notion of Divine jealously offended her, and "that's when the search for something more than doctrine started to stir within me."

Rightly Dividing Oprah's Truth

I believe Oprah's rejection of Biblical doctrine has led to her acceptance of the doctrines of demons as 1 Timothy 4:1 says will occur in the last days: "Now the Spirit expressly says that in latter times some will depart from the faith, giving heed to deceiving spirits and doctrines of demons."

The rejection of Biblical doctrine is the reason for the current great apostasy or falling away from traditionally held Biblical truths. Journalists Richard Cimino and Don Lattin explain in their 1988 book, *Shopping for Faith*, that for many people "religious experience is replacing religious doctrine."

Oprah's rejection of religious doctrine—and her encouragement of others to do the same—has fostered a penchant for the lies of

New Spirituality. A popular saying among those who call for a liberal, ecumenical, one-world church is that "doctrine divides, but the spirit unites." And they're right, of course. The truth of Biblical doctrine *does* divide. It distinguishes true converts from false ones. A preference for un-doctrine also unites the unsaved in the spirit of anti-Christ.

Nevertheless, Oprah continues to sweep people into her congregation of New Spirituality through ever more pervasive means. Helen Schucman's teachings found in Oprah Winfrey the greatest promoter any thinker could hope for. The resulting stakes are high. Make no mistake: Biblical Christianity and New Spirituality will both lead people to God. In a sense, millions of ways *do* lead there. It's just that only one leads to God as Savior. All the others lead to Him as righteous Judge.

PART 3

COMPLIMENTS OF THE APOSTATE CHURCH

5

JULIUS WELLHAUSEN
(1844-1918)

In 1878, a German theology professor and author of numerous books "discovered" that the Bible was a book of stories but not the divinely inspired Word of God. He proclaimed his new truth to countless Germans and taught that the Bible could not be trusted, but human reason could. Known as Higher Criticism or German rationalization, this was the contribution to Germany's cultural demise offered by Julius Wellhausen.

It was also his contribution to the success of Adolf Hitler. David Breese explains:

> The initial effect of German rationalization upon a Christian culture was on the schools, churches, and scholarship of Europe....Even so, religion still continued in Europe. There were still large churches, burning candles, beautiful choirs, lovely stained glass windows, congregations...all of that was still there....The Bible was only empty pages written by men who were now dead, rather than revelation of the living God. European Christianity was destroyed from within while still possessing the external form by which it had been known for centuries...the leaders quoted everything but the Bible and preached everything but the gospel, and reality was gone....It was because of religious liberalism that Europe lost its soul.[70]

European Christianity was compromised and changed into a false religion from within as German rationalization led people into an essentially humanistic religion. Germany was Hitler's for the taking because absolute truth and the Gospel of Jesus Christ had long since been betrayed, and thus the German people believed that "the end justifies the means." In return for regaining their national pride and financial abundance, the people would grant Hitler his dream of hope and change. The masses went along, but, as has happened throughout history, God had a remnant that remained true to Him and His Word. A remnant is the group of Christians who stand firm in their Biblical convictions, even in the face of persecution and ridicule. It is often met with hostility not only by the world but by members of the postmodern, dominant, false church. The remnant can also encounter ridicule from family members. Matthew 10:36 declares, "a man's enemies will be those of his own household."

History screams that ideas have consequences, that worldview matters. Most Germans, including German Christians, willingly traveled the road to Hitler's hell, largely because they had lost the courage of their convictions. They had sold out to paganism, pragmatism, and a new gospel that promised everything and required nothing. David Breese sums it up this way:

> It is obvious that Europe, despite its vaunted intellectualism, was unable to defend itself against the arguments and subversions of Nazism, Communism, fascism, the world of the occult, and other diseased ideas. External results in the life of any nation are ultimately caused by the presence or absence of a spiritual core made of divine life and spiritual blessings.[71]

Does this not sound like churches, seminaries, Christian colleges, and some of the best-selling Christian authors in America?

Wellhausen's liberal philosophy eventually jumped the ocean, became popular on the East Coast, and has spread throughout the United States. Many American Christians seem all too willing to go down a path that will surely lead to the destruction of a once great nation. Incredibly, many self-professing Christians are not just following but leading the way over the cliff. A domineering false church is rising, largely due to pansies in the pulpit. These false teachers have turned the grace of God into lewdness, and they deny the only Lord God and our Lord Jesus Christ (Jude 3-4).

But now, as in Germany before us, God calls His remnant to contend for the faith and oppose the false teachers that have crept in unnoticed by most. As described in Revelation 14:12, the remanant are those who remain faithful to the cause of Jesus Christ even during great apostasy: "Here is the patience of the saints; here are those who keep the commandments of God and the faith of Jesus." Romans 11:5 also declares, "Even so then, at this present time there is a remnant according to the election of grace." Because of God's grace—not because of our good works—God has seen fit to save us unto Himself.

You know we have a problem when the Russian newspaper *Pravda* sees better than we do how America got where it is today. An April 27, 2009, article declared:

> Then their faith in God was destroyed, until their churches, all tens of thousands of different "branches and denominations" were for the most part little more than Sunday circuses and their televangelists and top protestant mega preachers were more than happy to sell out their souls and flocks to be on the "winning" side of one pseudo Marxist politician or another. Their flocks may complain,

but when explained that they would be on the "winning" side, their flocks were ever so quick to reject Christ in hopes for earthly power. Even our Holy Orthodox churches are scandalously liberalized in America.

Notice the term used in *Pravda*: "pseudo Marxist." Cultural Marxism is what most Americans know only as "political correctness," but it is the worldview of today's professors, leading educators, members of the media, numerous self-professing Christians, and almost every politician. Political correctness is a speech code the cultural elite have forced on America to deny the existence of God and His authority in all areas of life. Words have meanings, and words that reflect absolute moral truth based on the character and nature of God are considered bigoted, intolerant, and politically incorrect.The Bible says, "Blessed is the nation whose God is the Lord," but Germans turned to serving man and worshiping man's intellect instead of the Almighty God. As a result, they accepted Adolf Hitler's lies. America's courts, legislatures, executive branches, and the Church at large have fallen in love with similar deceptions. We've rejected the law of the Divine—the bedrock of our Constitutional Republic—in favor of moral relativism, situational ethics, and political correctness. The consequence is that most Americans have surrendered their heritage, their birthright, and their unalienable rights in exchange for the promise of free college, free healthcare, and whatever carrot can be devised to seduce them into slavery.

Our founders tried to warn us that the only workable option was God's moral law. Otherwise, martial law would be required from fork-tongued politicians who promise all the rights without any of the responsibilities. In general, the Church in America, like the Church in Germany, has not stood in the way of this change but has often been a willing proponent. We failed to guard our churches and seminaries, and the radicals penetrated every institution of the middle class, every institution that made us free and great. America is dying from within because of the religious Trojan horse crafted by Julius Wellhausen.

6

SØREN KIERKEGAARD
(1813-1855)

Whatever is right for you is right for you.

Although many Americans don't know the name Søren Kierkegaard, they know all too well his essential philosophy of life. In the mid-1800s Kierkegaard, who claimed to be a Christian, denied any consistent morality. Known as existentialism, his ideas suddenly gained steam in America a hundred years later. The central tenet of existentialism is that there is no absolute truth. "Christians" practicing existentialism introduced what is called neo-orthodoxy. The American version of this movement grew popular in the 1960s and virtually took over in the 70s and 80s. Again, David Breese sees how it happened:

> A careful neglect of Calvary, the blood of Christ, divine forgiveness, original sin, and other great Christian themes. Salvation becomes experience-oriented, theology becomes contextual, and ultimate truth becomes contradictory. They announce that Jesus Christ came into the world to bring economic liberation to the oppressed masses of the earth.[72]

There is really nothing new under the sun, and I contend that this neo-orthodoxy laid the foundation for what we now call the Emergent Church. It consists of post-modern radicals who could be characterized just as Dr. Breese explained neo-orthodoxy.

Worldview Weekend speaker and columnist Jason Carlson was once part of the small group that founded the Emergent Church, but he recognized their drift to heresy and got out. Today, Jason writes and speaks with conviction against the worldview of the Emergent Church. He outlines the tenets of Emergent Church this way:

- A highly ambiguous handling of truth.

- A desire to be so inclusive and tolerant that there is virtually no sense of Biblical discernment in terms of recognizing and labeling false beliefs, practices, or lifestyles.

- A quasi-universalistic view of salvation.

- A lack of a proper appreciation for Biblical authority over and against personal experience or revelation.

- Openness to pagan religious practices like Hindu yoga and incorporating them into the Christian life and Christian worship.

- Openly questioning the relevance of key historical Biblical doctrines such as the Trinity.

- An uncritically open embrace of the Catholic and Orthodox churches.

- An unbridled cynicism towards conservative evangelicalism and fundamentalism.

- A reading of Scripture that is heavily prejudiced towards a social gospel understanding.

- Little or no talk of evangelism or saving lost souls.

- A salvation by osmosis mentality, where if you hang out with us long enough you're in.

I've known several Christian leaders who argue that the Emergent

Church movement is simply a fad that will fade away. But that is like saying Secular Humanism, the New Age Movement, postmodernism, Gnosticism, pagan spirituality, or existentialism is a fad. While it's true the term Emergent Church may go away, the philosophies, theologies, values, and ideas that make up the movement are not new and will not go away until Christ judges the world and sets up His Kingdom that will endure forever. As Isaiah 40:8 declares, "The grass withers and the flower fades, but the Word of our God shall stand forever."

EC pastors sell millions of books and DVDs, and leaders have convinced millions of youth that all roads lead to God, that the social gospel is our highest calling, socialism is the economic philosophy that Jesus Christ embraced, homosexuality is the new civil rights, abortion is a matter of choice, pagan spirituality and Christianity are compatible, and proclaiming absolute truth is intolerant. Emergents believe the problem with Christianity in America today is narrow-minded evangelicals who oppose their emerging worldview because of our commitment to the divinely inspired Word of God—which the Emergents say is a man-made product.

Deconstructionism in the Culture and in the Church

Kierkegaard's existentialism proclaimed that "truth is subjective," a worldview very much alive today. "Existentialism is a philosophical movement that became associated with the philosophy of Jean-Paul Sartre (who rejected the name as too confining) and whose roots extend to the works of Søren Kierkegaard and Martin Heidegger."[73]

Martin Heidegger's existentialism and that of Kierkegaard's differed in some ways as did the existentialism of Kierkegaard and Nietzsche, but there is room for both on the highway of postmodern thinking. "Kierkegaard and Nietzsche differed radically, most famously in their approach to religion (Christianity in particular). Kierkegaard was devout while Nietzsche was a blasphemous atheist. But so, too, twentieth-century existentialism would include both religious and atheistic philosophers."[74]

Of course, once a person or society rejects absolute truth, the consequences of the downward spiral into moral relativism become increasingly brutal. Hitler greatly admired Nietzsche and liked to have his picture taken staring at a bust of Nietzsche. Heidegger was a member of the Nazi Party and an influential German philosopher who became rector of the University of Freiburg. In a 1933 article in the Freiburg student newspaper, he publically endorsed Nazism: "The German people must choose its future, and this future is bound to the Führer."[75]

Nietzsche may not have agreed with all that Hitler did, and while I am certain Kierkegaard would have absolutely rejected Hitler's worldview, Kierkegaard's dismissal of a Biblical worldview and commitment to subjective truth nevertheless set up a cultural slippery slope. We find that such slopes are often greased by professors, philosophers, intellectuals, and liberal theologians to the benefit of a dictator or tyrannical central government.

The wide way of existentialism is described by Walter Kaufmann in his book, *Existentialism: From Dostoevsky to Sartre*:

Existentialism is foreshadowed most notably by nineteenth-century philosophers Søren Kierkegaard and Friedrich Nietzsche, though it had forerunners in earlier centuries…. Although there are some common tendencies amongst "existentialist" thinkers, there are major differences and disagreements among them (most notably the divide between atheistic existentialists like Sartre and theistic existentialists like Tillich); not all of them accept the validity of the term as applied to their own work.[76]

Hubert Dreyfus puts Kierkegaard's particular contribution to the movement in succinct perspective: "Contemporary Heideggerians regard Søren Kierkegaard as, by far, the greatest philosophical contributor to Heidegger's own existentialist concepts."[77]

Nietzsche and Kierkegaard believed a person could not know truth, that we should embrace the mysticism of the world and reject absolutes. We can see this influence of Kierkegaard and Nietzsche on both the American culture and many of America's churches, seminaries, and Christian colleges.

Postmodernism, which is closely tied to existentialism, was introduced through the English departments of many American colleges and universities. The study of literature offered a convenient vehicle to teach the idea that one can never know what an author means to convey. Any interpretation is subject to each individual reader. As David Noebel notes:

> Postmodernism's most effective methodological tool is known as Deconstructionism, which means (1) that words do not represent reality, and (2) that concepts expressed in sentences in any language are arbitrary. Some postmodernists go so far as to deconstruct humanity itself. Thus, along with the death of God, truth, and reason, humanity is also obliterated.[78]

One of the most basic and successful methods of teaching reading—phonetically–has already been tossed aside by "enlightened" educators. "Whole Language" is now the instruction of choice for most public schools. And what is whole language? "Rethinking

Whole-Language," an article in the January 1994 issue of *The Executive Educator*, explains:

> The most basic principle of Whole Language, according to many laudatory books on the subject, is that illiterate people can best learn to read and write in precisely the same way they learned to speak....To develop writing skills, children are encouraged to "invent" the spellings of words and the shapes of letters they need for their compositions. In short, Whole Language demands that instruction be directed, unsystematic, and non-intensive. The second fundamental principle of Whole Language is that individual learners should be "empowered" to decide what written materials mean.[79]

Later, the article makes the crucial point, "Language never can communicate exactly what the author intended to convey."

In teaching kids to read, Whole Language proponents utilize relativism or postmodernism, as the *Executive Educator* article reveals:

> The founders of Whole-Language call reading a guessing game; in other words, the meaning of a written passage is generally anyone's guess. Whole-Language teachers urge students to use sentence context cues to guess at the identity of the various words they read. Students accordingly substitute, add, and omit words in sentences they read—as they see fit....As a student is at liberty to "reconstruct" the meaning of a reading selection in his or her own personal, idiosyncratic terms, differing interpretations of the author's intended meaning are encouraged. Whole-Language advocates dismiss concerns that such reading habits leave

students unprepared to examine an author's ideas and expression critically.[80]

You can imagine the results. Parents of children who have experienced the Whole Language approach have wondered why Johnny can't read, spell, sound out words, construct a simple sentence, or analyze the meaning of a story. Now you know.

The February 13, 1995 issue of *Forbes* reported the failure of Whole Language:

> Parents dislike Whole Language because it downgrades accuracy—children are allowed to approximate meaning— and also because it seems not to work: San Diego schools, for instance, found that the percentage of first-graders scoring above the median on a reading test dropped by half after 18 months of Whole Language instruction. And a study of two schools by University of Georgia professor, Stephen Stahl, shows that children at the school using traditional instruction far outperformed those at the Whole-Language school. Yet Whole-Language is increasingly inescapable: Many states have actually mandated its use.[81]

Postmodernists seek to deconstruct Western society by denying absolute truth even in the disciplines of reading and writing. Postmodernists within the American Church deconstruct Christianity—as did Kierkegaard—by proclaiming that the Bible is not the absolute, inerrant, divinely inspired Word of God. And the Emergent Church is gaining ground in spreading this false idea.

In rejecting traditional morality and values, existentialists uphold what they call an ethic of authenticity. You will also hear this phrase from the Emergent Church as they reject traditional, orthodox Christianity for an "authentic" Christianity.

There are other symptoms of deconstructionism as well. Deconstructionists tell us America was founded by rich white men who wrote our founding documents in order to control the masses and implement an evil capitalist worldview by which to enrich themselves at the expense the majority. Many deconstructionists within the Church add that rich white men also founded the Church as we know it and defended certain Biblical theology and doctrines in order to control and manipulate the masses while commercializing the Church for their own personal gain.

In *The Emergent Church: Undefining Christianity,* Pastor Bob DeWaay describes the worldview of Church deconstructionists:

> Deconstruction assumes that like the producer in the *Truman Show*, authorities have conspired to make us believe that the limited and constricted version of our "world" is all there is....In the minds of some in the Emergent Church those motives are "command and control" and the spread of white, Euro-centric male-dominated Christianity over others. Hints of such motives are ferreted out in written material.[82]

DeWaay also explains how this affects a person's reading of Scripture:

> Literary deconstruction has serious ramifications for the interpretation of Scripture....One can see the perverse affects of this postmodern approach to texts in many Bible studies that are far too common nowadays. A portion of Scripture is read and the question, "What does that mean to

you?" is posed. So rather than seeking the singular meaning of the Biblical author, the group shares various feelings about how they respond to the text. The authority of Scripture becomes a meaningless concept because the Bible no longer binds anyone to one valid meaning....Deconstruction also doubts that language corresponds to reality.[83]

Deconstructionism undermines a Biblical worldview in the areas of law, family, science, education, economics, history, and social issues, and replaces it with "social justice," a masking term for socialism, communism, and Marxism. By deconstructing the influence of the Bible and Biblical doctrine, the neo-orthodox create a "neo-evangelicalism" that is all-inclusive, pluralistic, and committed to a social gospel which is actually nothing more than socialism.

You'll recall that Alice Bailey and her demon predicted the "new order" would come about through the educational establishment and the apostate Church. Clearly, both institutions promote the same humanistic, postmodern worldview. Now let's add another piece to this worldview puzzle.

How will this false-dominant church be blended into the coming one-world religion? The answer is simple. With its rejection of Biblical authority, the false-dominant church is left with only one option, and that is pagan spirituality. Again, this trend can be traced to a modernist group of German theologians in the tradition of Wellhausen.

German theologian Jurgen Moltmann in the 1960s created what he called "a theology of hope," based largely on the philosophy of Friedrich Hegel. What makes this so critical is that Hegel had a huge influence on the German people, which helped to lay the foundation for Adolf Hitler. Yet, how many Bible-believing Christians are aware of the fact that Hegel's philosophies, as promoted by Moltmann, are now being promoted by some of America's most well-known "Christian" authors, pastors, and conference speakers? Pastor DeWaay reveals that the heretical teachings of the Emergent Church find their source in Moltmann:

> The Hegelian synthesis denies absolutes, such as absolute truth or knowledge, and instead claims that everything evolves as incompatible ideas merge into something new and better. Two incompatible opposites, such as good and evil, combine and evolve into an improved third option that surpasses both. Moltmann applied Hegel's synthesis to theology and eschatology, deciding that because incompatibilities were evolving into new and better things, God could not possibly allow the world to end in judgment. Instead of judgment, Moltmann set aside scripture to declare that the entire world and all of creation was heading toward paradise and progressively leaving evil behind.[84]

The Emergent Church, like many liberal, mainstream churches, has rejected the idea of the return of Jesus Christ and His judgment of the world. Instead they see it as their responsibility to build God's kingdom through utopian ideals of the redistribution of wealth, the social gospel, disarmament, and a world community committed to social justice and pluralism.

Involuntary Consensus

The Hegelian world uses a sinister methodology to insure its infiltration into groups—churches, schools, city councils, or wherever it is used. Called the Delphi Technique, I have personally witnessed its effect on a large group of parents at a school board meeting. It's not a pretty sight if you recognize what is happening. You realize that the group is being played as stupid—easily controlled and manipulated. The sad fact is, I saw it work well on an unsuspecting group of parents.

The Delphi Technique is a psychological manipulation to achieve acceptance of a desired, predetermined outcome by a group of "change agents" or "facilitators." Often the process starts in a meeting with the entire group. The ground rules are laid as to how participants will be asked for ideas and opinions. The facilitators also explain how to work as a group, be open-minded, and not dominate the discussion. Then the large group is divided into smaller, more controllable groups with each led by a pre-selected facilitator who manipulates the group to accept the predetermined conclusion, goal, plan, agenda, or outcome. The goal in the small group setting is to implement the Hegelian dialectic process of having two opposing ideas conflict so the group can be moved to the desired third option. Once everyone has gotten there, the group is praised for being "productive" and achieving consensus.

Those who oppose the predetermined outcome—the third option—are controlled by being told they are not showing proper respect for their fellow group participants by listening, dialoguing, and understanding the views of others. If the dissenter continues to object, he or she is made to feel like an extremist or that the person is monopolizing the discussion. I have even heard facilitators put a dissenter "in his place" by pointing out that going against a group of educators, business people, elected officials, and citizens who have invested many hours to bring the community plan together is arrogant.

The truth is, the "plan"—whether an educational, environmental, or sustainable development agenda—was not written by the public. While local people are made to think they helped draft the "local" plan, other "local" plans examined side by side from all across the country look almost identical. The reason is the lead organization behind it has already given local "change agents" a template for how their plan should read.

The federal government did this during the implementation of the federal education agenda, Goals 2000, during the Clinton Administration. The federal Department of Education sent an education plan to every state department of education and told them what their final state education plan must look like if they hoped to receive federal funds.

Thus all the parent, teacher and school board meetings held to develop local plans were simply a show to make parents and taxpayers believe they had written their local education plans to become part of the larger state education plan. However, state education plans throughout the nation were almost identical, including the outcomes children were expected to achieve. This is why outcomes such as "productive group participant," "understands positive health habits," understands diversity," "self-directed leader," "involved citizen," among others, appeared in almost every state education plan submitted to the federal government.

The *Education Reporter* warns parents and taxpayers about the Delphi Technique:

> The facilitator begins by working the crowd to establish a good-guy-bad-guy scenario. Anyone disagreeing with the facilitator must be made to appear as the bad guy, with the facilitator appearing as the good guy. To accomplish this, the facilitator seeks out those who disagree and makes them look foolish, inept, or aggressive, which sends a clear message to the rest of the audience that, if they don't want the same

treatment, they must keep quiet. When the opposition has been identified and alienated, the facilitator becomes the good guy—a friend—and the agenda and direction of the meeting are established without the audience ever realizing what has happened.

Next, the attendees are broken up into smaller groups of seven or eight people. Each group has its own facilitator. The group facilitators steer participants to discuss preset issues, employing the same tactics as the lead facilitator.

Participants are encouraged to put their ideas and disagreements on paper, with the results to be compiled later. Who does the compiling? If you ask participants, you typically hear: "Those running the meeting compiled the results." Oh-h! The next question is: "How do you know that what you wrote on your sheet of paper was incorporated into the final outcome?" The typical answer is: "Well, I've wondered about that, because what I wrote doesn't seem to be reflected. I guess my views were in the minority."

That is the crux of the situation. If 50 people write down their ideas individually, to be compiled later into a final outcome, no one knows what anyone else has written. That the final outcome of such a meeting reflects anyone's input at all is highly questionable, and the same holds true when the facilitator records the group's comments on paper. But participants in these types of meetings usually don't question the process.[85]

Believe or not, this process is even used in some churches and church denominational meetings.

So how do you confront the Delphi Technique? First, you need to let your conservative friends know about it so they can recognize it in action. Second, when in a meeting where it is being used, never lose your temper or get angry or hostile. Stay calm, professional, and ask questions instead of making statements. If the "facilitator" will not answer your question after several minutes of spinning, then simply ask your question again and keep politely asking it until it is answered or until the group sees the facilitator is hiding something.

The Delphi Technique is dishonest and based on lying to people. No surprise here, that once again we see every issue is a spiritual issue. Delphi is used in the spiritual battle by those who embrace evil and are committed to an anti-Biblical worldview. Satan himself is the father of lies, so we should not be shocked that those who do his bidding likewise use lies and deceit.

An Emerging Utopia

For several years, I have read and listened as major Emergent Church leaders embrace socialism and even Marxism. Thanks to the research of Bob DeWaay, I discovered how Moltmann came to Hegel's way of thinking. He studied a neo-Marxist by the name of Ernst Bloch, a devotee of George Hegel. DeWaay traces this connection:

> To most of us the idea that an atheist philosophy and Christian theology could both be valid is a contradiction. It certainly is to me. But what binds Moltmann and Bloch together is the philosophy of George Wilhelm Friedrich Hegel. The idea that contradictions, through the process of history, synthesize into a better future can be found in Moltmann's theology....Moltmann, by the way, uses the

term "emerging" often in his book as characterizing that which synthesizes from contradictions.[86]

One prominent Emergent leader, Pastor Jim Wallis, is a committed neo-Marxist who runs an organization called Sojourners. Wallis is also reportedly President Obama's spiritual advisor. According to Frontpagemag.com:

> The most notable of [Obama's] spiritual advisors today is his friend of many years, Rev. Jim Wallis. Rev. Wallis admits that he and Obama have "been talking faith and politics for a long time."[87]

In an article for my website, David Noebel explained why all Americans should be concerned about Wallis and his worldview agenda:

> First, Jim Wallis has had relationships with the communist Committee in Solidarity with the People of El Salvador (CISPES).

> Second, his "Witness for Peace" was an attempt to defend the Nicaraguan Sandinistas! Wallis, together with the Rev. Jeremiah Wright (Obama's former pastor of 20 years) "rallied support for the communist Nicaraguan regime and protested actions by the United States which supported the anti-communist Contra rebels" (*Family World News*, February 2009, p. 7).

> Third, Wallis and his Sojourners community of fellow-travelers believe Fidel Castro's Cuba, Hugo Chavez's Venezuela, Daniel Ortega's Nicaragua, and the other revolutionary forces "restructuring socialist societies" are the Communist

paradises the United States needs to emulate in order to establish "social justice." Writing in the November 1983 issue of *Sojourners*, Jacob Laksin notes, "Jim Wallis and Jim Rice drafted what would become the charter of leftist activists committed to the proliferation of Communist revolutions in Central America" (Laksin, "Sojourners: History, Activities and Agendas" in Discoverthenetworks.org, 2005).

The ugly truth is Wallis wishes to see the destruction of the United States as a nation and in its place "a radical nonconformist community" patterned after the progressive, socialist commune he established in Washington, D.C., in 1971 (Laksin, *Ibid*.).[88]

Noebel also outlines Wallis's impact on American evangelicalism:

> For years, Wallis has been in the forefront of the "evangelical" left and has been fêted at numerous evangelical colleges and seminaries. That seems to be the "in" thing right now! His publication *Sojourners* is piled high on these campuses for the reading pleasure of the naïve and foolish.

> Unbeknown to these colleges and seminaries is Wallis' Red background. He was the president of the radical Students for a Democratic Society (SDS) while at Michigan State University. The SDS was the youth arm of the League for Industrial Democracy—the American counterpart to the British Fabian Society founded to promote socialism throughout the West. One of the League's mentors for years was Norman Thomas, who argued that "the American people will never knowingly adopt socialism, but under the

name of liberalism, they will adopt every fragment of the socialist program until one day America will be a socialist nation without ever knowing how it happened" (Google, Norman Thomas quotes). Another prominent League mentor was John Dewey, a signatory of the atheistic, socialistic 1933 *Humanist Manifesto*. The SDS actually merits a chapter in Richard J. Ellis's work *The Dark Side of the Left: Illiberal Egalitarianism in America* published by the University of Kansas Press.

Are the Emergent Church leaders trying to create heaven on earth, a communist utopia? Bob DeWaay says indeed they are:

> As we shall see with the Emergent Church's theology, which is derived from Moltmann and others, a serious problem exists. The problem is that this hope is based on the idea that history is not headed toward cataclysmic judgment in which those who do not believe the Christian gospel are judged and lost for eternity but is headed toward the kingdom of God on earth with universal participation.[89]

Like many cults, false religions, and liberal mainstream churches, the Emergent Church, which has hijacked scores of once solid Bible-teaching churches, proclaims there will be universal participation in the kingdom of God. Universalism is exactly how we will see the false-dominant church in America blend with pagan spirituality.

DeWaay concludes his book by revealing that the Emergent philosophy is based primarily on the writings of Ken Wilber, an Emergent Church leader who, in turn, draws on the philosophy of Jurgen Moltmann and George Hegel:

We began by showing theologian Jurgen Moltmann to be the source of Emergent's eschatology. We will conclude by showing that Ken Wilber is the source of Emergent philosophy. Both their theology and philosophy contend that everyone must be headed toward a future utopia with God. Wilber describes a philosophical framework for the idea of "emergence" by describing an upward spiral, whereby everything is evolving into something better. Wilber is rather a mystical Darwin, promoting a "holistic" concept of evolution in which things are not only evolving physically but also spiritually. This spiritual evolution is the basis of "spiral dynamics," where the world evolves into a physical/spiritual paradise over time. What is most important to learn from this chapter is that Wilber's philosophy also has its roots in Hegel, the same philosopher from whom Moltmann drew his "theology of hope." In some sense, Hegel's belief in a synthesis where opposites like good and evil combine to form a better, third option is the root of both Wilber and Moltmann. These men, Moltmann and Wilber, and their belief in a world where everything gets better and ends in utopia, are the sources of the Emergent church. Really, there is nothing unique or special about the Emergent church. Emergent simply is what a church would look like if it rejected the scriptures and looked to Hegel as its prophet.[90]

Many within the Emergent Church are committed to being mystic Christians, which fosters their merger with pagan spirituality. Yoga, transcendental meditation, and walking the occultic "labyrinth" are increasingly popular practices in the Emergent, to say nothing of mainline, churches.

Even the secular media is taking notice. In the September 14, 2008 *Tennessean* newspaper (Nashville), the article "Meditation Goes Mainstream," reported:

> Joe Scott, 61, got hooked on meditation in yoga classes about 16 years ago. At the time, he was an opinionated workaholic who had a need to always be right. "I used to be a very angry, intense person," says Scott, who works in the quality assurance department at HCA. Thirty minutes of meditation first thing in the morning completely changed his life, says Scott, who also meditates with members of Self Realization Fellowship in Berry Hill, which incorporates readings from the Bible and the Hindu holy book in their Sunday services. For Carolyn Goddard of Nashville, she was drawn to centering prayer, a form of contemplative prayer, to deepen her connection with God. A Colorado monk revived this ancient ritual of "resting in God" in the 1970s as an alternative for Christians lured to transcendental meditation. Today, there are about 25 centering prayer groups that meet throughout Tennessee, with 13 in the Nashville area.
>
> Participants choose a sacred word to help them clear their mind of other thoughts. "You don't have to go outside the Christian tradition to find methods of meditation. It's part of our heritage, as well," says Goddard, who attends Christ the King Catholic Church and is an instructor with Contemplative Outreach of Middle Tennessee.
>
> "I was constantly driven and racing against deadlines," says Cassandra Finch of her former life as a Nashville television news reporter. "I didn't have time to chew my food or breathe

deeply. I kept it up for a while, but it was taking a toll on my body." She quit her job and cared full time for her father, who was dying from Parkinson's disease. After his death, she threw herself into meditation. "I discovered my true self through meditation," the 42-year-old says. "Often because we are so busy, we don't make time for self-discovery." A Christian who attends an interdenominational church and considers herself nondenominational, Finch has also been attending a Buddhist center to meditate.[91]

How all this could have started becomes clearer when you consider a *Christianity Today* November 2004 interview with Emergent pastor Rob Bell. It describes Bell's own journey:

The Bells started questioning their assumptions about the Bible itself—"discovering the Bible as a human product," as Rob puts it, rather than the product of divine fiat.[92]

And in one of his sermons posted on the internet, Bell connects the dots all the way to yoga:

[In Yoga] it's not how flexible you are, it's not whether you can do the poses, it's not how much you can bend yourself, it's can you keep your breath through whatever you are doing. And the Yoga Masters say this is how it is when you follow Jesus and surrender to God. If it's your breath being consistent, it's your connection with God regardless of the pose you find yourself in. That's integrating the divine into the daily.[93]

The ramifications of Emergent thinking affects even core doctrines such as salvation. How does Emergent pastor and best-selling author

Rob Bell define salvation? According to *Christianity Today* editor Andy Crouch, Bell describes salvation like this:

> Bell derides the "score card" approach to sin. Rather, he maintains that once you've converted, you're loved, you're accepted, you're forgiven, you're in. But he leaves the joy of this personal salvation with the message that being "in" means understanding poverty as the Savior did.[94]

(Silly me—I guess I took the Bible too literally when Jesus said being saved requires faith and repentance rather than having a proper knowledge of poverty.)

In an interview with *Relevant* magazine:

> Bell proposes some great ideas on living life the way God intended. He suggests what it might look like to bring heaven to earth, that heaven is a "now" thing, not a "someday" thing. He suggests viewing salvation as more than just a legal transaction. He suggests that maybe this whole thing is not just about us believing in God, but about God believing in us.[95]

While Bell is one of the strongest voices in the Emergent fraternity, he is by no means the only influential one. The 2007 National Pastors Conference promoted Emergent pastor Doug Pagitt's wife's Christian yoga classes:

> Join Shelly Pagitt for a time of prayer, stretching, and meditative reflection as you begin your day at the NPC. If possible, please bring a mat with you for the stretching time.

Emergents also find various ways to merge other disparate ideas. EC leaders Brian McLaren, Leonard Sweet, and Jerry Haselmayer declare in their book, *A is for Abductive—The Language of the Emergent Church*:

> Emergence theory incorporates into an intellectual and spiritual framework ancient and recent arguments for intelligent design (focusing on diversity and complexity) with certain aspects of evolution (natural selection and the fossil record). In this view, part of the goodness of Creation is an inherent potential to generate new possibilities so that more and more goodness can emerge.[96]

In his exposition of the Emergent Church heresy, Bob DeWaay comments:

> This is not a Biblical explanation of Creation followed by the Fall that explains both good and evil, but philosophical speculation after the manner of Ken Wilber. Goodness does not emerge; as Jesus said: "only God is good." But if you have a panentheistic or pantheistic system, God is part of the process, thus goodness can be deemed to "emerge."[97]

Rob Bell echoes McLaren, Sweet, and Haselmayer in *Velvet Elvis: Rethinking the Christian Faith*:

> For a mind-blowing introduction to emergence theory and divine creativity, set aside three months and read Ken Wilber's *A Brief History of Everything*[98]…Not only are we connected with creation but creation is going to move forward. It can't help it. It is loaded with energy. It's going to grow and produce and change and morph.[99]

DeWaay puts this view in perspective:

> Bell's description of the fall also is inadequate and more in
> line with panentheism. Rather than rebelling against God
> and transgressing His moral laws, Adam and Eve made a
> mess of the balance of things by falling out of harmony.[100]

At almost every turn, the Emergent mindset seems to be more
about us than about God. Bell explains our "personal power":

> God has given us power and potential and ability. God
> has given this power to us so we will use it well. We have
> choices about how we are going to use our power. The
> choices the first people made were so toxic because they
> were placed in the middle of a complex web of interaction
> and relationships with the world God had made. When they
> sinned, their actions threw off the balance of everything. *It
> is all one*, and when one part starts to splinter and fracture,
> the whole thing starts to crumble.[101] [Emphasis mine]

Alice Bailey and her demon said that the apostate Church would
be one of three institutions to lay the groundwork for the "new order,"
and the false-dominant church is laying the foundation for the great
rebellion prior to the coming and acceptance of the anti-Christ.

Lutheran scholar Frederic Bauer suggests where this all will lead:

> To a phase of western or world civilization that is innately
> religious but hostile to Christianity…or worse, a dominant
> but false church that brings all of its forces to bear against
> the truth of God's Word. [102]

This new church will, itself, become a persecutor of the remnant Bible-
believing Christians.

As long ago as 1898, Abraham Kuyper warned in the Stone Lectures at Princeton:

> Do not forget that the fundamental contrast has always been, is still and always will be until the end: Christianity and Paganism, the idols and the living God.

The rise of the Emergent Church brings to mind the words of the late Vance Havner regarding Satan's shrewdest strategy for getting his way in the world:

> The devil is not fighting religion; he is too smart for that. He is producing a counterfeit Christianity so much like the real one that good Christians are afraid to speak out against it.

The Emergent Church is really proclaiming Liberation Theology which is a mixture of liberal Christianity with Marxism.

Christians who have not "studied to show themselves approved" unto God and who are not committed to the Word of God, are at great risk for spiritual deception. And for those caught unaware, there will be an Emergent Church eager to welcome them. Kierkegaard would be smiling.

7

FRIEDRICH NIETZSCHE
(1844-1900)

"**P**ostmodernism" is a term so widely known these days that you might think it is simply a word that's become attached to a vast but vague set of contemporary ideas. But its origin is actually very traceable—right to the subject of this chapter. Friedrich Nietzsche, along with Michael Foucault, founded postmodern thought.

Postmodernism argues that truth and reality are created by man and not by God, that something is true "if it works for you." Truth is neither absolute nor binding over the entire globe, but merely situational and subjective. What's more, postmodernism is a dominant worldview in America today, largely because Friedrich Nietzsche is one of the most widely read authors on college campuses.

Nietzsche is best known for declaring "God is dead," but few know that he went on to say that not only is God dead but that "we have killed him." Nietzsche hated Christians. "Christianity has been the most calamitous kind of arrogance yet,"[103] wrote Nietzsche, and, "I call Christianity the one great curse, the one enormous and innermost perversion, the one moral blemish of mankind....I regard Christianity as the most seductive lie that has yet existed."[104] Nietzsche believed that Christianity made his fellow Germans weak, so he described himself as "The Anti-Christian Friedrich Nietzsche" or sometimes as just "The Antichrist" (also the title of one of his books—*Antichrist*).

So exactly why should Americans be concerned that Nietzsche's worldview is so popular? Let's start with his connection to Adolf Hitler.

Hitler was so enamored with postmodern thought that he visited

Nietzsche's museum to have his picture taken while staring at a bust of Nietzsche. Hitler declared, "Creation is not yet at an end. Man is becoming God….Man is God in the making."[105] And: "Do you really believe the masses will be Christian again? Nonsense! Never again. That tale is finished. No one will listen to it again."[106] He even passed the writings of Nietzsche along to his Italian counterpart, Benito Mussolini.

Hitler combined the survival-of-the-fittest worldview of Darwinian evolution with the "superman" concept of Friedrich Nietzsche and developed eugenics—the systematic elimination of individuals the State deemed to be the weakest links, the racially defective, and subhuman. Both Hitler and Nietzsche championed the eradication of guilt from the human conscience. Nietzsche elevated Darwin's survival of the fittest to the next level and proclaimed "that all life simply is will to power."[107] Whatever it takes, one should purpose to be a ruler, a master over the less desirable. Thus, in promoting his master-and-slave morality, Nietzsche, in his book *Beyond Good and Evil*, proclaimed the need to look beyond Christian definitions of good and evil to whatever it takes to gain power, part of which means endorsing cruelty when necessary to accomplish the goal. Nietzsche explained:

> We should reconsider cruelty and open our eyes…. Almost everything we call "higher culture" is based on the spiritualization of cruelty, on its becoming more profound: this is my proposition.[108]

"Master morality" means the strong rule over the weak. Nietzsche includes among the weak Christians with their compassion for the sick, aged, and vulnerable. Anyone who held to a fixed morality, he maintained, would make themselves slaves—and deservedly so.

Nietzsche thoroughly rejected the Christian worldview, its absolute truth, standards of justice and injustice, righteous and unrighteous. For Nietzsche, the only standard that matters is what puts and keeps someone in power. He believed "…that the demand of one morality for all is detrimental for the higher men…."[109] Notice that this is why today's cultural elite have set one standard for the masses and a completely different one for themselves.

In contrast to Nietzsche, why do Christians have such a strong commitment to the unborn, the sick, the disabled, and the elderly? Because we understand—as did America's Founding Fathers—that man is created in the image of God, and therefore every person has a right to life, liberty, and property. With the loss of the Christian worldview and the ever-increasing acceptance of Nietzsche's postmodernism, Christians and conservatives in America are at risk of being portrayed as enemies of the State—intolerant, out of touch, bigoted, extremist, or even domestic terrorists—all because their Biblical worldview conflicts with that of "the higher man," the cultural elite, or the master morality.

America's sick, handicapped, and elderly will also be at risk as man's intrinsic, God-given worth is replaced by a value measured only by what a person can do for the State. Once national healthcare is a reality and the majority of Americans come to see it as a right, only the threat of its removal will be needed to convince younger, postmodern generations that the lifeboat is too full, and it is time to toss the weak overboard.

I've predicted this for many years, and there are those who once believed I was talking foolishness. But Bloomberg news reported that in the early 2009 stimulus bill a new bureaucracy was created:

The National Coordinator of Health Information Technology

will monitor treatments to make sure your doctor is doing what the federal government deems appropriate and cost effective. The goal is to reduce costs and "guide" your doctor's decisions.

Medicare now pays for treatments deemed safe and effective. The stimulus bill would change that and apply a cost-effective standard set by the Federal Council. The Federal Council is modeled after a U.K board....This board approves or rejects treatments using a formula that divides the cost of treatment by the number of years the patient is likely to benefit. Treatments for young patients are more often approved than treatments for diseases that affect the elderly...."[110]

When this was added to the stimulus bill, U.S. Representative Dr. Charles Boustany Jr. (R., La.), who is also a heart surgeon, predicted that this would lead to "denying seniors and the disabled lifesaving care."[111]

On June 19, 2009, Betsy McCaughey, writing in *The Wall Street Journal* on the proposed healthcare bill of President Obama and U.S. Senator Ted Kennedy, declared:

While the house bill being pushed by the president reduces access to such cures and specialists, it ensures that seniors are counseled on end-of-life options, including refusing nutrition where state law allows it (pp.425-446). In Oregon, the state is denying some cancer patients care that could extend their lives and is offering them physician-assisted suicide instead.

The harshest misconception underlying the legislation is that living longer burdens society. Medicare data proves this is untrue. A patient who dies at 67 spends three times as much on health care at the end of life as a patient who lives to 90, according to Dr. Herbert Pardes, CEO of New York Presbyterian Medical Center.[112]

The Obama/Kennedy healthcare bill proposed cutting $500 billion dollars out of Medicare spending over ten years. And just how would that be achieved? It would be accomplished by denying care to elderly and disabled people—active euthanasia through the rationing of healthcare.

Dr. Ezekiel Emanuel, brother of White House Chief of Staff Rahm Emanuel, was appointed to two important government boards to assist in drafting and passing socialized medicine. Emanuel declared that healthcare should be saved for people the State deems are productive human resources and that it should not be given to those:

> ...who are irreversibly prevented from being or becoming participating citizens....An obvious example is not guaranteeing health services to patients with dementia.[113]

In a sad irony, many retired teachers will experience first-hand the inhumane consequences of the worldview they inculcated into their pupils through situational ethics courses. Americans will not likely escape the consequences of their duplicity or apathy. Whether parents, grandparents, uncles, aunts, elected officials, pastors, Sunday school teachers, journalists, butchers, bakers, or candlestick makers, they will find that Aristotle was correct when he said, "All who have meditated on the art of governing mankind have been convinced that the fate of empires depends on the education of youth."

Hitler understood that through socialized medicine he could further his goal of eugenics and active euthanasia. America is rushing toward government-sponsored, national healthcare at the time I am writing this book in September 2009. Hitler, too, expanded and centralized Germany's healthcare system, as Melchior Palyi explained:

> The ill-famed Dr. Ley, boss of the Nazi labor front, did not fail to see that the social insurance system could be used for Nazi politics as a means of popular demagoguery, as a bastion of bureaucratic power [and] as an instrument of regimentation.[114]

In another, perhaps more satisfying irony, Nietzsche went insane just a few months after writing his book *The Antichrist* and spent the next ten years out of his mind. The godless worldview of Nietzsche will lead individuals into self-inflicted insanity and despair and will cause nations to be ruled by madmen.

I fear the insane consequences of assimilating the worldview of Friedrich Nietzsche are coming soon to a country (very) near you.

PART 4

COURTESY OF THE EDUCATIONAL ESTABLISHMENT

8

JOHN DEWEY
(1859-1952)

O ne would hope that the person dubbed "the father of modern American education" would craft a system to preserve the high ideals of Jefferson, Washington, Adams, and other Founding Fathers in the hearts and minds of American children for generations to come. One would hope that. But one would be grievously disappointed.

The most influential education guru in American history was a Fabian Socialist, signer of the *Humanist Manifesto I*, founding member of the American Civil Liberties Union, and president of the League for Industrial Democracy—the American counterpart of the British Fabian Society.[115] As all of the above, John Dewey has wounded America to a degree that few other people have.

Dewey worked hard to refine his socialist pedigree. In 1928, he traveled to Russia to help implement the Karl Marx system of education and then returned to teach at Columbia University as the head of that university's department of education. Dewey supported the upstart Socialist Society in America while also being an honorary president of the National Education Association. He promoted Secular Humanism in his book, *A Common Faith*, and was the leading force behind bringing a group of German intellectuals from the "Frankfurt School" to America.

The Frankfurt School (Chapter 9) promulgated the worldview of Friedrich Nietzsche, and with the arrival of the school's "Pilgrims" in 1933, they set about to implement cultural Marxism in every area of American life under the disguise of political correctness. (I use the term "Pilgrims" to reflect the irony that our original Thanksgiving Pilgrims attempted a form of socialism that resulted in the deaths of so many of their community that they abandoned the idea in deference to pure capitalism after their first year in the New World.) The Frankfurt goal was the destruction of Christianity, the creation of chaos, and then the transition from cultural Marxism to traditional Marxism, i.e., socialism.

One of Dewey's most famous quotations sums up his philosophy, now prevalent in America's educational system and curriculum:

> There is no God and no soul. Hence, there are no needs for the props of traditional religion. With dogma and creed excluded, then immutable (unchangeable) truth is also dead and buried. There is no room for fixed, natural law, or permanent moral absolutes.[116]

Can you say, "Postmodernism"? The cross-pollination of ideas shared by the influencers in this book is obvious.

John Dewey, Karl Marx, Aldous Huxley, B. F. Skinner, and Benjamin Bloom were interested in a student's academic achievement only if it would in some way benefit the State. Before a student's cognitive knowledge could be used to its full potential, the student's attitudes, values, feelings, and beliefs must conform to that of the State. In his book, *My Pedagogic Creed*, John Dewey explains:

> I believe the true center of correlation on the school subjects is not science, nor literature, nor history, nor geography, but the child's social activities. . . . I believe that the school is primarily a social institution. . . . The teacher's business is simply to determine, on the basis of the larger experience

and riper wisdom, how the discipline of life shall come to the child. . . . All these questions of the grading of the child and his promotion should be determined by reference to the same standard. Examinations are of use only so far as they test the child's fitness for social life.

John Dewey and company were interested only in knowing where to place students in the social and economic hierarchy. Tests were to determine a child's area of worldview weakness. Once the weakness is determined, the child's attitudes, values, feelings, and emotions that don't fit the State's worldview are changed via the curriculum—as Bloom said, to change the student's fixed beliefs. Those who do not conform are punished by being channeled into dead-end, low-income jobs.

What the Deweyites (i.e., liberals) wanted, they have successfully accomplished with the help of legislators and liberal judges. As Dr. David Noebel explains in *Clergy in the Classroom*, humanists have ushered Christianity out the front door and the humanism of John Dewey in through the back door. So if you like where America's education system is headed, you can thank John Dewey.

9

THE FRANKFURT SCHOOL
(1864-1993)

As the chapter title and 129-year span of its life suggests—and unlike the rest of the influencers discussed in this book—the Frankfurt School is not a single individual. It is, however, comprised of a specific group of people whose philosophies merged into one overarching worldview which still burdens us today.

The writings of the Frankfurt School faculty and their disciples are abundant, and their goal can be summed up as the eradication of Christianity. Here is a list of the most influential faculty members, the last of whom died as the twentieth century approached its close:

Walter Benjamin	(1892-1940)
Franz Oppenheimer	(1864-1943)
Franz L. Neumann	(1900-1954)
Siegfried Kracauer	(1889-1966)
Theodor W. Adorno	(1903-1969)
Friedrich Pollock	(1894-1970)
Max Horkheimer	(1895-1973)
Herbert Marcuse	(1898-1979)
Erich Fromm	(1900-1980)
Karl A. Wittfogel	(1896-1988)
Alfred Sohn-Rethel	(1899-1990)
Leo Löwenthal	(1900-1993)

After growing similar thought patterns along separate tracks, a group of German intellectuals in 1923 started what has become known as the Frankfurt School. Dr. William Lind explains, though, that the originally intended name of the institute had to be eliminated in order to conceal from the public its true agenda:

> The intended name for the Frankfurt School was the Institute for Marxism. The Institute's father and funder, Felix Weil, wrote in 1971 that he "wanted the Institute to become known, and perhaps famous, due to its contributions to Marxism as a scientific discipline…." Beginning a tradition Political Correctness still carries on, Weil and others decided that they could operate more effectively if they concealed their Marxism; hence, on reflection, they chose the neutral-sounding name, the Institute for Social Research (Insitut für Sozialforschung).[117]

As we have seen, many of the 21 we look at are in some way connected back to each other. In the case of the Frankfurt School, we find that it was directly connected to Karl Marx, Sigmund Freud, George Hegel, and Friedrich Nietzsche. Dr. Lind writes:

> The Frankfurt School blended Marx with Freud, and later influences (some Fascist as well as Marxist) added linguistics to create "Critical Theory" and "deconstruction." These in turn greatly influenced education theory, and through institutions of higher education gave birth to what we now call "Political Correctness." The lineage is clear, and it is traceable right back to Karl Marx.[118]

According to the online *Britannica Concise Encyclopedia*:

> Intellectually, the school is most indebted to the writings of G. W. F. Hegel and the Young Hegelians…Karl Marx… Friedrich Nietzsche, and Sigmund Freud.

Frankfurt—American Style

In 1933, when the Nazis came to power in Germany, many members of the Frankfurt School conveniently found refuge in America at the invitation of John Dewey, who was on staff at Columbia University in New York. Dewey saw the opportunity to place these Marxists at leading colleges and universities around the country. He and his cohorts specifically targeted education and media as the means by which to inculcate their worldview into American culture.

Dewey had help from Edward R. Murrow in disbursing the Frankfurt School refugees. In 1934, Murrow became the Assistant Secretary of the Emergency Committee in Aid of Displaced German Scholars. Earlier, in 1932, Murrow had gained experience as the Assistant Director of the Institute of International Education, which was established through a grant from the Carnegie Endowment for International Peace, and he was well positioned for his later assignment. Murrow had been hired by Stephen Duggan, the director of IIE, who advised the Soviet government on issues related to their workers' colleges. Duggan was a crusader for the Communist agenda.

Murrow also joined the American Russian Institute, which had been founded with the help of John Dewey. The Institute sponsored lectures from individuals such as Anna Louise Strong, a well-known journalist who wrote books defending the Soviet system. Eventually, Murrow went to work for CBS, where he became the famed newscaster.

Murrow is perhaps best known for using his broadcasts to destroy U.S. Senator Joseph McCarthy, who was investigating the infiltration of Communists into education, media, and Hollywood. McCarthy had personality quirks that made him an easy target for marginalization, yet many experts now admit that McCarthy was correct in his view that Communists had infiltrated American education and the media. Murrow knew it to be true because he helped settle many of these Marxists in America, dropping them into influential positions. Murrow was out to destroy McCarthy before he could uncover the anti-American agenda of Dewey, Murrow, and their friends.[119]

One of the men Murrow brought to America from the Frankfurt School was Herbert Marcuse. The phrase "make love, not war" shouted during the counter-culture revolution of the 1960s was coined by Marcuse. The 1960s student rebels implemented strategies laid out by Marcuse in writings greatly influenced by Italian Communist Antonio Gramsci. They were inspired by Marcuse's Cultural Revolution proclamations such as:

> One can rightfully speak of a cultural revolution, since the protest is directed toward the whole cultural establishment; including the morality of existing society….[T]here is one thing we can say with complete assurance. The traditional idea of revolution and the traditional strategy of revolution has ended. These ideas are old-fashioned….[W]hat we must undertake is a type of diffuse and dispersed disintegration of the system."

Having achieved much that they set out to accomplish, many of the anti-American, flag burning, pot-smoking, pagan spiritualists of the counter cultural revolution are now college and university presidents, professors—and American textbook authors.

The author of the *Communist Manifesto,* Karl Marx called for a powerful central government, a punitive progressive income tax system, the merging of education with industrial production, the elimination of a free press, and much more. Thanks to many from the Frankfurt School, Marxism is alive and well in America, but this destructive worldview has been hidden from most Americans under terms that mask the reality of what is going on.

A New School of Language

When you hear "political correctness," what comes to mind? You probably think of PC words such as tolerance, diversity, multicultural-ism, and feminism. But what hides behind these terms?

Tolerance means that one person never expresses a judgment about someone else's ideas, beliefs, and values from a worldview of absolute truth. Tolerance demands that you not only accept another worldview, but that you value it—unless, of course, the worldview is Biblical Christianity. Tolerance is very intolerant of Bible-minded Christians.

Diversity or sensitivity training is about the normalization of the homosexual lifestyle.

Multiculturalism is not the study of many cultures but the criticism of Western Culture and its founding worldview of Christianity. Multiculturalism also desires to destroy patriotism.

Feminism is not about equal rights for women but about the destruction of a patriarchal society in favor of a matriarchal society. The goal of feminism is the destruction of the family by eliminating the husband and father as provider, protector, and principled leader of his home. Think of fathers like Charles Ingalls from *Little House on the Prairie*, John Walton from *The Waltons*, and Ward Cleaver from *Leave It to Beaver*. Each of these television programs presented what American society at one time expected and loved about the patriarch of the family. A father who did not shape and encourage his children to embrace and live out a Christian worldview through character and life choices was looked down on by society as being a dead-beat, a drunkard, a reprobate, or at least slothful.

Our society no longer has these high expectations, nor do we shun men who are not principled and present fathers. In today's television programs, the father is often not even in the picture, and, if he is, he certainly is not a leader trying to disciple his children in truth and right living. Often Dad is the whipping boy of the show, the stooge the children treat with disrespect or even contempt.

Feminism has accomplished its goals—the destruction of the American family through the destruction of the father and the resulting rise of the welfare state.

Political correctness is all about creating chaos by destroying the American family, replacing the role of the father with the role of the State, normalizing sexual perversion, and ridiculing traditional morals and virtues that stem from Christianity. The PC crowd uses this chaos to justify more government.

Political correctness, in general, is a masking term for cultural Marxism. An all-powerful and intrusive government that robs you of your freedoms is the ultimate goal of what you may know only as political correctness.

Although people regularly laugh about political correctness as if it is some kind of joke, losing your freedom of religion, freedom of speech, property rights, and parental authority is no laughing matter. Thought control is not funny, and many Christians already have been prosecuted under hate-crime laws for sharing the gospel and for publicly speaking out against homosexuality.

Alvin Schmidt describes another agenda behind political correctness when he writes:

The idea behind political correctness is the notion of

oppression. Women, blacks, Hispanics, and homosexuals are viewed as oppressed minorities due to the influence of Christianity and capitalism, bringing about the need for a revolution to overthrow their white, male, heterosexual, Euro-centric oppressors.[120]

And in his research paper "Political Correctness in Higher Education," T. Kenneth Cribb, Jr., outlines the problem among us:

> Perhaps the most disturbing aspect of the Politically Correct assault on the curriculum is that it has occurred at many of America's elite universities. Take, for example, the case of Stanford University, an institution that has long played a leadership role in American higher education. Stanford eliminated its long-standing Western civilization requirement in 1988 and replaced it with a multicultural program known as "Cultures, Ideas, and Values." Under this new program, freshmen at Stanford can just as easily study Marxist revolutionaries in Central America as they can Plato, Shakespeare or Newton. Because elite institutions such as Stanford set an example for the rest of American higher education, other universities eagerly adopt these devastating assaults on the curriculum. This "trickle-down" effect will have a long-lasting impact on the way future generations of Americans will be educated. One distinguished scholar recently lamented that "higher education is increasingly about acquiring attitudes and opinions that one puts on like a uniform."

Nearly 30 years ago, *U. S. News and World Report* noted that there were, even then, 10,000 Marxist professors teaching at America's colleges and universities.[121] That number today is much higher.

Tracking the growing trend, Georgie Anne Geyer, writing in a 1989 *Denver Post* article, reported that "the percentage of Marxist faculty numbers can range from an estimated 90 percent in some Midwestern universities."[122] Herbert London, writing in "Marxism Thriving on American Campuses," states in 1987 that:

> The strides made by Marxism at American universities in the last two decades are breathtaking....Every discipline has been affected by its preachment and almost every faculty now counts among its members a resident Marxist scholar.[123]

The way to combat political correctness is to expose it for the Marxism it really is. Equally important in defeating this anti-Christian, anti-American worldview is to not comply with its mandates. Call homosexuality what it is—sin. Expose feminism as being anti-family and anti-father. Show tolerance as moral relativism and intolerance toward those who don't conform to the politically correct dictates of tolerance. Reveal sensitivity training as an attempt to destroy freedom of speech and freedom of religion. Point out to your family and friends the impact that cultural Marxism has had and is having on American faith, families, and freedoms.

William Lind accurately describes how we have allowed this worldview to destroy America by failing to follow and teach a Biblical worldview to the next generation:

> In the United States of America our traditional Western, Judeo-Christian culture is collapsing. It is not collapsing because it failed. On the contrary, it has given us the freest and most prosperous society in human history. Rather, it is collapsing because we are abandoning it.[124]

By eradicating Christianity not only will the family fall and the Church become impotent, but capitalism and the free enterprise system that were birthed out of the Protestant Reformation will be destroyed.

The ultimate goal of cultural Marxism is to destroy Christianity in all areas of American life: law, science, economics, history, family, social issues, and education. The elimination of the Christian worldview from the culture will create the desired chaos. Once chaos has reached a fevered pitch, the public will cry out for government to solve the problem and people will accept socialism—and the outright rejection of the U.S. Constitution and our other founding documents. Then the cultural Marxists will have accomplished the transition from cultural Marxism to traditional Marxism—socialism—the economic philosophy of Karl Marx.

So, unless you desire to live in a country where the middle class has been eliminated—most will live in a socialistically enforced poverty of equals while a few remain wealthy—and where we are under the tyrannical thumb of a small group of cultural elitists who control every aspect of your life, then you had better speak up. Nothing is more powerful than the truth, nothing scares the elitists more than their worldview and agenda being exposed for what it really seeks to accomplish, and nothing would be more likely to make the faculty of the Frankfurt School turn over in their graves.

10

BETTY FRIEDAN
(1921-2006)

I f "tolerance" is the core value of political correctness, feminism is its most cherished cause, and the implications of our cultural devotion to feminism are monstrous. Feminism is not about equal rights for women but about the feminization of the American male, an ideology that is anti-family and anti-father—and virtually guaranteed to bring about the wholesale destruction of the American family.

The Frankfurt School staff knew that "Even a partial breakdown of parental authority in the family might tend to increase the readiness of a coming generation to accept social change."[125]

Dr. Gerald L. Atkinson, CDR, USN (Ret.), describes the attack on the American male through the propaganda of the Frankfurt School:

> The Frankfurt school studied the "authoritarian personality" which became synonymous with the male, the patriarchal head of the American family. A modern utopia would be constructed by these idealistic intellectuals by "turning Western civilization" upside down. This utopia would be a product of their imagination, a product not susceptible to criticism on the basis of the examination of evidence. This "revolution" would be accomplished by fomenting a very quiet, subtle and slowly spreading "cultural Marxism" which would apply to culture the principles of Karl Marx bolstered by the modern psychological tools of Sigmund Freud. Thus, "cultural Marxism" became a marriage of Marx

and Freud aimed at producing a "quiet" revolution in the United States of America. This quiet revolution has occurred in America over the past 30 years. While America slept! "The Authoritarian personality," studied by the Frankfurt School in the 1940s and 1950s in America, prepared the way for the subsequent warfare against the masculine gender promoted by Herbert Marcuse and his band of social revolutionaries under the guise of "women's liberation" and the New Left movement in the 1960s. The evidence that psychological techniques for changing personality is intended to mean emasculation of the American male is provided by Abraham Maslow, founder of Third Force Humanist Psychology and a promoter of the psychotherapeutic classroom, who wrote that, "...the next step in personal evolution is a transcendence of both masculinity and femininity to general humanness." The Marxist revolutionaries knew exactly what they wanted to do and how to do it. They have succeeded in accomplishing much of their agenda.[126]

Among the champions of feminism have been Gloria Steinem, Elizabeth Cady Stanton, and, most assuredly, Betty Friedan. Friedan was also co-founder of the National Organization of Women (NOW), one of America's most radical feminist organizations.

Out of Touch

Friedan's book, *The Feminine Mystique,* could be described as the Feminist Manifesto. Released in 1963, it was a major force behind the 1970s explosion of the radical feminist agenda. Like many of the people in this book, Friedan was an atheist who embraced Marxism. As Benjamin Wicker points out:

Before she published *The Feminine Mystique*, Friedan had spent years in Marxist-inspired agitation on behalf of mistreated lower-class workers—and the abstractness of her analysis is fundamentally Marxist.[127] She had been a Marxist since her college days at Smith in the late 1930s and early 1940s. In the years after, she belonged to, worked for, or wrote positively about a string of leftist organizations and publications—like the Popular Front, the Federated Press, UE News, Congress of American Women, Jewish Life—that had significant Communist membership or Soviet sympathies. Knowing that the call to revolution in *The Feminine Mystique* would be damaged if it was associated with the call to revolution in the *Communist Manifesto*, she hid her radical past.[128]

Benjamin Wicker believes Friedan's book is much longer than needed to convey her belief that "women who are only wives and mothers are secretly or openly miserable because they cannot venture outside the home and cheerfully maximize their potential as human beings in meaningful work, just as men do."[129] In critiquing her obsessive work, he asks an obvious and telling question: What makes Friedan think it is a guaranteed fact that men just can't wait to get up each morning to drive a truck, build a house, pave a road, paint a house, manage a store, fill out people's tax forms, write their wills, or work in a laboratory? Countless men rise dutifully each morning to do jobs they really don't enjoy and, in many cases, jobs they detest. But they do it for love of their families and for the purpose of providing for them. Many men long for the day they can retire and leave behind a job they long since stopped enjoying.

Just because Friedan doesn't want to acknowledge the self-sacrifice of such men does not mean they're not fulfilling a God-given role of protector, defender, and provider. Most women (my wife among them) are happy to have husbands who willingly and eagerly embrace this role so they can pursue their God-given role and passion of being wives and mothers.

When Melissa and I were married, we agreed it would be ideal to be married five years before having children. This would allow my wife to finish college and spend a few years pursuing her interest in being a hospital-based medical social worker in a large American city. Long before our five-year anniversary, though, my sweet wife—still in her mid-twenties—was eager to quit her job and have a family. A year after our first child was born, she returned to the hospital two days a week so we could keep our health insurance. (I've always been self-employed, and as those of you who are self-employed know, purchasing your own health insurance is rather expensive.) So, I cared for our son while she was at work. This lasted only a few months because *I* was not a good *mother*. While I aspire to be the best father in history, that's a different calling. Motherhood wasn't in my bones.

Melissa did not aim to be a working mother but a full-time, stay-at-home mom, despite Freidan's claim that women would rather be in the workforce than at home raising children and caring for their husbands. But what about that expensive health insurance that we would have to purchase if she quit? It was up to me. I had to take on more speaking engagements, which meant I had to do one of the things I hate more than anything in the world: I had to travel on airplanes. "Fear of flying" doesn't even begin to describe my attitude. It also meant leaving my wife and child behind more weekends when everyone else was having fun together, going to ball games and social functions. But Friedan would not understand that men often do what they don't want to do in order to provide for their families. To her, men live the dream life while women are stuck at home living a nightmare. I'm not sure what planet Friedan was on when she did her research.

Now after almost 20 years of marriage, my wife often thanks me for working hard enough to allow her to do what God has called her to do—and what she loves. She's thankful to have the choice to be a full-time mother, unlike some families where the husband is passive, unmotivated, and content to stay in a low-paying job that forces the wife back into the work force. In some cases, the wife makes a large salary while her boy-husband enjoys the toys and entertainment her money affords him, despite her real desire to be a full-time mother.

Thanks largely to Betty Friedan, feminists claim women do not like strong-willed men who have convictions and the courage of those convictions to lead their families. Reality suggests otherwise, however. Most women want exactly that.

One time, early in our marriage, my wife and I disagreed vehemently over something she wanted to do. I explained that I did not think traveling by herself several hundred miles to see her family and attend a family birthday party was safe. I added that, in a few weekends, I would be off the road and free to drive her. This went over like a ton of bricks, but I didn't back down. I love my wife and view her protection and security as one of my responsibilities. After a few hours' reflection, my wife agreed that I was correct, and she thanked me for not giving in to her. When I asked what she meant by that, she said, "One of the qualities that attracted me to you in the first place was that you are not a panty waist I could push around."

Now don't misunderstand me: I know I'm not always right. She's a smart woman and has her share of "right" times. What my story means is that wives want a husband who will lovingly lead, defend, protect, and provide for them—and not back down on vital issues of principle and protection. One consequence of the fall of man in the Garden of Eden was that the woman will challenge the man for leadership (Genesis 3:16). This does not mean that women really want it—even if they think they do—because if a woman takes the leadership position, she ultimately doesn't find it satisfying and usually ends up discontent with her man. What women really want in a marriage is the protection, provision, and servant leadership of a loving husband.

Whether people admit it or not, it is evident that there are God-ordained roles for men and for women—each complementing the other. This is what makes a great marriage great—the different and sometimes opposite but complementary gifts, abilities, insight, and interests of each spouse.

Spreading Bad Choices Around

The feminist agenda is simply that Friedan and friends do not want women to find fulfillment in being wives and mothers. My friend and staunch conservative Phyllis Schlafly explains that feminists are really dictators who want to leave women no choice but to follow a humanist, politically correct lifestyle:

> The feminists whine endlessly using their favorite word "choice" in matters of abortion, but they reject choice in gender roles. The Big Mama of feminist studies, Simone de Beauvoir, said, "We don't believe that any woman should have this choice. No woman should be authorized to stay at home to raise her children . . . precisely because if there is such a choice, too many women will make that one."

The feminists have carried on a long-running campaign to make husbands and fathers unnecessary and irrelevant. Most divorces are initiated by women, and more women than men request same-sex marriage licenses in Massachusetts so that, with two affirmative-action jobs plus in vitro fertilization, they can create a "family" without husbands or fathers.

Despite the false messages of the colleges and the media, most American women are smart enough to reject the label feminist, and only 20 percent of mothers say they want full-time work in the labor force. I suggest that women suffering from unhappiness should look into how women are treated in the rest of the world, and then maybe American women would realize they are the most fortunate people on earth.[130]

Schlafly, a Washington University Law School-educated lawyer, also describes in an article, "The Feminists Continue Their War Against Men," how feminist leaders feel about motherhood:

In 1970, Gloria Steinem told the Senate Judiciary Committee it is a "myth" to believe "that children must have full-time mothers. . . . The truth is that most American children seem to be suffering from too much mother, and too little father. Part of the program of Women's Liberation is a return of fathers to their children. If laws permit women equal work and pay opportunities, men will then be relieved of their role as sole breadwinner."

Articulating vintage feminism in the 1974 Harvard Educational Review, Hillary Clinton wrote disparagingly about wives who are in "a dependency relationship" which, she said, is akin to "slavery and the Indian reservation system." [131]

Schafly expands on this feminist notion of marriage and motherhood as slavery:

Then-ACLU attorney Ruth Bader Ginsburg wrote in her 1977 book *Sex Bias in the U.S. Code* that "all legislation based on the breadwinning-husband, dependent-homemaking-wife pattern" must be eliminated "to reflect the equality principle" because "a scheme built upon the breadwinning husband [and] dependent homemaking wife concept inevitably treats the woman's efforts or aspirations in the economic sector as less important than the man's." Feminist literature is filled with putdowns of the role of housewife and mother. This ideology led directly to feminist insistence that the taxpayers provide (in Ginsburg's words) "a comprehensive program of government-supported child care."[132]

The icon of college women's studies courses, Simone de Beauvoir, opined that "marriage is an obscene bourgeois institution." Easy divorce became a primary goal of the feminist liberation movement. Robin Morgan, one of the founders of *Ms. Magazine*, said that marriage is "a slavery-like practice" and that "we can't destroy the inequities between men and women until we destroy marriage." Three-fourths of divorces are now unilaterally initiated by wives without any requirement to allege that the cast-off husband committed any fault.[133]

In a political bait-and-switch that would make Karl Marx proud, once feminists achieved one of their goals of easy divorce, they did a complete turnaround on the importance of mothers raising their children. Again, Schlafly reports:

> As divorces became easy to get, the feminists suddenly did a total about-face in their demand that fathers share equally in child care. Upon divorce, mothers demand total legal and physical custody and control of their children, arguing that only a mother is capable of providing their proper care and upbringing, and a father's only function is to provide a paycheck. Gone are the demands that the father change diapers or tend to a sick child. Feminists want the father out of sight except maybe for a few hours a month of visitation at her discretion. [134]

Suddenly, the ex-husband is targeted as a totally essential breadwinner, and the ex-wife is eager to proclaim her dependency on him. Feminists assert that, after divorce, child care should be almost solely the mother's job, dependency is desirable, and providing financial support should be almost solely the father's job. What's behind this feminist reversal about motherhood? As Freud famously asked, "What does a woman want?" The explanation appears to be the maxim, Follow the money. Beginning in the mid-1980s, the feminists used their political clout to get Congress to pass draconian post-divorce support-enforcement laws that use the full power of government to give the divorced mother cash income proportional to the percentage of custody time she persuades the court to award, but unrelated to what she spends for the children or to her willingness to allow the father to see his children. Since the father typically has higher income than the mother, giving near-total custody to the mother enables the states to maximize transfer payments and thereby collect bigger cash bonuses from the federal government. When fathers appeal to family courts for equal time with their children, they are opposed by a large industry of lawyers, psychologists, custody evaluators, domestic-violence agitators, and government bureaucrats who make their living out of denying fathers their fundamental rights.[135]

In another article, "Understanding Feminists and Their Fantasies," Schalfy describes what today's feminists are up to with their millions of dollars:

• The National Organization for Women (NOW) lobbies for feminist and pro-abortion legislation, organizes protest rallies, initiates lawsuits, and always backs Democratic Party candidates and proposals. The NOW agenda supports all abortion rights including partial-birth abortion, gay and lesbian rights, worldwide legalization of prostitution, and unrestricted access to pornography in libraries. According to the guide, "NOW revels in attacking Christianity and traditional values, conservative ideas and men."

• The League of Women Voters abandoned its former credibility and became a federally funded lobby to expand the size of government so that it can accommodate expensive feminist programs. The League, which spent $4,620,246 in 2000, supports gun control, abortion access, universal health care, more environmental regulation, and increased power for the United Nations.

• The feminists use the YWCA to teach radical feminism to the next generation. The Girl Scouts went feminist after they took Betty Friedan on their board; they dropped "loyalty" from the oath, began a condom-friendly sex-ed program, and made belief in God optional.

• Most of the activist feminist organizations have 501(c)(3) sister groups with interlocking directors. They pursue the same agenda, including government-funded daycare, paid entitlements for family leave, unrestricted access to abortion, comparable worth, lesbian rights, affirmative action, universal health insurance, and anti-male implementation of Title IX. As the *Guide* states, "It's hard to see where NOW political lobbying ends and NOW Foundation education activity begins."[136]

The feminist agenda has made great headway. According to an article in the *Deseret News* posted July 4, 2009:

A recent survey by *Babytalk Magazine* found that many married ladies feel it might sometimes be easier to go the mommy route alone. Of these women, 76 percent liked the idea of not fighting with a partner over the best way to raise a child. Other pros to being single were not having the chore of keeping up a healthy marriage (69 percent), and not dealing with in-laws (30 percent). And single moms agree. Almost two-thirds of the unmarried moms felt that it would be harder to be a parent if there was a man in the house. Of the single ladies, 55 percent said that they feel relieved to not have to worry about working on a marriage too, and 38 percent said they feel freer to follow their own dreams.[137]

The bottom line is that feminism has been a tool of the humanists to destroy the family. Leading humanist Paul Kurtz said, "Humanism and feminism are inextricably interwoven."[138] Humanists and Communists have sought the destruction of the American family because they know that, for America, the family has been the instrument for passing on Christian values and a Biblical worldview—the source and foundation of our freedoms and Constitutional Republic.

Founding Father Jedediah Morse reveals the deep connection between our form of government and the Biblical institution of marriage:

> To the kindly influence of Christianity we owe that degree of civil freedom, and political and social happiness which mankind now enjoys….Whenever the pillars of Christianity shall be overthrown, our present republican form of government, and all blessings which flow from them must fall with them.[139]

With the help of the feminist movement in the late 1960s, as I've pointed out, divorce laws were liberalized. The resulting drastic increase in divorce began to break down the strength, respect, and permanency of the marriage covenant in the civil arena. No-fault divorce made separation fast and allowed couples to split up without admitting fault or accepting responsibility.

In the 1972 *Stanley v. Illinois* case, the U.S. Supreme Court ruled that custody laws that distinguished between married and unmarried fathers was "constitutionally repugnant." Fathers would be given the same rights and face no consequences for fathering a child outside of the covenant and contract of marriage. Thus, one of the main reasons for entering into the religious and civil covenant and contract of marriage was removed. Those who were married and those who were not married were given the same respect and legal standing.

Divorce and illegitimacy has undercut the institution of the family. What was to be the incubator for creating and nurturing self-governed offspring who would safeguard the republic is now relatively in shambles.

The postmodern belief that "freedom" is the right to do whatever works for you and makes you happy has actually destroyed our country. Our Founders saw freedom and the right to life, liberty, and property as a by-product of fulfilling one's responsibility to Divine laws. They did not believe in rights without responsibility.

To be fair, we cannot lay all of this trouble at the feet of the humanists or Betty Friedan and her radical gang of gals. The American people must own some of the responsibility. With the rise of divorce and illegitimacy among heterosexuals—even within the church—we have weakened the commitment that marriage is about producing offspring. To that extent, we have played right into the hands of the homosexual community that uses the high divorce and illegitimacy rate to say marriage has nothing to do with children and so homosexual marriages should be legally recognized.

Friedan and the cultural Marxists have used the civil law, courts, and the media to destroy the family, fathers, and make possible the rise of the welfare-nanny state. The break-up of the family has been the leading cause of generational poverty and the permanent underclass. This chaos is used by the radical left to convince the American people that we need more government and more intrusion into the family. Read on to see how little the Church is doing to stop it.

11

WILLIAM JAMES
(1842-1910)

Remember I promised you in the introduction of this book that I was going to rip away the prettily packaged lies and reveal the hidden truth so you can protect yourself and your children and grandchildren from the anti-God agenda? Well, pay close attention, because our opposition is marketing "community youth service" in such a way that even many Christian parents will think it a good thing and end up giving their children over to the State to be indoctrinated with a worldview contrary to a Biblical one and opposed to the values of their homes.

As we've discussed, word manipulation is standard fare among those who foist social transformation on people who would otherwise utterly reject their advances. This manipulation of words reached perhaps its greatest heights in the work of a late-nineteenth-century Harvard University professor of physiology, psychology, philosophy, and anatomy. As his professorial titles suggest, William James wrote on a wide variety of topics that still influence American culture. One essay, however, is of such overwhelming influence that it deserves to be the central focus of the story of the William James legacy.

"The Moral Equivalent of War" lays the groundwork for the insidious concept of organized national service. Much lauded in its Great Depression-era incarnation as FDR's Civilian Conservation Corps, "national service" is a principle for undermining competing social institutions—including the family and Church. Before digging into the specifics of James's writings, though, you'll want to know where his thinking comes from. And much of it will sound familiar.

Spiritual, Pragmatic—and Deceived

Remember Alice Bailey and the Tibetan? James wrote of sitting with a medium named Leonora Piper as she would go into a trance. After being with Piper on several occasions, James wrote that he believed "she has supernatural powers."[140] Predictably, spiritualism became one of James's topics of writing.

In *What Pragmatism Means* James reveals his commitment to a belief system based on the idea that truth is relative and situational. To him, truth is that which proves *useful* to the individual. And in *The Meaning of Truth* James writes, "…the pragmatist always means 'true for him who experiences the workings'."

Against this background, William James conceived "The Moral Equivalent of War." Christopher Chantrill, writing for *American Thinker*, reveals that the war James envisions is against the ideas and values that make up our worldview and all that our ideals reinforce—families, parental authority, private property ownership, and all God-given liberties—so they might be surrendered to the state:

> Ever since philosopher William James invented the concept of the "moral equivalent of war" our liberal friends have wanted to regard almost all conflicts between nations as misunderstandings that ought to be resolved by negotiation and diplomacy.

> Writing in 1906 William James worried about what to do if pacific socialists like him ever got to stop war and militarism. He wanted to conscript young men to battle social evils, not foreign foes.

What James neglects to realize is that when you conduct domestic politics using the moral equivalent of war metaphor you do not just conduct a War on Poverty or a war for Energy Independence. Wars are not conducted against an idea but against people. You end up making your fellow Americans into a hated enemy. You declare, in other words, a "moral equivalent of *civil* war" against people who disagree with your call to fight wars on poverty or who fail to grasp the Inconvenient Truth of the need to save the planet.

Our liberal friends are quick to worry about the dangers of "nationalism" and are ultra-sensitive about anyone questioning their patriotism. But they have no problem in questioning the motives of anyone that dares to oppose their militant campaigns for universal health care and gay marriage.[141]

President Carter referenced Williams James in an address to the nation on April 18, 1977, when talking about what he deemed an energy crisis:

Then I declared the energy effort to be the moral equivalent of war, a phrase coined by William James and suggested to me by Admiral Hyman Rickover.

Author David Boaz reveals that President Clinton was likewise influenced by James:

In 1988 the Democratic Leadership Council proposed an almost-compulsory national service program, which would entail "sacrifice" and "self-denial" and revive "the American tradition of civic obligation." Nowhere in the DLC paper on the subject was there any mention of the American tradition of individual rights. The proposal was described as a way to "broaden the political base of support for new public initiatives that otherwise would not be possible in the current era of budgetary restraint." In other words, it would be a way for government to hand out benefits by enlisting cheap, quasi-conscript labor. The last chapter of the paper was, inevitably, titled "The Moral Equivalent of War."

Then, in 1993 DLC chairman Bill Clinton became president and proposed his own national service plan, and darned if it didn't sound a lot like "the moral equivalent of war." He wanted to "rekindle the excitement of being Americans" and "bring together men and women of every age and race and lift up our nation's spirit" to "attack the problems of our time." Eventually, perhaps, every young person would be enlisted. For the moment, however, the president envisioned "an army of 100,000 young people. . . to serve here at home . . . to serve our country."[142]

Picking up the James theme, radical lesbian Margaret Mead viewed mandatory national service as a way to wage her war on the family and, more specifically, on marriage, as described by Doug Bandow in his article, "National Service: The Enduring Panacea":

In 1967, for instance, anthropologist Margaret Mead argued that universal service "would make it possible to assay the defects and the potentialities of every young American on the threshold of adulthood." The experience would have some unique impacts on women, she observed, since it "would replace for girls, even more than for boys, marriage as the route away from the parental home."[143]

In the ideal society she outlined, people would be homosexual when young, then switch to heterosexuality during the breeding years, then switch back.[144] Among the direct descendents of this notion of "universal service" are the Peace Corps and AmeriCorps.

Syndicated columnist Thomas Sowell expands on the anti-family, totalitarian goals of "community service":

> Professor Dewey, the godfather of "progressive" education, said it all, 70 years ago: "The great task of the school," he said "is to counteract and transform" the beliefs and values that the child brings from "the home and the Church."
>
> That is what the educational trends of the past two generations have been all about, whether the specifics were called "values clarification," "community service," "outcome-based education" or a thousand other pretty names. Once you look behind these glittering labels to the specific things that are said and done, the agenda becomes clear: Undermining the values and beliefs that parents have taught their children and replacing them with politically correct notions from the counter-culture.
>
> "Community service" is not about the community or about service. It is about using children for ideological agendas and using those agendas to insinuate the welfare-state view of the world on impressionable young minds.
>
> This is not about educating children. It is about using

children as cannon fodder in ideological battles and as guinea pigs for experiments. Children are also being used by the schools as entering wedges through which to invade the family itself and insinuate and impose the agenda of the anointed on the unwary.

Intruding into family privacy is the first step toward intruding into the family itself. Most parents have no idea how much personal family information is being collected from school children and fed into computer networks.

These networks can integrate medical, psychological, academic and social information from numerous sources to create an electronic dossier on each individual child—a dossier that can follow that child on through school and out into the adult world. Assurances about the confidentiality of such information are absolutely meaningless.

Even when the forms filled out by children or their families have no name on them, the forms themselves are pre-coded with identifying numbers that tell a computer whose form it is. Assurances that this information will never be given to any "unauthorized" individuals or organizations likewise mean nothing, because anyone they give it to will be called "authorized." It is one of the signs of our dumbed-down education that we are so easily taken in by people who play with words.[145]

Please understand that I am in favor of students being involved in ministry work. What I am opposed to is children being manipulated by the State to believe that the solution to poverty is redistribution of wealth and bigger government. I am also opposed to the attempt by humanists to create humanists out of our children and put them to work in government and humanist non-profits as their "agents of change."

Do not think for one minute that when students are taken into the inner city through a government community service program that they are going to be told that the reason many are homeless and suffer from extreme poverty is that ideas have consequences, that your worldview matters, and that sin has consequences. They will not be told that many of those living in poverty are unemployed and homeless because of illegal drug use and alcoholism. They will not be informed that the reason for generational poverty is rejection of God's standards and principles for sexuality.

The Bottom Line on Poverty

Psychiatrist Theodore Dalrymple, author of *Life at the Bottom: The Worldview That Makes the Underclass*, has spent years treating the poor in a slum hospital and prison in England. So just why is the condition of the underclass so oppressive? While Dr. Dalrymple's is not a Christian book, per se, he nevertheless arrives at the astounding conclusion that a misshapen worldview accounts for the plight of today's poor in Western countries:

> Patterns of behavior emerge—in the case of the underclass, almost entirely self-destructive ones. Day after day I hear of the same violence, the same neglect and abuse of children, the same broken relationships, the same victimization by crime, the same nihilism, the same dumb despair. If everyone is a unique individual, how do patterns such as this emerge?[146]

Dalrymple later answers his own question:

Welfare states have existed for substantial periods of time without the development of a modern underclass: an added ingredient is obviously necessary. This ingredient is to be found in the realm of ideas. Human behavior cannot be explained without reference to the meaning and intentions people give their acts and omissions; and everyone has a *Weltanschauung*, a worldview, whether he knows it or not. It is the ideas my patients have that fascinate—and, to be honest, appall—me: for they are the source of their misery.[147]

While there are a few true *victims* of poverty—children who suffer from their parents' bad choices (which all too many choose to repeat as adults)—the blame for poverty does not lie solely with those who make lifestyle decisions that lead to their status. Dr. Dalrymple asserts that the great facilitators of chronic indigence are liberal humanists and their worldview of "if it feels good do it": "most of the social pathology exhibited by the underclass has its origin in ideas that have filtered down from the intelligentsia."[148]

"Intelligentsia" is a synonym for the liberal, humanistic elite—educrats and social engineers. Propagation of the liberal, morally relativistic worldview has raged through the underclass most ruinously in the form of glaring sexual promiscuity. Remember what the humanist manifestos have to say about moral relativism, sex, and the pursuit of pleasure:

- *Humanist Manifesto I*: "…the quest for the good life is still the central task for mankind."

- *Humanist Manifesto II*: "We strive for the good life, here and now…neither do we wish to prohibit, by law or social sanction, sexual behavior between consenting adults. The many varieties of sexual exploration should not in themselves be considered 'evil'."

Dalrymple articulates the agonizing consequences reaped by the underclass because they embraced, however unwittingly, the worldview of humanists:

> Of nothing is this more true than the system of sexual relations that now prevails in the underclass, with the result that 70 percent of the births in my hospital are now illegitimate (a figure that would approach 100 percent if it were not for the presence in the area of a large number of immigrants from the Indian subcontinent).

> …The connection between this loosening and the misery of my patients is so obvious that it requires considerable intellectual sophistication (and dishonesty) to be able to deny it.

> The climate of moral, cultural, and intellectual relativism— a relativism that began as a mere fashionable plaything for intellectuals—has been successfully communicated to those least able to resist its devastating practical effects.[149]

Do ideas have consequences? Does your worldview matter? Liberals can enjoy the distinct satisfaction of seeing just how radically their "forward-thinking" ideas affect the world in which people live day by day.

I know from firsthand experience that Dr. Dalrymple's

observations are true. For five years, on the first Tuesday of each month, I traveled to the Union Gospel Mission in St. Paul, Minnesota, to speak and lead music for the nightly service before the mission's free supper. Except for the few mentally ill regulars left on the streets after the death of a parent who had cared for them, I met individuals that chose to be homeless. In fact, most have a home and parents, or even a wife and children, but they opt to live awash in drugs, alcohol, serial sexual encounters—in short, a life of no responsibility. Many men who showed up for the service (attendance required if they wanted the free meal) admitted that they choose to live as they do.

The mission chaplain told me numerous personal stories of habitual attendees who could return to their families if they would simply take responsibility for their actions, clean themselves up, get a job, and stop abusing drugs and alcohol. There were men, he explained, who at one time had been judges, doctors, attorneys, or businessmen who destroyed their lives through drugs and booze.

To be sure, Jesus promised that the poor will "always be with us." A key reason is man's sinful nature, and one all-too-common consequence of sin is poverty. But this will not be what your children will learn from the humanistic, State-sponsored youth service program that is specifically designed to manipulate their emotions, ignore the facts, and brainwash them into the belief that the solution is government-sponsored socialism and a rejection of free-market capitalism.

The humanist's love affair with socialism is deeply entrenched in the humanist mindset that denies anything like the all-too-evident tendency of people to do the wrong thing (the Christian worldview calls this "the sin nature of man"). In its Pollyanna fashion, socialism assumes the best about us, denying the reality that people routinely succumb to greed, selfishness, bitterness, dishonesty, and anger, that they are often awash in pride or envy, and that virtually anyone will be lazy if given the opportunity. All of these sinful human qualities undermine a system of economics based on equal work, equal income, and shared benefits. What "sin nature" requires is a system where overcoming these tendencies is in everyone's own best interests— namely, capitalism.

In his book *The Battle for Truth,* David Noebel explains the twisted thinking that makes people think socialism is viable:

> If one *denies* the inherent fallen nature of man, socialism becomes the most attractive economic system for creating a heaven on earth. For the Humanist, *there is no original sin* to stand in the way of creating a helping, sharing, co-operative community on earth. Therefore, the economic system best suited to promote the ethics of Humanism and amend the evils of capitalism is socialism.[150] [emphasis mine]

There are even some non-liberals who mistakenly allow that the Bible endorses socialism. While many people described in the New Testament Church shared their goods and livelihood, the key distinction is that theirs was a voluntary system, not a compulsory governmental system of sharing. Whenever government tries to equalize salaries or standards of living and education, productivity takes a nosedive.

The free enterprise system is the most equitable economic system available to our sin-prone humanity. Whereas socialism puts a few powerful elite in control of whether or not you have a job and how much money you make (for the benefit of the all-powerful State), capitalism offers to the individual control over his or her own earthly future, destiny, and wealth.

After understanding the miserable failure of humanistic socialism, the Christian worldview is the hope that is left—and a genuine hope it is. Christians must reach out to the underclass, seek to change hearts, renew minds, and reframe their deformed worldview by showing them their need for Christ.

Parents and grandparents, if your children or grandchildren are taken captive by the brainchild of William James, you cannot say I didn't warn you. You can see from the excerpts below from "The Moral Equivalent of War" just how expert James is at his "play with words" that captivate the unaware:

> All these beliefs of mine put me firmly into the anti-military party. But I do not believe that peace either ought to be or will be permanent on this globe, unless the states, pacifically organized, preserve some of the old elements of army-discipline. A permanently successful peace-economy cannot be a simple pleasure-economy. In the more or less socialistic future toward which mankind seems drifting we must still subject ourselves collectively to those severities which answer to our real position upon this only partly hospitable globe. We must make new energies and hardihoods continue the manliness to which the military mind so faithfully clings. Martial virtues must be the enduring cement; intrepidity, contempt of softness, surrender of private interest, obedience to command, must still remain the rock upon which states are built....

In other words, James hates the military but thinks his liberal friends can learn from the techniques armies use to build a cohesive group that rejects individual interests in deference to collective interests. He is also building the case for collectivism, the abandonment of individual property rights, and the redistribution of wealth. James continues:

> If now—and this is my idea—there were, instead of military conscription, a conscription of the whole youthful population to form for a certain number of years a part of the army enlisted against *Nature*…

By "nature" James is speaking of what he sees as man's natural tendencies toward the evil virtues of self-interest, self-preservation and independence instead of the collective good, or, as Karl Marx said, "From each according to his ability, to each according to his need."

James sees mandatory service as a way for America's youth to "get the childishness knocked out of them." What I see, however, is a system that seeks to dumb everyone down to the same level and to brainwash them into socialism and anti-Christian bigotry. James suggests the forms of desirable service:

> …to dishwashing, clotheswashing, and windowwashing, to road-building and tunnel-making, to foundries and stoke-holes, and to the frames of skyscrapers, would our gilded youths be drafted off, according to their choice, to get the childishness knocked out of them, and to come back into society with healthier sympathies and soberer ideas. They would have paid their blood-tax, done their own part in the immemorial human warfare against nature; they would tread the earth more proudly, the women would value them more highly, they would be better fathers and teachers of the following generation.

James proclaims that it is only a matter of time and skillful propaganda before the American people buy into his social justice:

But I have no serious doubt that the ordinary prides and shames of social man, once developed to a certain intensity, are capable of organizing such a moral equivalent as I have sketched, or some other just as effective for preserving manliness of type. It is but a question of time, of skillful propagandism, and of opinion-making men seizing historic opportunities.

Liberals can always claim they oppose injustice and cruelty, but no matter how pure their motives, socialism always ends in dehumanization. Human value is reduced to the level of whether individuals are productive or unproductive resources. James finally reveals his bottom-line belief that individuals are nothing more than human capital to be owned and controlled by the State for its own purposes:

We should be *owned*, as soldiers are by the army, and our pride would rise accordingly. We could be poor, then, without humiliation, as army officers now are. The only thing needed henceforward is to inflame the civic temper as past history has inflamed the military temper. H. G. Wells, as usual, sees the centre of the situation. "In many ways," he says, "military organization is the most peaceful of activities. When the contemporary man steps from the street, of clamorous insincere advertisement, push, adulteration, underselling and intermittent employment into the barrack-yard, he steps on to a higher social plane, into an atmosphere of service and cooperation and of infinitely more honorable emulations. Here at least men are not flung out of employment to degenerate because there is no immediate work for them to do. They are fed for better services. Here at least a man is supposed to win promotion by self-forgetfulness and not by self-seeking.

James also reveals an inexcusable ignorance of the benefits and good works wrought through free-market capitalism. Like most pencil-pushing, wind-bag professors, James never spent a single day building a company, producing a product, or making a payroll. Yet, he dares to tell us that working for the government instead of for yourself and your family is the higher calling. Such ignorant dribble reminds me of another college professor who never engaged in any free-market enterprise but called for America's youth to "go through the government to go to college and then go back into government." Professor Barack Obama declared, "Individual salvation depends on collective salvation."

Chief of staff to now-President Obama, Rahm Emanuel wrote *The Plan: Big Ideas for America* in 2006. His book calls for three months of compulsory, mandatory civil service for ages from 18 to 25. Wasting no time implementing his Machiavellian agenda, Obama signed into law "The Generations Invigorating Volunteerism in Education Act" (GIVE Act) in April 2009.

Volunteer Slaves

The program is voluntary so far, but I believe the proverbial nose of the camel is well inside the tent. Obama's intentions have been clear since long before his election. The Obama Administration would like to make the volunteerism bill mandatory, as stated on the Obama-Biden campaign website in 2008:

Obama will call on citizens of all ages to serve America, by developing a plan to require 50 hours of community service in middle school and high school and 100 hours of community service in college every year.[151]

Thankfully, the outrage was so great, the campaign removed the word "mandatory" from the website description. But "mandatory" is their goal, and future legislation is being created to accomplish that end. Meanwhile, even if service is not mandatory, many Americans are liable to give their children over to this government re-education program, lured by the promise of government money for education.

Within the provisions of the GIVE Act, not all volunteer activities are created equal. The statute forbids program participants from being involved in ministry or church work. The legislation states:

They cannot engage in religious instruction, conducting worship services, providing instruction as part of a program that includes mandatory religious instruction or worship, constructing or operating facilities devoted to religious instruction or worship, maintaining facilities primarily or inherently devoted to religious instruction or worship or engage in any form of religious proselytization.

Obama's commitment to what he calls "Universal Voluntary Public Service" is not new. In 1992, Mr. Obama was a founding board member of Pubic Allies, and Michelle Obama became executive director of the Chicago chapter of Public Allies in 1993. According to the Public Allies website:

President-elect Obama has trained several classes of Allies in community organizing, spoken at Public Allies Chicago events, and helped Senator Durbin secure an appropriation from the Department of Justice that successfully helped us better recruit and retain young men of color for our Chicago program and learn practices we are applying nationally.[152]

An article in the *The Chronicle of Philanthropy* explains that Michelle Obama went looking for Have-Nots to pit against Haves as encouraged by her husband's mentor, Saul Alinsky (Chapter 20):

> In looking for potential leaders, Public Allies still uses techniques that Ms. Obama pioneered in Chicago. Paul Schmitz, the group's chief executive—who worked with Ms. Obama after he started a Public Allies program in Milwaukee in 1994—recalled that she looked for leaders in unconventional places, like in the city's poorest neighborhoods.

> "In her first class, she had a Harvard graduate, she had a Northwestern [University] graduate," he said. "But she also had people who'd been incarcerated, she had women on welfare, people who'd been homeless, who'd been in gangs."[153]

And lest you think this is the agenda only of the Democrats, Republicans, too, have been pushing the William James agenda. Public Allies boasts of its non-partisan support and partnerships:

> In 1992, President George H. W. Bush identified Public Allies as a model for national service and funded our pilot program. Under President Clinton, we grew from a pilot to a national program, and under President George W. Bush, we more than doubled in size and were contracted to provide training and technical assistance to other grantees of the

Corporation for National and Community Service.[154]

The September 4, 2008 issue of *Investor's Business Daily* ran an editorial entitled "Michelle's Boot Camp for Radicals," which revealed:

Big Brother had nothing on the Obamas. They plan to herd American youth into government-funded reeducation camps where they'll be brainwashed into thinking America is a racist, oppressive place in need of "social change."

But its [Public Allies] real mission is to radicalize American youth and use them to bring about "social change" through threats, pressure, tension and confrontation—the tactics used by the father of community organizing, Saul "The Red" Alinsky.

"Our alumni are more than twice as likely as 18-34 year olds to . . . engage in protest activities," Public Allies boasts in a document found with its tax filings. It has already deployed an army of 2,200 community organizers like Obama to agitate for "justice" and "equality" in his hometown of Chicago and other U.S. cities, including Cincinnati, Los Angeles, Milwaukee, New York, Phoenix, Pittsburgh and Washington. "I get to practice being an activist," and get paid for it, gushed Cincinnati recruit Amy Vincent.

When they're not protesting, they're staffing AIDS clinics, handing out condoms, bailing criminals out of jail and helping illegal aliens and the homeless obtain food stamps and other welfare.

Public Allies brags that more than 80% of graduates have continued working in nonprofit or government jobs. It's training the "next generation of nonprofit leaders"—future "social entrepreneurs."

"It was too touchy-feely," said Nelly Nieblas, 29, of the 2005 Los Angeles class. "It's a lot of talk about race, a lot of talk about sexism, a lot of talk about homophobia, talk about -isms and phobias."[155]

On the Public Allies website, I found an expanded testimony of Nelly Nieblas, and sadly, she did not reject the worldview training. I believe she was emotionally and psychologically manipulated to reject her initial disgust and ultimately accept the organization's political correctness:

She [Nieblas] recalls changing her mind about Public Allies after participating in an exercise that was designed to show that some people face life with built-in advantages while others are less privileged. Participants were asked to take one step backward for each disadvantage they had experienced if, for example, their refrigerator had ever been empty while they were growing up. "By the end of the whole exercise I was hitting the wall," she says. "I broke down crying." Ms. Nieblas says the exercise forced her to recognize that her identity was something deeper than her résumé—which included a college degree and a year-long political fellowship in Washington.

One of those -isms is "heterosexism," which a Public Allies

training seminar in Chicago describes as a negative byprod-
uct of "capitalism, white supremacy, patriarchy and male-
dominated privilege."[156]

The *Investor's Business Daily* article concludes by stating that the
Obamas (like William James) hate the military yet want a military-style
boot camp to indoctrinate an army of radicals:

> The government now funds about half of Public Allies'
> expenses through Clinton's AmeriCorps. Obama wants
> to fully fund it and expand it into a national program that
> some see costing $500 billion. "We've got to have a civilian
> national security force that's just as powerful, just as strong,
> just as well-funded" as the military, he said.

> The gall of it: The Obamas want to create a boot camp
> for radicals who hate the military—and stick American
> taxpayers with the bill.[157]

Mandatory volunteerism has a generational goal as well as the
immediate plan to control American youth. It is looking for future
leaders for the socialist, utopian regime. The GIVE Act includes
funding for selected students to go on to an intensive training program
conducted by Alinsky-like organizations, such as Public Allies (see
Chapter 20). This training lasts several months, and those involved are
provided with healthcare, a stipend, and money for their education.

The Chronicle of Philanthropy, reporting on Public Allies in an April
2008 article entitled "Fired Up and Ready to Grow: Youth Group's
Obama Link Raises Its Profile Nationwide," reports:

> More than 2,200 young people ages 18 to 30 have
> graduated from its program, which provides leadership

training and 10-month apprenticeships at charities—and more than 80 percent of them have continued working in nonprofit or government jobs, the group says....Public Allies participants receive average stipends of $1,500 a month...and an AmeriCorps educational grant of $4,725 if they complete the program.[158]

Students that complete this program are encouraged to make their career choices in either government work or far-left non-profits. One 25-year-old Public Allies trainee that is doing an apprenticeship at the Social Development Commission, an antipoverty group:

...hopes to use her AmeriCorps educational grant to study sociology...She says Public Allies has taught her that leadership is something that is earned. "The community organizer in me realizes I have to organize my community first to get them to understand there is a problem before I can step up on a podium and declare myself their leader." [159]

Bill Clinton, like the Obamas, supported a similar Saul Alinsky-style boot camp when he was governor of Arkansas. His Governor's School was a six-week summer program, founded in 1979, touted as a model for educational reform. In a revealing documentary about the governor's program, one former student, Steve Roberts, reveals the hidden agenda behind this prestigious school:

They're taking the best, the cream of the crop...the leaders in our next generation and pushing them into the values that Governor Clinton has—that the leftist media has—the values that go totally against what this nation was founded on. This is what I was exposed to. There wasn't any warning, there wasn't anyone that said, "Okay, now you're going to have to take all the values that you grew up with and put them on the shelf and be exposed to this." If my parents had known what was going on there, they wouldn't have let me go.[160]

Shelvia Cole, a psychologist and concerned mother, describes how the students were isolated from their families and their values:

For those six weeks…they were not allowed to go home except for July the Fourth. They are discouraged from calling home and talking on the phone. They can receive mail, but they are encouraged to have as little contact with the outside world as possible. So it's a closed campus.[161]

Killie Wood, another former student, explains what one guest speaker told them:

Students, do me a favor. Totally ignore your parents. Listen to them, but then forget them. Because you need to start using your own stuff.[162]

In an effort to tear down the students' authority figure system, instructors try to convince the students that "You are the elite." Mark Lowery, former director for Governor's School publicity, came out against the program many years ago. He says students are told by instructors:

The reason why you're not going to be understood when you go home—not your parents, your friends, your pastor, or anybody—is because you have been treated to thoughts that they can't handle.[163]

The purpose of such propaganda is to develop an intellectual and cultural elitism that gives kids the right to say, "We know better than you."

In the governor's program documentary, Lowery states:

> I think the whole intent of the Governor's School in taking 350 – 400 students per summer, is to pick out the four, five or six students that could be political leaders and then to mold their minds in this more liberal and humanistic thinking....The greatest influence of the Governor's School is to promote the thought...that to be considered intellectual by your peers...you have to be a liberal thinker....[This is] not teaching...but indoctrination.[164]

How was this indoctrination fostered? Among other techniques, liberal, anti-Christian values were promoted by forcing students to watch explicit pornographic movies about the gay lifestyle. (Remember, this was a taxpayer-funded program!) Another approach appears in a video promoting the Governor's School as students are seen lying on the floor while a teachers asks them, "Are you ready to divorce yourself from your bodies?"

One of the leading goals of youth service is to brainwash students into the worldview of Saul Alinsky, (Chapter 20) which includes pitting the Haves against the Have-nots in order to stir up a protest movement for the re-distribution of wealth. Alinsky believed all of society's problems could be blamed on capitalism. Although the alternative to capitalism is socialism, in true William James word manipulation style, proponents call it "social justice."

Larry Grathwohl was an FBI informant who penetrated the Weather Underground, a group of radical, 1960s hippies like Bill

Ayers, friend of President Obama. The Weather Underground was involved in more than 30 bombings here in the United States, including a bombing of the Pentagon. Mr. Grathwohl stated that Bill Ayers and his friends often talked about what they would do when they finally brought about the communist agenda. Although they figured they'd have to re-educate 100 million people, they guessed that 25 million wouldn't succumb to the brainwashing and would have to be exterminated.

Today Ayers is busy writing the brainwashing curriculum while his old friend President Obama is championing the legislation that will federally fund the brainwashing used in the national youth service envisioned by William James. Phyllis Schlafly, in her article "Bill Ayers's Scary Plans for Public Schools," warns:

> From his prestigious and safe university position, Ayers has been teaching teachers and students in rebellion against American capitalism and what he calls "imperialism" and "oppression." The code words for the Ayers curriculum are "social justice," a "transformative" vision, "critical pedagogy," "liberation," "capitalist injustices," "critical race theory," "queer theory," and of course multiculturalism and feminism.

> That language is typical in the readings that Ayers assigns in his university courses. He admits he is a "communist street fighter" who has been influenced by Karl Marx, as well as Che, Ho and Malcolm X.

> Ayers speaks openly of his desire to use America's public school classrooms to train a generation of revolutionaries who will overturn the U.S. social and economic regime. He teaches that America is oppressive and unjust, socialism

is the solution, and wealth and resources should be redistributed.

In Ayers's course called "On Urban Education," he calls for a "distribution of material and human resources." His left-wing notions would be very compatible with those of Barack Obama, who publicly told Joe the Plumber that we should "spread the wealth."

Ayers's books are among the most widely used in America's education schools. Ayers even uses science and math courses as part of his "transformative" political strategy to teach that the American economic system is unjust.

Unfortunately, Ayers's far-out education theories are already having an effect in education schools. One after another, teachers colleges are using their courses to promote socialist notions of wealth distribution, "social justice," diversity and environmentalism, and to punish students who resist this indoctrination by giving them low grades or even denying them graduation.

You might assume that Ayers's political ideas would put him on the outer fringe of the left-wing education establishment. However, his peers recently elected him to serve as vice president for curriculum in the American Education Research Association, the largest organization of education school professors and researchers.[165]

Ayers is also a friend of Hugo Chavez, the communist leader of Venezuela, and in a 2006 speech in Venezuela, he declared, "Education is the motor-force of revolution."

Throughout history, communist and Marxist leaders have declared that they need two things for a successful revolution. The first is some kind of crisis, such as a financial crisis, and the second is the youth of the middle class. The William James, Dewey, Bush 41, Clinton, Bush 43, and Obama youth service agenda falls right in line with the goal of former Assistant U.N Secretary General Robert Muller who, in his *World Core Curriculum*, called for:

> Assisting the child in becoming an integrated individual who can deal with personal experience while seeing himself as a part of "the greater whole." In other words, promote growth of the group idea, so that group good, group understanding, group interrelations and group goodwill replace all limited, self-centered objectives, leading to group consciousness.[166]

To achieve his world-changing agenda, William James understood the need to shape the worldview of young, impressionable minds toward humanism, the end of capitalism, the ouster of parental authority, and the demise of a Constitutional Republic. His moral equivalent of war continues to destroy America from within. If in the end we are as James wanted, "*owned*, as soldiers are by the army," then we will have no one to blame but ourselves due to our ignorance and intellectual laziness. As Hosea 4:6 says, "My people are destroyed for lack of knowledge."

12

ALFRED KINSEY
(1894-1956)

Alfred Kinsey earned his Ph.D. from Harvard University in entomology—the study of insects—and became a world-class expert on the gall wasp,[167] so perhaps it is no surprise that his later research on human sexuality was little more than a "sting operation" designed to hoodwink and titillate gullible people into believing their fantasies. Kinsey, who was strongly committed to Darwinian evolution, released his most famous books, *Sexual Behavior in the Human Male*, in 1948 and *Sexual Behavior in the Human Female* in 1953. Far from being scientific studies, Kinsey's writings were outright sexual propaganda that sought to convince Americans that all sex is "outlet" sex and equally okay, regardless of whether it is between people of the same sex, the opposite sex, adults with children, or humans with animals.

His "research" included collecting data from adult men who had raped and molested as many as 300 children ranging in age from 2 months to 15 years. Kinsey personally watched and kept detailed notes. This data was then compiled into charts and tables that claimed to record the sexual stimulation of children, including infants.

Kinsey believed it was vital for children to engage in sex by age 6, before they picked up "cultural taboos" based on "religion."[168] He did not think people should be classified as homosexual or heterosexual, and one of his specific propaganda goals was to normalize homosexuality, bisexuality, pedophilia, and other sexual perversions. In fact, the extensive research by people such as Dr. Judith Reisman reveals that Kinsey, though married, was a homosexual and a sado-masochist.

Kinsey kicked off the sexual revolution, and the war on Biblical sexuality continues to this day through sex education curricula based on his perversions. (And believe me when I say perversions—of the most unimaginable kinds. Because I want this book to be for ages 13 through adult, I'll spare the sordid details, but if you'd like to do your own in-depth research, you'll find more on the websites of organizations like Concerned Women for America and of Dr. Judith Reisman. Dr. Reisman has written several books on Kinsey and is an often-quoted expert on the impact of Kinsey's worldview on America. She has also been a guest on my radio program and a columnist for worldviewtimes.com.)

Sex for Kids

Kinsey claimed that children are born sexual but that religious tyranny suppresses their otherwise natural sexual activity. He believed that as long as a child gave "consent," [169] it was completely normal and healthy for adults to engage in sexual activity with children.

This thinking has played out in some bizarre ways. For instance, an eighth-grade curriculum that a concerned parent in South Dakota personally placed in my hands told its young, impressionable readers that "Children are not necessarily harmed or disturbed by a child molester." Although numerous attempts have been made by parents, educators—even a member of Congress—to eliminate federal funding of any sex education curriculum based on the perversion of Kinsey, the pro-Kinsey lobby, Hollywood, and the liberal media have mischaracterized, marginalized, and demonized anyone who sought to expose Kinsey's demented worldview and how taxpayers pay for its wide distribution.

My friend and Worldview Weekend speaker Bob Knight has long been a courageous warrior for children and a Biblical worldview applied to family and sexuality. He has appeared on numerous national radio and television programs as a "token" member of the religious right. While many hosts have tried to set up Knight for ridicule, they often find themselves speechless at the documentation Knight brings to their shows. In 2002, for instance, The University of Minnesota Press published *Harmful to Minors: The Perils of Protecting Children from Sex* by Judith Levine. It reveals that the influence of Kinsey has not been diminished on the liberal left, as Knight describes the book's message:

> Judith Levine makes the argument that children are being unjustly denied the opportunity to have sex with adults and each other, and she blames the "Religious Right," "religion," and "ignorance."

> Levine cites the Sexuality Information and Education Council of the United States (SIECUS) as a key influence in her work, along with other child-sex advocates such as James Kincaid, author of *Child Loving: The Erotic Child and Victorian Culture*. She also positively cites the 1998 article in the American Psychological Association's (APA) flagship publication *Psychological Bulletin* that urged people to use "neutral" terms such as "adult-child sex" and said that not all adult-child sex is harmful and some might even be beneficial. The APA article was denounced by Congress, the American Psychiatric Association, and by many American Psychological Association members.

Harmful to Minors, published by the University of Minnesota Press, makes the case that children are capable sexual partners, are entitled to sex, and benefit from having sex with adults as long as the children consent to it. The real problem, the author says, is societal "hysteria" surrounding the issue of child sexuality. When children consent, the experience can be positive, she says. In an interview with the *Minneapolis Star-Tribune*, Levine said she admired the approach used in the Netherlands, where the age of sexual consent was lowered to 12.

In her book, Levine declares:

Sex is not harmful to children. It is a vehicle to self-knowledge, love, healing, creativity, adventure, and intense feelings of aliveness. There are many ways even the smallest children can partake of it.[170]

So who is now helping to fund and promote the worldview of Alfred Kinsey to American adults and, most objectionably, to American children through sex-education curriculum? The natural partner to Kinsey's model, Margaret Sanger's (Chapter 22) Planned Parenthood organization, as well as SIECUS.

The Kinsey Institute created SIECUS in 1964 with the explicit goal of incorporating Kinsey's philosophy into sex-education material.[171] Dr. Mary Calderone, who was medical director for Planned Parenthood, became the first SIECUS president. Wardel Pomeroy, who was Kinsey's co-author on both his male and female sex books, served on the founding board. With SIECUS under their direction, the Kinsey ideology began pouring into the sex-education programs promoted by Planned Parenthood.[172]

The movement also embraces Kinsey's belief that moral standards regarding sex result only from "cultural conditioning," not from timeless guidelines for right and wrong.[173] In 1991, SIECUS published *Guidelines for Comprehensive Sexuality Education*, which requires Kinseyan-trained teachers to convey "sexuality literacy" in public classrooms.[174]

In addition to influencing educational curriculum, Kinsey personally worked to reduce penalties for sex offenders. With Columbia University law professor Herbert Wechsler, he promoted the American Law Institute's Model Penal Code (1955). Most states cite the code—which is based largely on Kinsey's findings—as the blueprint to ease penalties for sex offenses, resulting in less protection for women and children from sexual predators.[175]

In 1949, Kinsey testified before the California General Assembly's Subcommittee on Sex Crimes, urging them to liberalize sex offense statutes. He argued specifically for granting immediate paroles to suspected child molesters and warned that societal "hysteria" does more harm to children than the actual molestations.[176]

Since their publication, Kinsey's reports and data have been discredited by many experts, including one of his friends at the time, liberal humanist and psychologist Abraham Maslow. Bob Knight reveals:

> Dr. Maslow had discovered that human sexuality studies tended to attract exhibitionists and practitioners of unconventional sex. This increased the reporting of illicit behaviors such as promiscuity and homosexuality.[177] Before the publication of his reports, Kinsey had arranged for Dr. Maslow to test his volunteers for bias. After evaluating

students from Indiana University, Maslow concluded that Kinsey's sample was unrepresentative of the general population.[178] Kinsey dismissed Maslow's finding and terminated his relationship with him. No mention of this study ever appeared in the Kinsey reports.[179]

Kinsey's research has been declared "junk" science and not credible by numerous professional groups such as the American Board of Pediatrics. His treatment of children reminds me of another man, committed to Darwinian evolution, who in the name of science also experimented cruelly on children—Adolf Hitler.

Fantasy Research, Fanciful Results

Some of the subjects used by Kinsey to study sexual behavior certainly skewed his reports toward his own personally desired outcome and agenda. For example:

- A quarter to nearly half of Kinsey's subjects were prisoners, hardly reflective of the general population.

- Over 1,400 of his subjects were sex offenders.

- His subjects were overwhelmingly single when less than a third of the population was single during the 1950s, and they were also predominantly college educated.

- He classified prostitutes and cohabiting females as "married" women, and then claimed that 26 percent of married women committed adultery. Of course his deceptive definition of married was buried in the details of the lengthy book and didn't end up in popular versions of the research.[180]

Kinsey made extreme claims, such as approximately 70% of males had had sex with prostitutes and that 37% of all males had homosexual experiences between adolescence and old age, with 10% being exclusively homosexual for periods of up to three years between the ages of 18 and 25. This is the source for the fraudulent estimate that 10% of the population is "gay."[181] To the contrary, a 2003 Canadian government survey indicates an incidence of homosexuality at less than 1.5% of the population.[182]

Revealing the connection between Kinsey and the radical feminists also is not difficult. Homosexual goals are furthered through the feminist agenda that seeks to feminize men, to destroy the institution of family, to undermine the role of fathers in the lives of their children, and to promote lesbianism, bi-sexuality, transgenderism, and any other perversion du jour.

There are many reasons why humanists, homosexuals, feminists, and other radicals seek to destroy the traditional family and traditional Biblical values, including their own sinful rebellion against God and His character and nature, the desire to recruit more participants into their perversion, the will to see their deviant lifestyle normalized in hopes eliminating their guilty consciences (if their consciences have not been seared, which keeps them from even feeling guilty any longer). Finally, as David Noebel explains, many believe cultural evolution demands the destruction of old traditions:

> The concepts of biological and cultural evolution dictate that the traditional concepts of marriage and family have outlived their usefulness. As the human species and culture progress, old traditions become outdated and must be replaced by new concepts that will continue the evolutionary process.[183]

Feminist Gloria Steinem has stated in an article that, while Kinsey's work was "far from perfect," it was a "big step forward" for women. "The Kinsey report," she contends, "is a little like the Bill of Rights. It only is powerful if we use it." And, "If it exists only on paper, then it has little importance. It depends on what is done with it now."[184]

In keeping with Steinem's thinking, I have a great idea of what should be done with the work of insect-expert-turned-sex-researcher Kinsey: Throw it in the trash. Then let's demand that elected officials of all political persuasions stop funding school curriculum based on Kinsey's destructive perversion and worldview propaganda.

13

ALDOUS HUXLEY
(1894-1963)

S ix U. S. states offer a career exploration test that asks these true/
false questions:

• I have taught a Sunday school class or otherwise take an
active part in my church;

• I believe in a God who answers prayers;

• I pray to God about my problems;

• I read the Bible or other religious writings regularly;

• I believe in life after death;

• I believe that God created man in His own image;

• If I ask God for forgiveness, my sins are forgiven.

While it could be argued that such questions merely help determine a student's fitness for a career in Christian ministry, it does not
take much imagination to see how they could be equally well used to
screen a person out of certain occupations in the name of finding the
"proper place" to assign each student. Certainly, if the authorities who
determine this proper place take their cues from Aldous Huxley, the
test results will be anything but benign.

Big Government, Big Brother

Best known as the author of *Brave New World*, Huxley outlines steps
toward total social transformation. His stated goals are having an

ominous impact on America's educational system:

1. Rewrite history to discredit nationalism and promote globalism.

2. Teach thinking skills based on feelings and experience, not facts and reason.

3. Encourage loyalty to peers and teachers, not family and churches.

4. Immerse students in global beliefs and values.

5. Block opposition to the new global paradigm.

6. Condition students to serve a "greater whole."

Huxley's classic story of government oppression, *Brave New World*, explains this motivation for government control:

A really efficient totalitarian state would be one in which the all-powerful executive political bosses and their army of managers control a population of slaves who do not have to be coerced because they love their servitude....To bring about the revolution we require...enabling government managers to assign any given individual to his or her proper place in the social and economic hierarchy. Round pegs in square holes tend to have dangerous thoughts about the social system and to infect others with their discontents.[185]

In other words, those who do not agree with the State's worldview ("standards") will not be allowed to pursue positions of power or influence either socially or economically.

This philosophy has been in the process of being implemented at both state and federal levels for many years, despite that fact that individuals such as Lynn Cheney, I, and others have been warning about the danger it poses to individual liberty and free markets. Many Americans believe the government education system is a planned failure and intellectual slavery. Why? If children are not well educated, they can be easily controlled.

As we saw in Chapter 8, John Dewey believed the goal of school is to determine where students fit in the social and economic hierarchy—the modernist version of a caste system—consistent with Huxley's worldview. Today, many courses and tests are used to determine how a child's attitudes, values, and feelings line up with the state's outcomes, benchmarks, or preferences.

Many of the national standards proposed under the federal education legislation Goals 2000, for example, had little to do with cognitive data. The October 20, 1994 *Wall Street Journal* included an article by Lynne Cheney titled, "The End of History," in which Cheney describes the new national standards for history:

> Imagine an outline for the teaching of American history in which George Washington makes only a fleeting appearance and is never described as our first president. Or in which the foundings of the Sierra Club and the National Organization of Women are considered noteworthy events, but the first gathering of the U.S. Congress is not. Alexander Graham Bell, Thomas Edison, Albert Einstein, Jonas Salk and the Wright brothers make no appearance at all. The midnight ride of Paul Revere also went unmentioned and Lincoln's "Gettysburg Address" is only mentioned once. Yet, the American Federation of Labor is mentioned nine times.[186]

In 1997, then-Governor Roy Romer of Colorado, while serving as a board member of the Goals 2000 panel, was asked how to enforce national standards. He replied:

> I believe if you were to get all employers of this country saying that we would not hire anybody unless we see a high school graduate certificate that has on it the results of this potential employee's record....Then I think this nation will come to the realization that there is no job for them, there is no life for them....There is the motivation.[187]

As big government and big business merge through corporate fascism, the meshing of education and labor becomes much easier. Chester Finn, former assistant secretary of education and author of federal education legislation, has recommended a system of rewards and punishments based on federal government standards:

> Perhaps the best way to enforce this standard is to confer valuable benefits and privileges on people who meet it, and to withhold them from those who do not. Work permits, good jobs and college admission are the most obvious, but there is ample scope here for imagination in devising carrots and sticks. Driver's licenses could be deferred, so could eligibility for professional athletic teams. The minimum wage paid to those who earn their certificates [of mastery] might be a dollar higher.[188]

A recent incident in Nevada demonstrates how this is already in play. In Las Vegas, Darcy Tucker was pulled out of a geography class—without her parent's consent—to be given a computerized assessment of career possibilities. Although Darcy aspires to become a veterinarian, the test said she ought to be a bartender or waitress, and it spat out a list of courses she should take to that end. Darcy's mother objected, "The school stepped on my toes as a parent. It is my job to direct my child's career path, and it would not be in her best interest to be a bartender."[189] On the other hand, it just might be in Nevada's best interest—given the insatiable hospitality needs of the gambling and entertainment industry—but that shouldn't matter to Darcy.

Another contemporary Huxlian movement is school-to-work legislation. Mark Tucker, president of the National Center on Education and the Economy, has helped his organization lead the charge in passing school-to-work laws at state and federal levels. In the February 4, 1998 issue of *Education Week*, Millicent Lawton quoted Tucker as encouraging government control of individual destinies:

> State higher education systems would deny admission to those who didn't have the certificate [of mastery], and state leaders would prod employers to express a preference for hiring job applicants who had the certificate. Both conditions would serve as powerful incentives for students.[190]

This sort of thinking has troubling roots. Whether socialist, communist or Marxist, the foundation of all these philosophies is the humanist worldview. In his book, *Character and Destiny*, Dr. D. James Kennedy explains:

> Humanists are socialists by nature. Like Karl Marx, they see private property as primitive and selfish, nationalism and pride of country as dangerous, and allegiance to any power other than the socialist state should be illegal. Ideas,

ethics, and the means of production belong to the state. For supporters such as Paul Kurtz, B. F. Skinner, John Dewey, Francis Crick, Isaac Asimov, and the other signers of the [humanist] manifesto, communism and state socialism were the only logical solutions to mankind's problems. In the first edition of that thin volume, they wrote, "A socialized and cooperative economic order must be established to the end that the equitable distribution of the means of life be possible...."[191]

The danger in this thinking goes beyond just its influence on contemporary public school education. The day may be fast approaching when holding to and expressing a Biblical worldview in America will cost you a degree, a promotion, or even your job. A few years ago, my brother was informed that in order to get his license to practice law renewed in the state of Minnesota, he would have to take a course on diversity—and particularly the acceptance of homosexuality. After weeks of fighting this requirement, he was finally allowed to take a course on feminism with which he disagreed but which was not as offensive. Although my brother was prepared to leave Minnesota and set up his practice in another state, the dangerous trend he encountered seems to be going nationwide:

> The State Bar of Arizona is considering whether to require new attorneys to swear they will not let their views on sexual orientation get in the way of providing legal services. Mat Staver, founder of Liberty Counsel and dean of Liberty University's Law School, is concerned.

> "I believe that this is a major threat to the practice of law," he contends. "This is an attempt to literally license those

out of business and to revoke the license of those who, in fact, have traditional moral values."

Staver believes the campaign is going nationwide and will be a tool used by homosexuals to hold back Christian lawyers. "If they then can hold over your head the license and the ability to practice law, that will be a devastating blow to those of us who believe in traditional family values," he points out.[192]

I began writing about this in the early 90s and since then have asked thousands of adults in live seminars to raise their hands if they have ever had to take a politically correct diversity program in order to receive or renew a professional license of some sort. Hundreds have said they have. One air conditioner technician was required take a diversity class in order to get his license renewed to work with Freon! Another man, a federal aviation employee, told me that in order to be promoted he had to take a diversity course, and the list goes on and on.

President George H. W. Bush once said we need to be a nation of students, and the globalists work hard to make that a reality. Our young people are indoctrinated through school and volunteerism, and if authorities can ever make it mandatory, adults, too, will be routinely indoctrinated through diversity programs tied to career growth.

The Multiple Realities of Aldous Huxley

Huxley spent the last years of his life experimenting with mind-altering drugs in an attempt to find some kind of esoteric or hidden truth. Harvard professor, psychologist, and promoter of psychedelic drugs Dr. Timothy Leary recalls, in a piece titled "Flashback," a conversation he had with Huxley. Huxley said:

These brain drugs, mass produced in the laboratories, will bring about vast changes in society. This will happen with or without you or me. All we can do is spread the word. The obstacle to this evolution, Timothy, is the Bible.[193]

To which Leary responded:

We had run up against the Judeo-Christian commitment to one God, one religion, one reality, that has cursed Europe for centuries and America since our founding days. Drugs that open the mind to multiple realities inevitably lead to a polytheistic view of the universe. We sensed that the time for a new humanist religion based on intelligence, good-natured pluralism and scientific paganism has arrived.[194]

While I don't think there's anything brave about it, the new world is upon us.

14

BENJAMIN BLOOM
(1913-1999)

Although it received tremendous exposure early in its public life, the term Outcome-Based Education has long since been abandoned because parents figured out what it was all about, and it wasn't good. Parents realized it meant they would no longer have much to say about the "base" for their children's education, and the outcomes they saw didn't make them very happy. So naturally, the purveyors of OBE abandoned the offending concepts.

Not!

By this point in our study, you should be able to guess what they did instead. If you guessed that they came up with new names for the same ol' same ol', you would, of course, be absolutely correct.

Creative Labels for a Broken Idea

Hiding OBE has become a full-time job for many educators. To keep parents and the public confused, OBE proponents cloak their educational approach in different terms. Here is a list of the most common ones:

> Mastery Learning
> Results Oriented
> Total Quality Management
> Quality Schools
> Essential Schools
> Transformational Education
> Reformed Education, Restructured Education

Competency Based Education
Break the Mold 21st Century Schools
Exit Based Teaching
High Standards
Performance Based Learning
High Level Learning
Mastery Teaching
Formative Testing
Correctives Teaching
Extensions Learning
Summative Evaluations
Credentialing Curriculum
Advancement Teaching
Results-Based Curriculum

Tracing the ancestry of the term through the newspeak maze would bring you back to the one that the tops the list above. The original concepts behind OBE came from the "Mastery Learning" plans of Benjamin Bloom.

Even "Mastery Learning" once fell on hard times, and so began the many attempts to disguise it. William Spady, one of OBE's most well-known gurus, devised a cover-up and encouraged educators to do away with the old terminology:

> I pleaded with the group not to use the name "mastery learning" in the network's new name because the word "mastery" had already been destroyed. I argued that we had about five years before they destroyed the term "outcomes," but at least we could get a start.[195]

At a February 1994 conference sponsored by Free World

Research in Des Moines, Iowa, Dr. William Coulson, a longtime colleague of psychologist Carl Rogers, quoted Dr. Rogers's approach to manipulating words: "Change the name of [the reform policy] as fast as necessary to stay ahead of the critics." Now that OBE has been unmasked, the spin doctors of the educational elite are out in full force using many different names to disguise Outcome-Based Education.

Regardless of what it is called, Bloom's approach is based on the socialist premise that no one can be better than anyone else. Instead of redistributing wealth and destroying capitalism, though, they are redistributing grades and destroying the acquisition of knowledge.

Socialism has been tried many times and has proven a total failure. Why then are we teaching America's children socialism in and through education?

Socialism will never succeed because it is based on a false concept of equality. Equality of outcomes among vastly different individuals cannot happen. Whenever government tries to equalize salaries, the standard of living, or education, productivity takes a nosedive. The fantasy world mentality of socialism sets a dangerous precedent for any public school student. Why? Because OBE never permits a child to fail.

In order for the outcomes to be equal, however, the standard must be lowered to ensure that all students, regardless of ability, can reach the benchmark. If you want everyone to slam dunk, you have to lower the basket. Children are robbed of the valuable lessons of determination and persistence learned from failure. Failure can be used to teach children to dig in and double or even triple their efforts in order to reach a goal. In *Schools Without Failure*, William Glasser, one of OBE's promoters, reflected this mentality: "We have to let students know there are no right answers, and we have to let them see that there are many alternatives to certainty and right answers."[196]

Glasser takes his cues directly from one of the most notorious agents of change ever involved in the American educational system, Benjamin Bloom. In his book, *Taxonomy of Educational Objectives*, Bloom calls for the "thorough going-through and reorganization of attitudes and values."[197]

Bloom taught that the highest form of intelligence has been reached when an individual no longer believes in right or wrong. Bloom proclaimed that the purpose of education and the schools is to change the thoughts, feelings, and actions of students. In another of his books, *All Our Children Learning*, Bloom discloses what he believes is the ultimate goal of education:

> The curriculum may be thought of as a plan for changing students' behavior and as the actual set of learning experiences in which students, teachers, and materials interact to produce the change in students.[198]

In other words, Bloom was espousing corrective thought control. What kind of "correction" does Bloom desire? Simply that students question everything taught them—except, of course, what he teaches—and that they learn to remove moral absolutes from the foundation of their thinking. Teaching based on feelings, not facts, and encouraging loyalty to peers and teachers, not family and churches, is exactly the goal of Outcome-Based Education.

Remember Aldous Huxley's idea that "a really efficient totalitarian state would be one in which the all-powerful executive political bosses and their army of managers control a population of slaves"?[199] Bloom's Mastery Learning gives us just such a generation. Outcome-Based Education has not only produced a nation of compliant slaves but a generation enslaved to a humanist worldview. It is a generation that does not believe in absolute truth but does believe that to be considered an intellectual you must be liberal and must hold tolerance as the highest "virtue."

An Elite Group of Thinkers

So what is Bloom's final objective? To change the students into exactly what he is: a humanist and elitist. Bloom's goal is to tear down a child's traditional authority figures and replace them with a new one: the State group consensus.

And how does Bloom plan to do this? By making students believe they have been exposed to superior thought that is beyond the ability of most people—particularly the child's parents—to understand. Students are fed lies that go something like this:

> Do not expect to be understood by your parents, pastor, or even some of your friends. You are part of an elite group of thinkers. If you truly want to be an intellectual thinker, you have to be a liberal thinker. You can't believe in the old standard of right or wrong. You must decide for yourself what is right and what is wrong based on your own feelings, beliefs, and ideas. It is okay to challenge and question the things your parents or society have taught you. That is all part of becoming part of a rare group of leaders and achievers.[200]

This is also why our federal government has been pushing for mandatory volunteerism. Congress has authorized billions of dollars for mandatory brainwashing by putting children in emotional, liberal, bleeding-heart situations void of reason and logic in which the desired outcome is the student's acceptance of government intervention in every area of life. This will usher in a society based on "fairness" and the redistribution of wealth.

Am I over-stating the case? I don't think so, as Bloom's own words demonstrate:

> The careful observer of the classroom can see that the wise teacher as well as the psychological theorist use cognitive behavior and the achievement of cognitive goals to attain affective goals. . . . [A] large part of what we call "good teaching" is the teacher's ability to attain affective objectives through challenging the student's fixed beliefs.[201]

And where did the students get the "fixed beliefs" that must be challenged? For millions, it is through their parents and churches. Most of us would respond: All the more reason why those fixed beliefs should remain fixed, instead of being torn down and replaced by some liberal, socialist, humanist, elitist educrat like Benjamin Bloom.

Bloom's thinking fits right in with others we've studied. As you'll recall about Alice Bailey, her demon friend, the Tibetan, proclaimed that the one-world religion and the "new age" or "new order" would be implemented through the dominant false church, Freemasonry *and the education establishment*:

> The three main channels through which the preparation for the new age is going on might be regarded as the Church, the Masonic Fraternity and the educational field. All of them are as yet in relatively static condition, and all are as yet failing to meet the need and to respond to the inner pressure. But in all of these three movements, disciples of the Great Ones are to be found and they are steadily gathering momentum and will before long enter upon their designated task.[202]

If Bailey were alive today, she would see that these three institutions have not been static in recent years and are now clearly promoting the same demonic worldview agenda to which she was committed.

To achieve globalism, one of the goals of the education establishment is to teach children to think as a group and to accept group values that are pre-determined by the State. Collectivism is crucial for the accomplishment of the new order. Again, according to Bailey:

> This coming age will be as predominantly the age of group interplay, group idealism and group consciousness as the Piscean Age has been one of personality unfoldment...for the will of the individual will voluntarily be blended into group will.[203]

Discovered: New Meanings for Old Words

Today's educational elite mask the true nature of the outcomes, "high standards," and a host of other goal-related terms. Benjamin Bloom called them "higher order thinking skills." As with the term OBE itself, whatever the goals are called, parents need to know that the terms have specific, underlying meanings, and they usually aren't what you think. For example: what do you think when you hear the term, "critical thinker"? Do you want to be considered one? Do you want your child or grandchild to be considered a critical thinker? Before you answer that question, you need to ask: who is defining the terms?

Dr. Raymond English, one of the educational elite, gave a speech before the National Advisory Council on Educational Research and Improvement on April 2, 1987, in which he defined critical thinking as follows:

> Critical thinking means not only learning how to think

for oneself, but it also means learning how to subvert the traditional values in your society. You're not thinking critical if you're accepting the values that mommy and daddy taught you. That's not critical.

Some of the other "outcomes" they want your child to achieve can be found in the statement of purpose of almost every school district. Here is a sampling:

Involved citizen, quality producer, self-directed learner, productive group participant, understand diversity, understand positive health habits, deliberate on public issues and interpret human experience.

Do you think students would be considered "self-directed learners" if they listened to their parents, pastor, youth pastor, or grandparents?

"Understanding diversity" means accepting and valuing every lifestyle anyone chooses to practice. "Understanding positive health habits" is nothing more than passing a "safe sex class."

In the early 90s, America embraced the U.N. global education agenda, largely inspired by Robert Muller. This agenda in America came to be called America 2000 and was introduced by President George H. W. Bush in an April 1991 speech at the White House:

Nations that stick to stale old notions and ideologies will falter and fail. So I'm here today to say, America will move forward....New schools for a new world....Re-invent— literally start from scratch and reinvent the American school....Our challenge amounts to nothing less than a revolution in American education.[204]

Although Bush 41 could not get the legislation through Congress, the legislation was finally passed as Goals 2000 through the subsequent efforts of President Bill Clinton and his administration. As chairman of the National Governors Association, Governor Bill Clinton had helped draft this education agenda, and he was in the White House Rose Garden when it was unveiled by then-President George H. W. Bush. After migrating through the Clinton Administration, the agenda emerged with yet another name change under President George W. Bush when it became known as No Child Left Behind.

Lamar Alexander, former governor of Tennessee and U.S. secretary of education for President George H. W. Bush, revealed that the book by René Dubos entitled *A God Within* "changed his thinking the most."[205] Dubos was also a board member of the futuristic organization Planetary Citizens. A small excerpt from Dubos's book reveals his worldview that so impacted the secretary of education:

> The earth is literally our mother, not only because we depend on her for nurture and shelter but even more because the human species has been shaped by her in the womb of evolution.... Our salvation depends upon our ability to create a religion of nature.[206]

As the first President Bush's secretary of education, Lamar Alexander aggressively promoted the global education agenda America 2000 to the American people. Many corporations bought into this education agenda and lobbied for its passage. See how easy it is to spot the education establishment and occultism/pagan spirituality connections back to the government-corporate complex? At the writing of this book, Lamar Alexander is the Republican U.S. senator from Tennessee. With Republicans like Alexander, who needs Democrats?

Rush to Failure

The education agenda is picking up steam under President Obama. On July 24, 2009, the U.S. Department of Education announced that the "centerpiece of the Obama Administration's education reform efforts" in its "$4.3 billion Race to the Top" will include "adopting internationally benchmarked education standards." The U.S. Department of Education press release said the Obama Administration will be pushing strategies for "Adopting internationally benchmarked standards and assessments." States will be encouraged to adopt these international education standards by being rewarded with additional federal funds. While Republican and Democrat administrations come and go and the U.S. Congress flips back and forth from Democrat to Republican control, the U.N. agenda moves forward unabated.

John Dewey admitted that the purpose of school is not to create educated students but to change their values and prepare them for their place in life. Benjamin Bloom admitted that the goal of his educational philosophy is to change a student's "fixed beliefs." The goal of Robert Muller is based on the same worldview of humanists Dewey and Bloom, and his goal was to use the U.N. to convince national leaders to embrace a humanistic worldview so as to usher in the New Order. The late Norman Cousins, former president of the World Federalist Association, wrote the foreword to one of Robert Muller's books in which he admits that Muller has helped to further the "values" of Dewey, Bloom, and other humanists:

> Whatever the uncertainties of the future may be,… the oncoming generations will…need to have special knowledge, certainly; but they will need something far more important: an intense awareness of the conditions under

which the values essential to the future of mankind can be created and maintained. They will need living examples of the conspiracy of love that…will be essential to man's salvation. Robert Muller is involved in such a conspiracy.[207]

The liberal media are known for attempting to characterize and marginalize conservative authors and researchers for using the terms "conspiracy" and "New World Order." However, the hard facts reveal that authors, researchers, talk-show hosts, and conference speakers such as myself are simply quoting the agenda clearly stated and described by individuals such as Norman Cousins, Alice Bailey, Henry Kissinger, Benjamin Bloom, and countless others.

I can hardly say this emphatically enough: *Americans must stop being so trusting and understand that educational policy makers in Washington, DC and at the state departments of education are individuals who have betrayed a public trust.*

In his 1964 book *Stability and Change in Human Characteristics*, Bloom shows that this sad state of affairs has been a long time in coming:

Efforts to control or change *human behavior by therapy*, by education, or by other means will be inadequate and poorly understood until we can follow behavior over a longer period.[208] [Emphasis mine]

"Control" is where we see the worldviews of Benjamin Bloom and behavioral psychologist B. F. Skinner merging. This, at least in part, is why Skinner is next on our list of individuals destroying America from the grave.

15

B. F. Skinner
(1904-1990)

In 1972, Burrhus Frederic Skinner—behavioral psychologist, author, and professor at Harvard University—was given the Humanist of the Year Award by the American Humanist Association. It was a well-deserved honor.

An avowed atheist, Skinner was one of the early promoters of using a machine for "remediation." Its purpose was to aid in developing programmed learning or corrective thought control. A behavioral psychologist, Skinner believed man is controlled by stimuli from the environment and, therefore, can never make a decision in which he exercises free will. He explained why this belief is so central to his approach to psychology: "the hypothesis that man is not free is essential to the application of scientific method to the study of human behavior."[209] At least he made his assumption clear.

He even predicted the results his presupposition would lead to:

> We must expect to discover that what a man does is the result of specifiable conditions and that once these conditions have been discovered, we can anticipate and to some extent determine his actions."[210]

In other words, once the right stimuli, or the right conditions, are discovered, the one in charge of the stimuli can control anyone. According to Skinner in *Beyond Freedom and Dignity*, his vision postulates a new sort of Have's and Have-not's:

> [Man] plays two roles: one as a controller, as the designer of

a controlling culture, and another as the controlled, as the products of a culture.[211]

As long as environment is controlled, he proclaimed, behavior can be controlled.

According to the *New World Encyclopedia*:

Skinner is popularly known for his controversial books *Walden Two* and *Beyond Freedom and Dignity*. *Walden Two* describes a visit to an imaginary utopian commune in the United States in the 1940s. In this community, the productivity and happiness of the citizens is far in advance of that in the outside world, due to their practice of scientific social planning and the use of operant conditioning in the raising of children.

Walden Two, like Thoreau's *Walden,* champions a lifestyle that does not support war, foster competition and social strife. It encourages a lifestyle of minimal consumption, rich social relationships, personal happiness, satisfying work, and leisure.

Beyond Freedom and Dignity advanced the thesis that social concepts such as free will and human dignity (by which Skinner meant belief in individual autonomy) were obsolete, and stood in the way of greater human happiness and productivity.[212]

Creating a utopia—even in a writer's imagination—in a small-scale, controlled community is difficult, so building it in reality on a national scale requires a quantum leap in methodology. Nowhere is the leap better prepared for by the influencers in this book than in our educational system.

The Obsolete Teacher

As school curriculum has been re-engineered by the likes of Benjamin Bloom, the job of teacher is being transformed by the work of B. F. Skinner—transformed to the degree that some believe the role of the teacher is *disappearing* from America's classrooms. Bloom's "higher order thinking skills" and the behavioral psychology of B. F. Skinner have met in today's computer programs. The result is classrooms that no longer require a teacher, merely a facilitator to indoctrinate children with the desired government worldview. One observer noted, "Our teachers will be reduced to computer disc DJs."[213]

In a publication titled "Technology and Outcome-Based Education in Minnesota," the Minnesota Department of Education describes this changing role:

> Machines are becoming the information givers of our society. Since professional information givers of the past may quickly be replaced by these machines, teachers need to define themselves, and act as diagnosers, prescribers, creative climate makers, instructional designers, coaches, and learning facilitators. . . . Teachers must stop functioning as information givers, putting learners in rows, trying to transmit information through worksheets and lectures.

Sidestepping teachers is made easier with the OBE mindset in which excuses are built into the system to allow students to underachieve. In an effort to bolster their argument for the continued use of the Whole-Language approach to reading, for instance, educators have decided some readers are "genetically indisposed toward learning phonics."

The teacher-as-facilitator model is merely an idea that has "come of age." As early as 1968, the "education reform movement" laid the groundwork for its future policies. A report from an educational conference at the time reveals the agenda of the educational elite:

> The teacher will have disappeared, and his place will be taken by a facilitator of learning, focusing attention on the prime period of learning . . . from infancy to age six or eight. . . . He [the student] will never be graduated.

Social engineers call this "life-long learning."

In a 1969 speech before the 22nd Annual Teachers Education Conference at the University of Georgia, Dean Corrigan predicted that Skinner's "teaching machines will pace a student's progress, diagnose his weaknesses and make certain that he understands a fundamental concept before allowing him to advance to the next lesson."

Programming Humans

While computers are a tremendous asset to our society and to education, technology has the potential to facilitate the "Big Brother" thinking of bureaucrats who see education and schools as a way to control society. Within the framework of B. F. Skinner's worldview, computers can, in a hunter-becomes-the-hunted twist, be used to program people.

Skinner believed in Darwinian evolution and saw little difference between humans and animals:

> Skinner argued that the so-called humanistic characteristics of species, which presumably set *Homo sapiens* off from the

rest of living evolutionary products, are in fact an illusion, created over history to give humans a sense of security. In fact, for Skinner, to be human meant to be in control, to understand and use environmental contingencies to self benefit.[214]

Skinner and Karl Marx had the same mindset that dominates today's social engineers, who believe a perfect world or utopia can be created by establishing the right environment through proper conditioning, programmed learning, corrective-thought control, coercion, brainwashing, and manipulation. Dr. Skinner was so skilled at behavioral programming that he trained pigeons during World War II to pilot and detonate bombs and torpedoes. In *B. F. Skinner, The Man and His Ideas*, author Richard Evans quotes Skinner: "I could make a pigeon a high achiever by reinforcing it on a proper schedule."[215] Skinner believed that by using the teaching machines he developed to reinforce desired behavior in animals, he could also program humans.

The New World Encyclopedia makes the education connection:

> Skinner's work has also been applied to the field of education. He formulated principles of programmed learning, in which reinforcement of small, incremental steps with immediate reinforcement, or reward, for the correct responses would presumably lead to learning not only of sensori-motor responses but also of verbal responses and conceptual knowledge. In fact, his ideas have been successfully incorporated in "teaching machines" as well as computer assisted instruction.[216]

Alienating Children from Parents

Professor Kenneth Goodman, former president of the International Reading Association, wrote to President Jimmy Carter denouncing programs based on the philosophies of B. F. Skinner. Many were being funded by the U.S. Department of Education, and Goodman explained to the president exactly what B. F. Skinner's programmed learning was all about:

> In behavior management, outcomes are assumed or arbitrarily determined and the behavior of human learners is shaped, conditioned, reinforced, extinguished, rewarded or punished until the learners achieve the target behavior.[217]

Under Mastery Learning and Outcome-Based Education, teachers are expected to track, record, and correct improper attitudes, values, feelings, and emotions of their students—an impossible task unless the teacher has help. Today computers and specialized software can track and correct students who exhibit the politically incorrect responses, even without the aid of a teacher.

Why do the agents of change want to track the beliefs of our children? One reason is to aid the diabolical quest to inculcate into our children the elite's "higher minded" beliefs and values. And this must not be hindered by the beliefs of the child's parents. When children exhibit wrong attitudes and beliefs—likely those instilled by their parents—remediation, corrective thought control, and re-programming will be the order of business. The computer is the fastest and most effective means by which to track both a student's moral and character development to correct his or her wrong developmental behavior.

Using Eskimos to Mold Beliefs

In 1963, under contract with the U.S. Office of Health, Education and Welfare, the National Education Association managed the Technological Development Project. It published a statement of what it was working on:

Another area of potential development in computer applications is the attitude changing machine. Dr. Bertram Raven in the Psychology Department at the University of California in Los Angeles is in the process of building a computer-based device for changing attitude. This device will work on the principle that students' attitudes can be changed effectively by using the Socratic method of asking an appropriate series of leading questions logically designed to right the balance between appropriate attitudes and those deemed less acceptable.[218]

In the 1970s, a controversial social studies program called *Man: A Course of Study* was introduced into many American schools, and it is still in use. What was the purpose of this program? The stated purpose was "to help children by exploring in depth the lifestyle of an obscure Eskimo tribe."

But who designed the course? Why Eskimos, and how was it supposed to help children?

A team of experimental psychologists under Jerome S. Burner and B. F. Skinner created the course to mold children's social attitudes and beliefs along lines that set them apart and alienated them from the beliefs and moral values of their parents and local community. That was the assessment by Congressman John Conlan of Arizona on April 9, 1975, on the House floor.

Rep. Conlan hit the nail on the head. Skinner's programmed learning focuses on setting children apart and "alienating them from the beliefs and moral values of their parents"—particularly if those parents have attempted to instill in their children a Biblical worldview.

Forcing Students into Line

Eventually, every school child will be working on his or her own computer, on individualized projects and assignments. Why? Because every child will have different attitudes, values, feelings, and emotions that need remediating. What will really be happening, of course, is that every student will have varying shades and types of political incorrectness that must be changed.

According to the educational elite, every child is sick and in need of help. Dr. Pierce, professor of education and psychology at Harvard University, explains the challenge each student presents:

> Every child who enters school at the age of five is mentally ill because he enters school with an allegiance toward our elected officials, our founding fathers, our institutions, the preservation of this form of government that we have, patriotism, nationalism, sovereignty. All this proves that the children are sick, because a truly well individual is one who has rejected all of those things, and is what I would call the true international child of the future.[219]

Curriculum will be designed to correct this "mental sickness." Of course the question that arises is: What makes every five-year-old in America sick? Could it be the five years of love and attention the child has received from his parents? Yes, in fact, that is exactly what "experts" think makes children sick. Dr. Pierce says they come to school with a set worldview—one with which he disagrees. This worldview that Dr. Pierce finds so sickening, of course, came from the child's parents.

What Pierce really objects to is parental authority and influence, Judeo-Christian values, the traditional American family, and the Biblical worldview.

Research journalist Geoffrey Botkin notes that this is where the computer comes into play:

> In coming stages...the government can determine how to remediate, or fix, the way the child thinks with custom software for every child....[The software] can create custom individualized computer drills that can force every student into line.[220]

In the October 1999 *Education Reporter*, Phyllis Schlafly reported that the state of Massachusetts has developed a computer tracking system to follow personal data on every student in the state. The Massachusetts Department of Education calls it the Student Information Management System. According to Schlafly, "SIMS will eventually allow students to log onto any personal computer and access customized homework pages and personal homework folders."

While this may sound great to some, the potential for abuse by the state is so real that it sounds frightening to me. If my concern seems unwarranted or perhaps extreme, there is reason to believe that thought control is exactly what the educrats in Washington have in mind.

Collecting Data about Your Child

The April 15, 1970 *Washington Star* featured an article titled, "Set Up Data Banks, Allen Urges Schools" by John Matthews. Matthews quotes then-U.S. Commissioner of Education James Allen as encouraging local school systems to have a central diagnostic center:

> . . . to find out everything possible about the child and his background. . . . (The Center) would know just about everything there is to know about the child—his home and

family background, his cultural and language deficiencies, his health and nutrition needs and his general potential as an individual.

Allen suggests that professionals would write a "prescription" for the child "and if necessary, for his home and family as well." And how would the professionals determine which children need a prescription? According to Allen's plan, each child would "be evaluated before 6 years of age, then again at 11 and 15."[221]

Later that same year, the *Dallas Morning News* on December 12, 1970 reported in "School Survey to Begin," an article by Karen Elliott:

By 1972, administrators expect to have complete computerized records on each of the 180,000 students in the district. When this is completed. . .they will begin compiling information on Dallas teachers and on students' home life and socioeconomic background.

That was almost 40 years ago! The collection of student information has only increased, due both to the public's sheep-like acceptance of the practice and to improved technology that makes it easier than ever. Phyllis Schlafly's 1999 article in *Education Reporter* offered an update on the progress of tracking students:

The Massachusetts Department of Education (DOE) will begin issuing ID numbers to about one million public school children this fall through a computerized tracking system called the Student Information Management System (SIMS). The system will require school districts to provide at least 35 bits of information on each student, including scores on the Massachusetts Comprehensive Assessment System (MCAS) tests, career plans, race, and other personal data.

The *Massachusetts Eagle-Tribune* reported on August 22 that SIMS will create permanent records that will follow students throughout their years in public school. Information that formerly remained with the individual school districts will now be under state jurisdiction.

The Massachusetts Department of Education's own handbook points out that SIMS data may be shared with other state or local agencies without consent, and that it will be possible for federal agencies to subpoena the state for information.

Michael Sweeney, a lawyer and school committeeman in Lawrence, Massachusetts, called the process of identifying all the state's school children "outrageous" and termed it "Big Brotherism." He noted that, "a third of the information they are collecting is totally unnecessary. Any time the government starts centrally collecting information, people should worry."

Perhaps your response is, "Well, I don't have to worry because I don't live in Massachusetts." But Schlafly reports:

Massachusetts officials point out that their state is not the only one introducing such a system. "About 20-25 other states have implemented or are developing similar systems."

In a television documentary on America's educational system, Geoffrey Botkin discovered that even in 1978 the Institute of Electrical and Electronic Engineers warned about the unlawful political abuse of electronics technology, a warning that was ignored. In 1994, IEEE published a summary of the abuses that had occurred by then:

1. The collecting of psychological, medical, sociological data on students and their families without their knowledge or consent via the NAEP, the National Assessment of Educational Progress.

2. The "going on line" of the education supercomputer, the Elementary and Secondary Integrated Data System in 1989. This system linked the U.S. Department of Education with all 50 state education departments.

3. Promoting the above under the rubric of "educational restructuring" under names like Outcome-Based Education while withholding from the public the nature and extent of the data collection.

America's social engineers will stop at nothing to achieve their goal of reprogramming our youth. "Withholding from the public" is a favorite strategy for concealing their methods of collecting data about our children. B. F. Skinner would probably approve heartily of the conditioning we've received to think that "what we don't know won't hurt us."

16

CHARLES DARWIN
(1809-1882)

Given that Adolf Hitler fully embraced the worldview of Charles Darwin, at this point in our discussion it would be tempting to ask, "Need I say more?" On the other hand, if the chapters in this book were placed in order of importance of influence, Darwin would be number one.

The spectacular scope and intensity of Darwinism's influence on virtually every arena of thought is breathtaking. The acceptance of Darwin's worldview and the associated "science" paved the way for acceptance of every one of the people named in this book. If rising to Darwin's level of impact was the standard for induction into the Destructive Ideas Hall of Fame, he would be the only one to qualify for admittance.

In a sense, Darwin "started it all." His *Origin of Species* and *The Descent of Man* crystallized the worldview he would come to stand for.

Survival of the Eugenicists

The Descent of Man is essentially a call to embrace eugenics, which Darwin euphemistically called "survival of the fittest." Although Darwin initially described a farm animal breeding program, he eventually made it clear he was talking about human "evolution" as well. The legacy of this one idea has led to the deaths of millions. Eugenicists, as defined by Dr. George Grant, are:

> the practitioners of an odd pseudo-science who sincerely
> believe that if human civilization were to survive, the physi-

cally unfit, the materially poor, the spiritually diseased, the racially inferior, and the mentally incompetent had to be eliminated.[222]

Here's how Darwin put it:

> With savages, the weak in body or mind are soon eliminated; and those that survive exhibit a vigorous state of health…. We civilized men, on the other hand, do our utmost to check the process of elimination; we build asylums for the imbecile, the maimed, and the sick; we institute poor-laws; and our medical men exert their utmost skill to save the life of every one to the last moment. There is reason to believe that vaccination has preserved thousands, who from a weak constitution would formerly have succumbed to small-pox. Thus the weak members of civilized societies propagate their kind. One who has attended to the breeding of domestic animals will not doubt that this must be highly injurious to the race of man. It is surprising how soon a want of care, or care wrongly directed, leads to the degeneration of a domestic race; but excepting in the case of man himself, hardly anyone is so ignorant as to allow his worst animals to breed.[223]

Darwin spins this into his prescription for how to assure the continuing upward progress of mankind:

> If…various checks…do not prevent the reckless, the vicious and otherwise inferior members of society from increasing at a quicker rate than the better class of man, the nation will retrograde, as has occurred too often in the history of the world. We must remember that progress is no invariable rule.[224]

Now consider Hitler writing in *Mein Kampf*:

Every crossing between two breeds which are not quite equal results in a product which holds an intermediate place between the levels of the two parents. This means that the offspring will indeed be superior to the parent which stands in the biologically lower order of being, but not so high as the higher parent. For this reason it must eventually succumb in any struggle against the higher species. Such mating contradicts the will of Nature towards the selective improvements of life in general. The favourable preliminary to this improvement is not to mate individuals of higher and lower orders of being but rather to allow the complete triumph of the higher order. The stronger must dominate and not mate with the weaker, which would signify the sacrifice of its own higher nature. Only the born weakling can look upon this principle as cruel, and if he does so it is merely because he is of a feebler nature and narrower mind; for if such a law did not direct the process of evolution then the higher development of organic life would not be conceivable at all.[225]

Dr. Erwin Lutzer in his book, *Hitler's Cross,* illuminates the Darwin/Hitler connection:

Hitler also accepted Charles Darwin's theory of "the survival of the fittest" and asserted that man had every right to be "as cruel as nature." Detailed lectures were given in schools and to SS troops to prove the inferiority of the Jews. Aryan skulls were compared with those of Jewish ancestry to prove on a scientific basis that the latter were hopelessly inferior. Only the "fittest" had the right to survive."[226]

Naturalism and Its Consequences

Darwin was committed to naturalism, the belief that all that exists is the natural world. To him, there is no spiritual world, no Creator God. This worldview brings with it serious consequences:

- If there is no God or Creator, then everything happens by chance or by mistake.

- If there is no God, then man was not created in His image.

- If there is no God, then there is no right or wrong.

- If there is no God, there is only the natural world.

- If there is no God, then man does not have an eternal soul and there is no life after death.

- If there is no God, life has no meaning.

- If there is no God, man does not have a free will, for he is the product of his environment.

Yale University history professor Donald Kagan points out the consequences of a worldview that says "God is dead." Often called nihilism and based largely on the writings of Friedrich Nietzsche, it permeates our culture:

> [A] vulgar form of Nihilism has a remarkable influence in our educational system through our universities. The consequences of the victory of such ideas would be enormous. If both religion and reason are removed, all that

remains is will and power, where the only law is that of tooth and claw.[227]

Hitler, Stalin, and Mussolini demonstrate the destruction that results when a leader doesn't believe in God, life after death, heaven, hell, or a judgment day on which he will be held accountable by the righteous Judge. In their atheistic worldviews, they were the highest authority. As a result, Hitler killed as many as six million Jews and five million non-Jews during his Holocaust, and while Stalin was dictator of the Soviet Union, he killed some 20 to 40 million people. The twentieth century was the most murderous of any century in history, due largely to tyrants and dictators who did not acknowledge any authority higher than themselves. The *Congressional Record* noted that 135 million people were killed by Communists in the twentieth century.[228]

Our Founders so believed in the importance of elected officials believing in a deity higher than government that Benjamin Rush, known as the Founding Father who promoted the establishment of schools in America, said:

> Such is my veneration for every religion that reveals the attributes of the Deity, or a future state of rewards and punishments, that I had rather see the opinion of Confucius or Mohamed inculcated upon our youth than see them grow up wholly devoid of a system of religious principles. But the religion I mean to recommend in this place is that of the New Testament.[229]

Benjamin Rush understood that religion—or a belief in God—made for great citizens. He also knew that if America's future educators were not firm in their belief in the Deity who rewards good and punishes evil, then our republican form of government would not last.

In 1925, the American Civil Liberties Union defended evolution in the now-famous Scopes trial. Building on the momentum started by that case, the ACLU has fought hard through the years to keep creationism from being taught in America's public schools. The ACLU, with the aid of the NEA and other liberal groups, has been tremendously successful in their censorship of facts and reality.

Since the ACLU and NEA both are liberal organizations founded and supported by well-known humanists, we should not be shocked by their contempt for the creationist worldview. Evolution, as outlined in the *Humanist Manifesto I, II,* and *2000,* is a major religious doctrine or tenet of Secular Humanism. Instead of a belief in God as the basis for their religion, humanists believe in nature or "natural science." Thus, a humanist is said to believe in naturalism.

The humanists' point in promoting naturalistic evolution is to create an intellectually sophisticated way to deny the existence of God. I would contend, however, that believing in evolution requires more blind faith than believing in God. Dr. D. G. Lindsay agrees and describes the blind religion of evolution this way:

> Evolution is a religion that attributes everything to "nature." It demands a faith that is totally blind. Since the evolutionist believes nature and its laws are the guiding force in the universe, he is totally at odds with the Christian faith and the essential miraculous aspect of creation. The miraculous events of the Bible deviate from the known laws of nature, or at least from our understanding of them. However, the evolutionist is blind to the fact that his religion, evolution, violates every known law for its own existence, making

atheistic evolution more incredible (miraculous) than the Christian faith.[230]

The Presupposition Matters

Man, for the humanist, is his own "higher power." The humanist rejects God and so must accept biological evolution because the alternative is to say there is a supernatural Creator and intelligent designer. If there is such a Creator, then He is the author of the laws of nature, and we are accountable to Him. But being accountable to anyone other than self is not acceptable to the humanist. As a result, humanists reject out of hand any and all evidence that challenges their desired reality.

The liberal, then, who chooses to have faith in evolution does so not because of compelling intellectual honesty but because the alternative requires accountability to God. This renders the liberal agenda a house of cards, for if a liberal acknowledges God, then abortion is murder, homosexuality is a sin, and sex outside of marriage is fornication. Most humanists refuse to admit to God's existence—regardless of the sound reasoning and evidence to the contrary—because of their commitment to self-idolatry and pride. But the Bible paints a clear picture of these people in Psalm 14:1: "The fool says in his heart, 'God does not exist'." Only a fool could look at the historical, archaeological, prophetic, philosophical, and scientific evidence and deny God's existence.

I admit to looking at everything through the presupposition that "in the beginning, God," but the humanist must admit that they start with "in the beginning, matter." This means a humanist considers only theories that don't contradict his presupposition. As the *Humanist Manifesto II* states:

We find insufficient evidence for belief in the existence of a supernatural; it is either meaningless or irrelevant to the question of the survival and fulfillment of the human race. As non-theists, we begin with humans not God, nature not deity.

That means any field of inquiry is limited for humanists. If something calls into question the original presupposition (that there is no God), it is rejected, even if it means having "faith" in an idea, belief, or theory that is mathematically impossible, or even if it contradicts known scientific facts and laws of physics. As long ago as 1929, Professor D. M. S. Watson, one of the leading biologists and science writers of his day, explained that the real goal behind evolution is to reject the alternative—a belief in God:

> Evolution [is] a theory universally accepted not because it can be proven by logically coherent evidence to be true, but because the only alternative, special creation, is clearly incredible.[231]

Professor Richard Lewontin, a geneticist and self-proclaimed Marxist, reveals why the dogmatic humanist continues to accept the lie of evolution despite its improbability and the unscientific propositions on which it is built:

> We take the side of science in spite of the patent absurdity of some of its constructs, in spite of its failure to fulfill many of its extravagant promises of health and life, in spite of the tolerance of the scientific community for unsubstantiated just-so-stories, because we have a prior commitment, a commitment to materialism. It is not that the methods

and institutions of science somehow compel us to accept a material explanation of the phenomenal world, but, on the contrary, that we are forced by our a priori adherence to material causes to create an apparatus of investigation and a set of concepts that produce material explanations, no matter how counter-intuitive, no matter how mystifying to the uninitiated. Moreover, that materialism is an absolute, for we cannot allow a Divine Foot in the door.[232]

I sincerely appreciate Prof. Lewontin's candor. Few humanists are so clear-headed in understanding and articulating what they really try to achieve by promoting purely naturalistic explanations for everything. Evolution is not based on science, despite what most evolutionists will tell you. Dr. Robert A. Millikan, a physicist and Nobel Prize winner, was equally clear when he stated in a speech before the American Chemical Society, "The pathetic thing about it is that many scientists are trying to prove the doctrine of evolution, which no science can do."[233]

Yes, *pathetic* is a good word. It is quite pathetic when you consider the mental gymnastics a humanist must perform to defend the presupposition that there is no intelligent designer for the universe and that spontaneous, macro-evolution is scientific. Although the humanist typically mocks as unscientific those who believe in a Creator God, they are the ones who ignore facts and instead create preposterous theories when the science at the foundation of their worldview is proven to be unscientific and mathematically impossible.

Scripture says, "The heavens declare the glory of God, and the sky proclaims the work of His hands" (Ps. 19:1), and a discussion of Darwin offers a natural time to look at various aspects of creation that reveal this glory and announce God's existence.

Happily for some in the scientific community, the remarkable discoveries of the past few years have caused some scientists to reject the lie of evolution and explore evidence for an "intelligent designer." The complexity of the human body and the orderliness of the universe are so overwhelming that these researchers no longer believe everything we see and know happened by chance. They may not quite be ready to say, "God is," but at least they acknowledge the necessity of an intelligent designer of some sort.

So, the issue is not that one worldview (theism) requires faith while the other (atheism) does not—*both do*. The question is: Which worldview is based on a more *rational* faith? And to that, the answer is clear.

There is far greater evidence for the existence of God as Creator than for the notion that everything came about by random chance. To accept the idea of a Creator God, you need to have faith in only one thing—an all-knowing, all-powerful Being. The astonishing complexity of creation is consistent with the infinitely knowledgeable, omnipotent Creator. Only such a One could have created the universe as we know it. On the other hand, to believe in spontaneous evolution, you must have faith in billions upon billions of mathematically improbable and scientifically impossible occurrences.

The real goal of evolution is not to gain knowledge about how the world came to be. The primary purpose is to explain away the existence of God. Atheists just don't want to admit that Someone could be so powerful and unimaginably intelligent as to put together the cosmos as we know it. It's too . . . well . . . humbling.

They have Darwin to thank for giving them a way out.

PART 5

AND NOW FROM THE GOVERNMENT-CORPORATE COMPLEX

17

KARL MARX
(1818-1883)

As a young man, Marx was dismissed from several universities for his radical, revolutionary views. An atheist and a Secular Humanist, he wrote the *Communist Manifesto* with his friend Friedrich Engels. Marx did not believe in the spiritual world or life after death, only in the natural, material world. He valued people only for what they could do for the State. Is it any wonder, then, that the worldview of Marx—Communism—has been responsible for the murder of more than 100 million people?

Marx hated the free market and capitalism—and their roots in the Protestant Reformation—perhaps because he was a lazy slob who wanted other people to take care of him. He lived largely off his friend Friedrich Engels, who drew an income from the family business. How perversely ironic is that? Marx spread his hatred of capitalism while drawing his livelihood from the fruits of capitalism. Isn't that always the mode of operation for those who follow the economic philosophy of Communism, the most virulent form of socialism?

Marx was such a reprobate that out of his six children, three died of starvation while still infants, two others committed suicide, and only one lived to become an adult. The Marx family was often hounded by creditors. Yet, when Marx received a gift of 160 pounds (about $500), he neglected to pay his bills, his rent, or to buy food for his starving family. Rather, he went on a two-month drinking binge with his intellectual buddies while his wife and infant children were evicted from their apartment. Marx, the parasite, also spent his wife's inheritances from her mother and uncle, causing his family to live on the edge of financial ruin for years.

Among the many infectious ideas Marx promoted was his hatred for the traditional family. Instead, he favored "a system of wives in common." Needless to say, Marx did not have a great marriage, and when his wife died, Marx didn't even attend her funeral. And not only was he a negligent husband and father, Marx was such an uncaring, arrogant bully that he had few friends. Even those who agreed with his teachings did not like him as a person. As a result, when he died, fewer than a dozen people attended his funeral (what goes around, comes around).

Dialectical Godlessness

The basis of Marxism is atheism. As Marx said, "Religion is the sigh of the oppressed creature, the sentiment of a heartless world, as it is the spirit of spiritless conditions. It is the opium of the people."[234]

While a student at the University of Berlin, Marx was greatly influenced by German philosopher George W. F. Hegel mentioned in Chapter 6. Hegel's dialectics taught a synthesis through which opposites like good and evil can combine for a better, third option. The dialectic is a theoretical construct which Marx tried to apply to the natural world. Lenin recognized what Marx was doing and wrote of the "great Hegelian dialectics which Marxism made its own, having first turned it right side up."[235]

David Noebel, in his book *Understanding the Times,* describes the Dialectical Materialism of Marx this way:

> The dialectic says that in everything there is a thesis (the way things are) and an antithesis (an opposition to the way things are), which must inevitably clash. The result of

the struggle and merging that comes from the clash is the synthesis, which becomes the new thesis. This new thesis will eventually attract another antithesis, and produce a new synthesis.[236]

Noebel also explains the Marxist hope for what dialectics will achieve:

[D]ialectics perceives the developmental process as an upward spiral. Simply stated, dialectics see change or process due to conflict or struggle as the only constant, and this change and conflict always lead to a more advanced level.[237]

This explains why so many humanistic politicians call for change and why they invite conflict. Neo-Marxist Saul Alinksy (Chapter 20), called for agitating to the point of conflict because he believed in the dialectic process. In his 1971 book, *Rules for Radicals,* Alinsky writes of the dialectic process without naming it as such:

The organizer is constantly creating new out of the old. He knows that all new ideas arise from conflict; that every time man has had a new idea it has been a challenge to the sacred ideas of the past and the present and inevitably a conflict has raged.[238]

…The job then is getting the people to move, to act, to participate; in short, to develop and harness the necessary power to effectively conflict with the prevailing patterns and change them. When those prominent in the status quo turn and label you an 'agitator' they are completely correct, for that is, in one word, your function—to agitate to the point of conflict.[239]

As I document in this book, variations on the ideas and values of Marx and Hegel influence the thinking of many of America's political, educational, occult, and Church leaders. Barack Obama, for instance, studied Alinksy and taught his strategies while a community organizer in Chicago. It is part of the spiritual battle I described in Chapter 2.

You'll recall from Chapter 3 that, Alice Bailey, under the influence of a demon, wrote that Lenin, Hitler, Stalin, Mussolini, and other such tyrants were "agents of destiny, creators of the new order and the initiators of the new civilizations; they are destroyers of what must be destroyed before humanity can go forward along the Lighted Way."[240]

And what is it they have to destroy? The answer is Christianity. The Biblical worldview is the "forces of evil" the Hierarchy (demonic realm) is battling.

De-Christianizing the World: A Firsthand Account

This obsession to obliterate Christianity manifests itself in many ways. Pastor Richard Wurmbrand was imprisoned for 14 years in Romania for preaching the Gospel while he also railed against Communism. After his freedom was purchased he found his way to America.

A month after his arrival in America in 1966, he testified before the United States Senate, and it has been reported that Wurmbrand's testimony was the most-sold government document for the next three years. His testimony is available online (http://members.cox.net/wurmbrand/communist.html), and if you read it, you'll understand why it is so popular. His testimony warns that Communism cannot tolerate Christianity, and the Communist strategy in America is to infiltrate religious institutions and use them to further the Communist cause. Wurmbrand pleaded with Americans to oppose Communism in any form:

...The church can never have a peaceful coexistence with atheism. Everybody would laugh if I would say that health can peacefully exist with the microbe of tuberculosis, that the FBI can coexist peacefully with gangsters, that the church can peacefully exist with drunkenness, but communism and atheism is much worse than drug addiction and drunkenness. You drink a little wine and the next day it passes, but communism poisons youth and our children since 50 years. How can there be peaceful existence with this on the side of churchmen and the church leadership I cannot understand.

Pastor Wurmbrand explained that Communists do not really care whether or not people become Communists per se but only that they do not oppose Communism. Pointing out the unBiblical ideas and values of Communism leads to cruel and murderous actions against the dissenter. In outlining the Communist approach, Wurmbrand explained that churches don't need to teach Communism, only a liberal Christianity that allows for the acceptance of what Communists want to accomplish:

Rumanian Communists are very interested in the fact that you have here in the States, something like 300,000 [liberal clergy] on their side. They can't very well win them for Communism, but they can win them for a leftwing Christianity which supports Communism.

In addition to his Congressional testimony, Wurmbrand wrote several books cautioning against embracing Communism. Unfortunately, Wurmbrand's warnings have largely gone unheeded, and we are now suffering the consequences.

A Strange Spiritual Partnership

Leftwing Christianity that rejects a Biblical worldview and proclaims a liberal social gospel is a partner to Communism, whether knowingly or not. Thus, Communism has many partners in America—even among some of America's most popular "Christian" authors and conference speakers.

FBI founder and director, J. Edgar Hoover, in his 1958 book *Masters of Deceit* explains why Communists put their people in as the heads of churches and other such organizations:

> To make a known Party member president of a front would immediately label it as "communist." But if a sympathizer can be installed, especially a man of prominence, such as an educator, minister, or scientist, the group can operate as an "independent" organization.

Even Russia's once State-controlled Communist newspaper understands that most of America's churches are a joke and are partially responsible for America's demise. To underscore the point, I'll repeat an exerpt from an April 2009 *Pravada* article I cited in Chapter 5:

> Then their faith in God was destroyed, until their churches, all tens of thousands of different "branches and denominations" were for the most part little more then Sunday circuses and their televangelists and top protestant mega preachers were more than happy to sell out their souls and flocks to be on the "winning" side of one pseudo Marxist politician or another. Their flocks may complain, but when explained that they would be on the "winning" side, their flocks were ever so quick to reject Christ in hopes

for earthly power. Even our Holy Orthodox churches are scandalously liberalized in America.[241]

Marx would be pleased to know how many of America's religious citizens have accepted certain aspects of his worldview, all of his worldview, or simply see no real threat in the wide acceptance of his worldview. Marx was openly hostile toward any religion that did not promote man as God:

• "Man is the highest being for man....The criticism of religion ends with the teaching that man is the highest being for man...."[242]

• Man "looked for a superhuman being in the fantastic reality of heaven and found nothing there but the reflection of himself."[243]

• "Religion is the sigh of the oppressed creature, the sentiment of a heartless world, as it is the spirit of spiritless conditions. It is the opium of the people."[244]

Marx and Engels wrote the *Communist Manifesto*, first published in 1848. Its core teaching can be summed up in what is often called the Ten Planks of the *Communist Manifesto*:

1. Abolition of property in land and application of all rents of land to public purposes.

2. A heavy progressive or graduated income tax.

3. Abolition of all right of inheritance.

4. Confiscation of the property of all emigrants and rebels.

5. Centralization of credit in the hands of the State, by means of a national bank with State capital and an exclusive monopoly.

6. Centralization of the means of communication and transport in the hands of the State.

7. Extension of factories and instruments of production owned by the State; the bringing into cultivation of waste-lands, and the improvement of the soil generally in accordance with a common plan.

8. Equal liability of all to labor. Establishment of industrial armies, especially for agriculture.

9. Combination of agriculture with manufacturing industries; gradual abolition of the distinction between town and country, by a more equal distribution of the population over the country.

10. Free education for all children in public schools. Abolition of children's factory labor in its present form. Combination of education with industrial production.

While serving as chief of police for Salt Lake City, Utah, Cleon Skousen wrote a 1961 best-selling book, *The Naked Communist,* in which he lists 45 goals of the Communist Party. Having served 16 years at the FBI, Skousen was a serious student of his Communist enemies. The January 10, 1963 *Congressional Record* lists these 45 goals:

1. U.S. acceptance of co-existence as the only alternative to atomic war.

2. U.S. willingness to capitulate in preference to engaging in atomic war.

3. Develop the illusion that total disarmament by the U.S. would be a demonstration of moral strength.

4. Permit free trade between all nations regardless of Communist domination.

5. Extension of long-term loans to Russia and Soviet satellites.

6. Provide American aid to all nations regardless of Communist domination.

7. Grant recognition of Red China. Admission of Red China to the U.N.

8. Set up East and West Germany as separate states in spite of Khrushchev's promise in 1955 to settle the Germany question by free elections under supervision of the U.N.

9. Prolong the conferences to ban atomic tests, because the U.S. has agreed to suspend tests as long as negotiations are in progress.

10. Allow all Soviet satellites individual representation in the U.N.

11. Promote the U.N. as the only hope for mankind. If its charter is rewritten, demand that it be set up as a one-world government with its own independent armed forces.

12. Resist any attempt to outlaw the Communist Party.

13. Do away with loyalty oaths.

14. Continue giving Russia access to the U.S. Patent Office.

15. Capture one or both political parties.

16. Use technical decisions of the courts to weaken basic American institutions by claiming their activities violate civil rights.

17. Get control of the schools. Use them as transmission belts for socialism and current Communist propaganda. Soften the curriculum. Get control of "teacher" associations. Put the party line in textbooks.

18. Gain control of all student newspapers.

19. Use student riots to foment public protests against programs or organizations which are under Communist attack.

20. Infiltrate the press. Get control of book review assignments, editorial writing, policy-making positions.

21. Gain control of key positions in radio, TV and motion pictures.

22. Continue discrediting American culture by degrading all forms of artistic expression. An American Communist cell was told to "eliminate" all good sculpture from parks and buildings, substitute shapeless, awkward and meaningless forms.

23. Control art critics and directors of museums. "Plan is to promote ugliness, repulsive, meaningless art."

24. Eliminate laws governing obscenity by calling them "censorship" and violation of free speech and free press.

25. Break down cultural standards of morality by promoting pornography and obscenity in books, magazines, motion pictures, radio and TV.

26. Present homosexuality, degeneracy and promiscuity as "normal, natural, healthy."

27. Infiltrate the churches and replace revealed religion with "social" religion. Discredit the Bible and emphasize the need for intellectual maturity which does not need a "religious crutch."

28. Eliminate prayer or any phase of religious expression in the schools on the grounds that it violates the principle of "Separation of Church and State."

29. Discredit the American Constitution by calling it inadequate, old-fashioned, out of step with modern needs, a hindrance to cooperation between nations on a worldwide basis.

30. Discredit the American founding fathers. Present them as selfish aristocrats who had no concern for the "common man."

31. Belittle all forms of American culture and discourage the teaching of American history on the grounds that it was only a minor part of "the big picture." Give emphasis to Russian history since the Communists took over.

32. Support any socialist movement to give centralized

control over any part of the culture—education, social agencies, welfare programs, mental health clinics, etc.

33. Eliminate all laws or procedures which interfere with the operation of the Communist apparatus.

34. Eliminate the House Committee on Un-American Activities.

35. Discredit and eventually dismantle the FBI.

36. Infiltrate and gain control of more "unions"!

37. Infiltrate and gain control of "big business"!

38. Transfer some of the powers of arrest from the police to social agencies. Treat all behavioral problems as psychiatric disorders which "no one but psychiatrists" can understand and treat.

39. Dominate the psychiatric profession and use mental health laws as a means of gaining coercive control over those who oppose Communist goals.

40. Discredit the "family" as an institution. Encourage promiscuity and easy divorce.

41. Emphasize the need to raise children away from the "negative" influence of parents. Attribute prejudices, mental blanks and retarding of children to suppressive influence of parents.

42. Create the impression that violence and insurrection are legitimate aspects of the American tradition, that students and special-interest groups should rise up and use "united

force" to solve economic, political or social problems.

43. Overthrow all colonial governments before native populations are ready for self-government.

44. Internationalize the Panama Canal.

45. Repeal the Connally Reservation so the U.S. cannot prevent the World Court from seizing jurisdiction over domestic problems. Give the World Court jurisdiction over "Nations and Individuals" alike.[245]

Who's Behind All This?

Like many communist/socialist radicals of today—and like Alice Bailey—Marx, as a teenager, wrote about his Christian faith and his Christian convictions. As a young student, he claimed that Christ was in his heart. But it is clear that Marx-the-adult held to nothing remotely like true faith and repentance in Jesus Christ. No, his worldview was quite opposite of that.

After Richard Wurmbrand offered his gripping testimony to Congress, he went on to found Voice of the Martyrs in support of Christians suffering for their faith. He also wrote several books about Karl Marx in which he documents the satanic influence underlying Marxism. He clearly reveals that Karl Marx was involved in Satanism.

In one of his poems, Marx declares:

> Thus heaven I've forfeited,
> I know it full well.
> My soul, once true to God,
> Is chosen for hell.[246]

In another, he exclaims:

> I wish to avenge myself against the One who rules above.[247]

Elsewhere, Marx claimed to have a pact with the devil, as Marx's biographer explains:

> He had the Devil's view of the world, and the Devil's malignity. Sometimes he seemed to know that he was accomplishing works of evil.[248]

A letter to Karl from his father dated March 2, 1837 reveals that his own father was fearful that his son was under demonic influence.[249]

The End-Game of Communism

Satan has used socialism, communism, and Marxism in an attempt to build his "new order"—his own kingdom—by seeking to destroy Christianity, free nations, national sovereignty, and law based on the character and nature of God. The devil has used dictators committed to Marxist/Leninist philosophies to kill countless Christians. Why? Because, in the end, it is only committed Christians who build God's Kingdom, making them Satan's greatest obstacle.

Satan encourages in every way possible the violation of the Ten Commandments. The obliteration (stealing) of private property, for instance, forces service to the State alone in order to survive. This fulfills the enemy's plan that people ultimately are not really serving the State but the one who stands behind the State—Satan himself. Jesus Christ points out in John 10:10 that "the thief does not come except to steal, and to kill, and to destroy." Satan—and his tool of the Communist State—is a thief. He loves communism, socialism, and Marxism because any version of such a government does, indeed, steal, kill, and destroy.

Later in John 10:10, Jesus offers the good news: He came so

we would have eternal life. This is a precious promise for the untold numbers of Christians and Jews who have refused to worship at the altar of Satan—and serve the State—with the result that they have been imprisoned or murdered.

Christians can take hope that God's Kingdom will come and crush Satan's dominion as foretold in the book of Daniel. Until that day, believers must realize that to not oppose socialism, communism, and Marxism is to agree with a satanic plan that fuels injustice, cruelty, anti-family values, and anti-Christian worldviews.

One final quote captures the essence of what Marx believed and what he thought should be done about it: "The idea of God is the keynote of a perverted civilization. It must be destroyed."[250] He was dead wrong, but that doesn't change the reality that the worldview of Marx is alive and well in America and around the world. The influence of Marx's ideas is overwhelming, and his vile legacy lives on despite the indisputable failure of his atheistic, communistic worldview wherever it has been tried.

18

John Maynard Keynes
(1883-1946)

John Maynard Keynes is likely the world's best-known economist. Yet, Keynesian economics can be recognized by its values that are contrary to much of what makes for healthy financial living for individuals or nations—love of debt and hatred of savings. The wholesale implementation of his ideas caused the Great Depression to be much deeper and last much longer than was necessary. He believed that during an economic downturn or recession, government should borrow or inflate the currency and dump large amounts of cash into the economy by being the primary source of spending and employment. The end results are inflation and the devaluation of currency.

A socialist, Keynes was a member of the British Fabian Society. Fabian Socialism was birthed in London in 1883 and is best defined as "desiring Socialism through evolution instead of revolution." Many members of America's two dominant political parties are committed to Keynesian economics, and many are likewise Fabians.

The true goal of Fabian Socialism is not merely socialism but globalism. Fabianism dovetails well with corporate fascism, the merging of big government and big business. In my second book, published in 1995, I predicted that America would move toward corporate fascism rather quickly. We have, as you can see now, and the pace is increasing.

Capitalistic Socialism?

Humanist Richard Rorty picks up a Keynesian theme by arguing that traditional socialism will not work, but a form of government similar to corporate fascism—welfare-state capitalism—will do nicely:

> Most people on my side of this...cultural war have given
> up on socialism in light of the history of nationalization
> enterprises and central planning in Central and Eastern
> Europe. We are willing to grant that the welfare-state
> capitalism is the best we can hope for. Most of us who were
> brought up Trotskyite now feel forced to admit that Lenin
> and Trotsky did more harm than good.[251]

David Noebel says this welfare-state capitalism is what we now
call "interventionism":

> Rorty is suggesting that an interventionist approach to
> economics works best. Interventionism is not a totally state-
> planned economy nor a completely free market economy,
> but a combination of the two, where the state plays a role
> in redistributing wealth created in a partially or mostly free
> market environment.[252]

In the end, Fabian Socialists don't really want to own it if they
can control it, and all they need to control it is a financial crisis that
allows them to change laws, inflate the currency, and buy stock
in corporations. Whether you call it nationalizing an industry or
corporate fascism, the result is the same—the death of freedom and
private property rights.

John Strachey, a one-time Communist, entered the British Fabian
Society in 1943 and become war minister in the Labor Government of
Great Britain in 1950. He explains Keynesian economics this way:

> The positive part of Keynes' work was a demand that
> capitalism should now be regulated and controlled by a

central authority....The principal instruments of its policy should be variations in the rate of interest, budgetary deficits and surpluses, public works and a redistribution of personal incomes in equalitarian direction. This positive side of Keynes' work requires an authority to do the regulating, and that authority can be, in contemporary conditions, nothing else but the government of a nation state.[253]

Keynes himself admitted that by:

...a continuous process of inflation, governments can confiscate, secretly and unobserved, an important part of wealth of their citizens. By this method, they not only confiscate, but confiscate arbitrarily: and while the process impoverishes many, it actually enriches some. The process engages all of the hidden forces of economic law on the side of destruction, and does it in a manner that not one man in a million can diagnose.[254]

The American institution used to inflate our currency has been the Federal Reserve. While it has achieved that unspoken goal, the Federal Reserve has failed to accomplish what it was supposedly created to do. According to economics writer Walter Williams:

The justification for the Federal Reserve Act of 1913 was to prevent bank failure and maintain price stability. Simple before and after analysis demonstrates that the Federal Reserve Bank has been a failure.

In the century before the Federal Reserve Act, wholesale prices fell by 6 percent; in the century after they rose by 1,300 percent. Maximum bank failures in one year before

1913 were 496 and afterward, 4,400. During the 1930s, inept money supply management by the Federal Reserve Bank was partially responsible for both the depth and duration of the Great Depression.[255]

Many Warnings

Americans cannot say they were never warned about the dangers of a central bank such as the Fed. As long ago as 1832, President Andrew Jackson worked to abolish the Bank of the United States, which operated much like today's Federal Reserve. In his farewell address, Jackson cautioned Americans never again to allow the creation of a central bank. Less than a century later, though, we ignored his warning and created the Federal Reserve System in 1913. I've noted below a portion of Jackson's farewell address. Read it, and see if it you don't agree with me that we are suffering the consequences of which he warned when our elected officials created the Federal Reserve and eventually ceased to back our currency by gold or silver:

> In reviewing the conflicts which have taken place between different interests in the United States and the policy pursued since the adoption of our present form of Government, we find nothing that has produced such deep-seated evil as the course of legislation in relation to the currency. The Constitution of the United States unquestionably intended to secure to the people a circulating medium of gold and silver. But the establishment of a national bank by Congress, with the privilege of issuing paper money receivable in the payment of the public dues, and the unfortunate course of legislation in the several States upon the same subject, drove from general circulation the constitutional currency

and substituted one of paper in its place.

It was not easy for men engaged in the ordinary pursuits of business, whose attention had not been particularly drawn to the subject, to foresee all the consequences of a currency exclusively of paper, and we ought not on that account to be surprised at the facility with which laws were obtained to carry into effect the paper system. Honest and even enlightened men are sometimes misled by the specious and plausible statements of the designing. But experience has now proved the mischiefs and dangers of a paper currency, and it rests with you to determine whether the proper remedy shall be applied.

The paper system being founded on public confidence and having of itself no intrinsic value, it is liable to great and sudden fluctuations, thereby rendering property insecure and the wages of labor unsteady and uncertain.

The corporations which create the paper money cannot be relied upon to keep the circulating medium uniform in amount. In times of prosperity, when confidence is high, they are tempted by the prospect of gain or by the influence of those who hope to profit by it to extend their issues of paper beyond the bounds of discretion and the reasonable demands of business; and when these issues have been pushed on from day to day, until public confidence is at length shaken, then a reaction takes place, and they immediately withdraw the credits they have given, suddenly curtail their issues, and produce an unexpected and ruinous contraction of the circulating medium, which is felt by the whole community. The banks by this means save themselves, and the mischievous consequences of their imprudence or cupidity are visited upon the public. Nor does the evil stop here. These ebbs and flows in the currency and these indiscreet extensions of credit naturally engender a spirit of speculation injurious to the habits and character of the people.

My humble efforts have not been spared during my administration of the Government to restore the constitutional currency of gold and silver, and something, I trust, has been done toward the accomplishment of this most desirable object; but enough yet remains to require all your energy and perseverance. The power, however, is in your hands, and the remedy must and will be applied if you determine upon it.

Our growth has been rapid beyond all former example in numbers, in wealth, in knowledge, and all the useful arts which contribute to the comforts and convenience of man, and from the earliest ages of history to the present day there never have been thirteen millions of people associated in one political body who enjoyed so much freedom and happiness as the people of these United States. You have no longer any cause to fear danger from abroad; your strength and power are well known throughout the civilized world, as well as the high and gallant bearing of your sons. It is from within, among yourselves—from cupidity, from corruption, from disappointed ambition and inordinate thirst for power—that factions will be formed and liberty endangered. It is against such designs, whatever disguise the actors may assume, that you have especially to guard yourselves. You have the highest of human trusts committed to your care.

In March 2009, Dr. Noebel described Keynesian economics to my radio audience. Notice how much his warning sounds like that of President Jackson:

Keynesianism, or interventionism, or socialism, is contrary to nearly every aspect of the Christian worldview in economics. Today, Keynesianism is called interventionism. Interventionism is where the government itself gets involved in the economic sphere and passes laws that destroy what we would call sound, basic economics. And what we had with Fannie Mae and Freddie Mac and the whole deal of going now into debt by trillions is nothing more or nothing less than Fabian, Keynesian economic philosophy. So this is what every Christian needs to get a handle on, Brannon, or we are finished as a nation. Austrian economics was just basically classical economics. I mean, come on. For 6,000 years, the economics of the world was basically money, sound money. You've got to have something that you can judge by, and even though over the history of the world for the last 6,000 years we've tried various things, they always ended up with gold and silver as being the standard of money. And you could judge it. The dollar itself comes from the word *thaler,* which was a measurement of what an ounce of silver would entail, or a percentage of a gold piece would entail….in fact, the U.S. Constitution identifies money as gold and silver.

Keynesian economics is unBiblical for many reasons, but even a quick reading of the Ten Commandments reveals two. The Commandments against stealing and coveting are broken when the government covets what you own and seeks to steal it from you through inflation. Further, in Deuteronomy 25:13-16 God declares His hatred of unjust weights and scales that are used to cheat people. Our government and the Federal Reserve use the "unjust weights and scales" of monetization (printing money) of our national debt to steal from Americans for the government's self-serving financial gain and harvesting of power.

Note, too, that according to the Bible, mere consumer confidence is not considered adequate backing for a currency. Haggai 2:8 proclaims, "The silver is mine, and the gold is mine, saith the LORD of hosts." Real wealth is not stored or found in paper but in gold and silver.

Like so many other losers on our list, Keynes was also a blatant pervert. Zygmund Dobbs, who conducted research for the book *Keynes at Harvard*, describes Keynes and his socialist buddies this way:

> Singing the Red Flag, the highborn sons of the British upper-class lay on the carpeted floor spinning out socialist schemes in homosexual intermissions . . . .The attitude in such gatherings was anti-establishmentarian. To them the older generation was horribly out of date, even superfluous. The capitalist system was declared obsolete and revolution was proclaimed as the only solution. Christianity was pronounced an enemy force, and the worst sort of depravities were eulogized as 'that love which passes all Christian understanding.' Chief of this ring of homosexual revolutionaries was John Maynard Keynes. . . . Keynes was

characterized by his male sweetheart, Lytton Strachey, as "a liberal and a sodomite, an atheist and a statistician." His particular depravity was the sexual abuse of little boys.[256]

Joan Robinson, a Marxist economist who worked with Keynes, declared that "the differences between Marx and Keynes are only verbal." I contend that many elected officials at the state and federal level are Fabian socialists committed to bring about a social revolution in America by deliberately creating an environment in which chaos and crisis can flourish for the purpose of bigger government—and to move us toward globalism.

The Opportunity in a Crisis

Dr. Noebel wrote a March 2009 article for my website, worldviewtimes. com, in which he documented that there were then some 123 known socialists in the U. S. House of Representatives:

> The legislators involved in this socialistic undertaking belong to one or more radical House organizations: the Progressive Democrats of America (6 House members), the Congressional Progressive Caucus (74 House members), the Congressional Black Caucus (43 House members), and the Democratic Socialists of America. Incidentally, the Democratic Socialists of America do not identify their House members since they consider all members of the Congressional Progressive Caucus part of their membership due to the fact that "they both shared operative social democratic politics."[257]

Pulitzer Prize-winning author James MacGregor Burns promotes globalism, and in his 1984 book, *The Power to Lead,* he reveals that a crisis will be what causes the American people to reject our founding documents, give up our sovereignty, and embrace globalism. The globalists/socialists are intentionally creating just such a crisis:

> Let us face reality. The framers [of the Constitution] have simply been too shrewd for us. They have outwitted us. They designed separated institutions that cannot be unified by mechanical linkages, frail bridges, tinkering. If we are to "turn the founders upside down" we must directly confront the constitutional structure they erected.

> Others might press for major constitutional restructuring but I doubt that Americans under normal conditions could agree on the package of radical and "alien" constitutional changes that would be required. They would do so, I think only during and following a stupendous national crisis and political failure.[258]

Days before Barack Obama was sworn into office as president of the United States, Nobel Peace Prize winner and former secretary of state for President Nixon, Henry Kissinger, gave an interview on CNBC at the New York Stock Exchange. Speaking of President-Elect Obama, Kissinger said:

> His task will be to develop an overall strategy for America in this period when, really, a new world order can be created. It's a great opportunity, it isn't just a crisis.

The crisis is a great opportunity? Barack Obama's White House chief of staff, Rahm Emanuel, told business leaders in a November 2008 meeting that the financial crisis presents "an opportunity to do things you could not do before." Emanuel has also said, "you never want a serious crisis to go to waste."

It sounds as if Kissinger, Obama, and Emanuel are singing from the same song sheet. But there's another voice in the chorus Americans should find alarming. Mikhail Gorbachev, the last leader of the Soviet Union, is president of the International Foundation for Socio-Economic and Political Studies in Moscow and has been pushing one-world religion and one-world government ideas for years. Remarkably, Gorbachev has conducted much of his work right here in America from an office in San Francisco.

On January 1, 2009, Gorbachev wrote a column in the *International Herald Tribune* in which he seemed gleeful over the financial crisis and the "opportunity" it provides for furthering the globalist agenda:

> The G-20 summit meeting in Washington foreshadowed a new format of global leadership, bringing together the countries responsible for the future of the world economy. And more than just the economy is at stake....The economic and political balance in the world has changed. It is now a given that a world with a single power center, in any shape or guise, is no longer possible. The global challenge of a financial and economic tsunami can only be met by working together.[259]

Working together for what purpose? Gorbachev reveals:

> A new concept is emerging for addressing the crisis at the national and international levels. If current ideas for reforming the world's financial and economic institutions are consistently implemented, that would suggest we are finally beginning to understand the importance of global governance.[260]

On the heels of Gorbachev's New Year's comments, a January 8, 2009 Associated Press article by Emma Vandore reported on a two-day meeting hosted by French president Nicolas Sarkozy. The event roster included former British prime minister Tony Blair, who has been calling for a one-world interfaith dialog for years and who used the platform to promote a new financial order based on "values other than the maximum short-term profits." Sarkozy argued that:

> In the 21st Century, there is no longer a single nation who can say what we should do or what we should think....We cannot accept the status quo....In the capitalism of the 21st century, there is room for the state.[261]

When the State moves in, capitalism ceases to be capitalism, and that is exactly the goal. The demise of capitalism brings the fulfillment of the humanist and socialist dream: global government.

In a January 12, 2009 article in the *International Herald Tribune* entitled "A Chance for New World Order," Henry Kissinger declared:

> As the new U.S. administration prepares to take office amid grave financial and international crises, it may seem counterintuitive to argue that the very unsettled nature of the international system generates a unique opportunity for creative diplomacy.... An international order can be permanent only if its participants have a share not only in building but also in securing it. In this manner, America and its potential partners have a unique opportunity to transform a moment of crisis into a vision of hope.[262]

In a twist of irony—or perhaps in a plan well laid and patiently implemented since 1883—the British Fabian Socialists are going to dominate America's financial system. Dick Morris's April 7, 2009 article, "European Socialism to Run Our Financial System," explains:

> On April 2, 2009, the work of July 4, 1776 was nullified at the meeting of the G-20 in London.
>
> The joint communiqué essentially announces a global economic union with uniform regulations and bylaws for all nations, including the United States. Henceforth, our SEC, Commodities Trading Commission, Federal Reserve Board and other regulators will have to march to the beat of drums pounded by the Financial Stability Board (FSB), a body of central bankers from each of the G-20 states and the European Union.
>
> The mandate conferred on the FSB is remarkable for its scope and open-endedness. It is to set a "framework of internationally agreed high standards that a global financial system requires."
>
> Now we may no longer look to presidential appointees, confirmed by the Senate, to make policy for our economy. These decisions will be made internationally.
>
> And Europe will dominate them. The FSF [Financial Stability Forum and precursor to the FSB] and, presumably, the FSB, is now composed of the central bankers of Australia, Canada, France, Germany, Hong Kong, Italy, Japan, Netherlands, Singapore, Switzerland, the United Kingdom, and the United States plus representatives of the World Bank, the European Union, the IMF, and the Organization for Economic Co-operation and Development (OECD).

The Europeans have been trying to get their hands on our financial system for decades. It is essential to them that they rein in American free enterprise so that their socialist heaven will not be polluted by vices such as the profit motive.[263]

The developments in Europe represent what I believe is the revived Roman Empire predicted in Daniel 2:41-43. This sort of prophecy reveals the remarkable, supernatural nature of God's Word. Scripture repeatedly predicts what inevitably comes to pass. We are now watching the fulfillment of Scripture as Europe increases and America decreases.

Secular journalists that once laughed at the idea of a world government are now writing on the issue themselves. In the December 9, 2008 *Financial Times*, Gideon Rachman shared his concern in "And Now for World Government":

I have never believed that there is a secret United Nations plot to take over the US. I have never seen black helicopters hovering in the sky above Montana. But, for the first time in my life, I think the formation of some sort of world government is plausible.

A "world government" would involve much more than co-operation between nations. It would be an entity with state-like characteristics, backed by a body of laws. The European Union has already set up a continental government for 27 countries, which could be a model. The EU has a supreme court, a currency, thousands of pages of law, a large civil service and the ability to deploy military force.

So could the European model go global?[264]

Rachman then lays out three reasons why he thinks it is plausible, and one of them is our global financial crisis.

Rachman's worries are well founded. On July 10, 2009, Bloomberg announced in "Medvedev Shows Off Sample Coin of New 'World Currency' at G-8":

> Russian President Dmitry Medvedev illustrated his call for a supranational currency to replace the dollar by pulling from his pocket a sample coin of a "united future world currency."

> "Here it is," Medvedev told reporters today in L'Aquila, Italy, after a summit of the Group of Eight nations. "You can see it and touch it."

> The coin, which bears the words "unity in diversity," was minted in Belgium and presented to the heads of G-8 delegations, Medvedev said.

> The question of a supranational currency "concerns everyone now, even the mints," Medvedev said. The test coin "means they're getting ready. I think it's a good sign that we understand how interdependent we are."[265]

Along with a few other observers, I've predicted for years that a global crisis would be used to implement the freedom-robbing tyranny of global governance, and now here we are.

Two Tracks to Globalism Merge

There have been two tracks to globalism for many years—political and spiritual. Now the two tracks have become one as politicians use religion to promote globalism and religious leaders become partners with politicians and promote the United Nations.

In July 2009, Pope Benedict XVI issued a 30,000-word encyclical, and this time even the *New York Times* understood the seriousness of what the Pope was calling for:

> Pope Benedict XVI on Tuesday called for a radical rethinking of the global economy, criticizing a growing divide between rich and poor and urging the establishment of a "true world political authority" to oversee the economy and work for the "common good"....Indeed, sometimes Benedict sounds like an old-school European socialist, lamenting the decline of the social welfare state and praising the "importance" of labor unions to protect workers. Without stable work, he noted, people lose hope and tend not to get married and have children....Benedict also called for a reform of the United Nations so there could be a unified "global political body" that allowed the less powerful of the earth to have a voice, and he called on rich nations to help less fortunate ones.[266]

Just as Alice Bailey said would occur, many Church leaders—even pastors and "Christian" authors—promote globalism and pagan spirituality. This has been coming from the Vatican and Catholic leaders for some time and has now affected Protestants as well. Just as I now speak out against the agenda of these Protestant leaders, some of my Catholic friends are laudably doing the same about the Vatican and other Catholic globalists. Many Catholics have even called in to my radio program to thank me for exposing globalists in both the Protestant and Catholic worlds.

Secularists see a useful parallel in Church influence. Former U.N.

Secretary General Dag Hammarskjold noted that there are "two Popes on this planet, a spiritual Pope in Rome and a civilian Pope in New York, namely, the Secretary-General of the UN."[267]

Even President Obama's science czar, John Holdren, envisions a "planetary regime." Cliff Kincaid of Accuracy in Media and columnist at worldviewtimes.com reviewed a paper by Holdren:

> That Holdren endorsed the concept of a "planetary regime" is shocking, considering that he is now a top White House official. In fairness, however, it doesn't seem much different from Pope Benedict XVI's endorsement of a "World Political Authority," which was included in his recent encyclical. Devotion to some form of world government seems popular in religious and government circles these days, especially in the age of Obama.[268]

Globalism has always been tied to occultism, so don't be surprised to see more and more politicians calling for globalism and embracing pagan spirituality. And don't be surprised when you hear politicians using New Age language. A few years ago, for example, Henry Kissinger appeared on the *Charlie Rose Program* and declared "we have to bring about together with other countries a different consciousness of what a world order is." New Agers have been using "consciousness" and "world order" language for years.

Tony Blair, the former prime minister of Great Britain and member of the Fabian socialist Labor Party, is another example of a politician who uses the language of pagan spirituality. As he tours the world promoting the Tony Blair Faith Foundation, he has given numerous interviews about globalism and the need for the religions of the world to "come together." Blair mobilizes young people between the ages of

18 and 25 to become "Faith Act Fellows." His website encourages them:

> The newly selected Faith Act Fellows are representative of Christian, Jewish, Muslim and Buddhist faiths and hail from across the US, Canada and UK. From Saskatoon to Michigan to Belfast they will work in interfaith pairs, reaching up to tens of thousands of people of faith, informing them about the devastating impact of malaria and the opportunities open to faith communities to work together to save millions of lives.[269]

Blair was featured speaker at the leadership conference of seeker-friendly, megachurch Pastor Bill Hybels in a Chicago suburb in August of 2009. Pastor Rick Warren, author of *The Purpose Driven Life*, has also endorsed the Tony Blair Foundation. In a statement on Blair's website, Warren explained:

> I honestly don't know of anyone better suited for this challenge. It's why I agreed to serve on the Advisory Board. The Tony Blair Faith Foundation's potential for doing good is staggering.[270]

A columnist for worldviewtimes.com put the leadership conference in perspective with her article, "When Evangelicals Dine with the Wicked":

> Blair is one of the chief players on the globalistic, one-world religion agenda. *The Tony Blair Faith Foundation* screams "unity" with every sentence, and not biblical unity. Blair states, *"God's Spirit moves through us and the world at a pace that can never be constricted by any one religious paradigm. Be very wary of people who think theirs is the only way."*

Members of his board include a Zen Buddhist, a Hindu from Minnesota, an Anglican, Rick Warren, a Rabbi, and others. A goal is to "heal the divisiveness in the world." This feeds into the end-time ecumenical effort predicted in the Bible.

Just as troubling is the appearance of rock star Bono. His U2 band was blatantly Satanic. Bono is seen [on a video on the internet] holding an upside down cross and singing praises to Charles Manson with the song *Helter Skelter*. Did Bono have a conversion experience? If he did, he has not changed the name of his music affiliation, which remains U2 from the days of blatant Satanism.

His efforts are directed at social change and he, too, is trying to build a bridge to all faiths. He also states, *"I stopped going to churches and got into a different religion. That's what being a rock-and-roll band is: Showbiz, shamanism, and music is worship."* U2's 2005 Vertigo tour promoted Bono's New Age, all-faith agenda. The word 'coexist' appeared on a giant screen—the 'c' represented by the Islamic crescent, the 'x' by the Star of David, and the 't' by the Christian cross. Then the big screen displayed the favorite mantra/lie of the Emergent/New Age Church, "Everything you know is wrong." Bono led the audience in a chant, "Jesus, Jew, Mohammed—all true!"[271]

Many "evangelicals" today are promoting a social gospel which is really nothing more than socialism. They call for bigger government, a more involved United Nations, the redistribution of wealth, and the Gospel is not mentioned for fear of offending someone. This is not so shocking since Bill Hybels, Rick Warren, Jim Wallis, and dozens of other "evangelicals" have all signed on to a document produced by the Yale Center for Faith that asserts that Christians and Muslims worship the same God. Strangely, Muslims themselves do not even believe that the God of the Bible is Allah. As you continue to watch events unfold you may find yourself shocked at who jumps on the pluralism bandwagon in the move towards a one-world religion.

The Societal Impact of Socialism

George Bernard Shaw represented the Fabian point of view by calling for "the socialization of the means of production, distribution, and exchange" to bring about an equal distribution of goods and services to all members of society and to make the State "the ALL of social well-being." The State "subsumes all economic life of the nation."[272]

In his *Intelligent Woman's Guide to Socialism,* Shaw details what happens to a culture once socialism is fully implemented:

> Socialism means equality of income or nothing, and that under Socialism you would not be allowed to be poor. You would be forcibly fed, clothed, lodged, taught, and employed whether you like it or not. If it were discovered that you had not the character and industry enough to be worth all this trouble, you might possibly be executed in a kindly manner; but whilst you were permitted to live you would have to live well.[273]

And just where will we find the money to feed, clothe, lodge, and teach everyone? Cuba has been trying this for years, and everyone in Cuba—whether doctor or sanitation worker—gets a check for about $10 each month from the government. The government-guaranteed poverty of Cuba is standard fare for socialism. The only ones who prosper are those in the ruling class. Castro has ruled over a nation of slaves who work in fields and factories to fund a lavish lifestyle for him, his military, and other favorites in his police state.

A friend of mine who has traveled to Cuba many times to speak at pastors' conferences describes the extreme poverty and tyranny that results from socialism. Many of the pastors to whom he ministers have been repeatedly imprisoned for speaking against the government or for proclaiming the Gospel beyond the walls of their church.

Notice that Shaw says that when the socialist system or new world order is fully in place, those that don't have the "character" to go along with their dictatorship will be "kindly" executed. I believe when America has fully implemented a government-run, national healthcare system, those that do not have the "character" to go along could easily be denied medical care and could find their lives snuffed out. If you think this sounds unrealistically extreme, then you don't understand the evil, tyrannical, and vindictive nature of socialism.

Russian author Fedor Dostoyevsky warned of the consequences of socialism: "The future kingdom of socialism will be a terrible tyranny of criminals and murderers. It will throw humanity into a true hell of spiritual suffering and poverty."

As Dr. David Noebel explains, the goal of Fabian socialists and the Keynesians that promote it is not only the destruction of capitalism but the destruction of Christianity as well:

> Socialists are united in their desire to see capitalism destroyed, either forcefully or gradually, and most would rejoice if Christianity were destroyed along with it. Socialists and liberals generally see in Christians "an infallible marker of mental retardation."[274]

Until they can completely transform America into a welfare-State Capitalism, politicians will take advantage of the wealth generated by capitalism to gain votes by redistributing it to the masses. Noebel describes their scheme:

> Today's Fabians/Progressives/Radicals allow their capitalist enemies to create wealth, but acquire it by taxing them instead of slaughtering them (Marx's "reign of terrorism on the bourgeoisie"). They are then free to distribute the wealth among the economically disadvantaged, the intellectual elites, and the superior governing classes.
>
> Such (re)distribution of wealth ensures the favorable vote of the masses being fed, entertained, housed (with sub-prime loans) and doctored. ACORN (Association of Community Organizations for Reform Now) and socialism fit hand-in-glove just as Fannie Mae and Freddie Mac fit Barney Frank, Maxine Waters, and Chris Dodd to a "T."
>
> Most Americans are totally unaware that the U.S. House of Representatives crawls with a large, well-organized assembly of socialist organizations. These organizations are dedicated to (a) bringing about the destruction of the capitalist economic system (portrayed as greedy, conservative, religious, and/or filthy rich) and (b) slowly but surely bringing production, education, food, and health care under the complete control and regulation of the federal government.[275]

Even though Fabians do not endorse the violent, radical tactics of communists, they will nevertheless defend communists as allies in their march toward globalism. President Obama and many that have served in his administration and in Congress are disciples of the Fabian socialists:

> Fabians worked for world revolution not through uprising of the workers but through indoctrination of young scholars. The Fabians believed that eventually these intellectual revolutionaries would acquire power and influence in the official and unofficial opinion-making and power-wielding agencies of the world. Then they could quietly establish a socialistic, one-world order.[276]

Fabian socialists have been disciplined and committed for years to converting individuals to their worldview, and nothing has worked better or more surreptitiously than Keynesianism.

19

CHRISTOPHER COLUMBUS LANGDELL
(1826-1906)

"Twentieth-century jurisprudence is based on a Darwinian worldview. Life evolves, men evolve, society evolves, and therefore laws and the constitution's meaning evolves and changes with time."[277] This observation by constitutional and legal scholar John Eidsmoe reflects the modern legal formulation known as "legal positivism."

In his book, *Christianity and the Constitution*, Eidsmoe reviews the writings of the Critical Legal Studies movement—a group of radical lawyers, law professors, and law students—and summarizes legal positivism this way:

- There are no objective, God-given standards of law, or if there are, they are irrelevant to the modern legal system.

- Since God is not the author of law, the author of law must be man; in other words, law is law simply because the highest human authority, the state, has said it is law and is able to back it up by force.

- Since man and society evolve, therefore law must evolve as well.

- Judges, through their decisions, guide the evolution of law (i.e., judges "make law").

- To study law, get at the original sources of law, the decisions of judges; hence most law schools today use the "case law" method of teaching law.[278]

Hence, legal positivism is simply moral relativism—the belief that there is no such thing as moral absolutes—applied to the law. According to relativists, there is no standard of right or wrong for all people in all places at all times. Moral relativism often flies under the more appealing term "pragmatism" and as such is closely tied to situational ethics, the belief that individuals should be free to do whatever seems best to secure the most desirable outcome for themselves in any given situation.

Tracing the development of the positivistic approach to law brings us to the next influencer on our list, Christopher Columbus Langdell. This philosophy of 'positivism', was introduced in the 1870s by Harvard Law School Dean Christopher Columbus Langdell (1826–1906) when he applied Darwin's premise of evolution to jurisprudence. As a result, Secular Humanism and its penchant for moral relativism—along with Langdell's misapplied Darwinism— has now become the postmodern foundation on which America's courts and law schools are built.

Langdell's thought was further advanced by Dean Roscoe Pound and Supreme Court Justice Oliver Wendell Holmes, Jr. Holmes was a student of Langdell's at Harvard and argued that there is no fixed moral foundation for law: "The felt necessities of the time, the prevalent moral and political theories . . . have a good deal more to do than the syllogism [legal reasoning process] in determining the rules by which men should be governed."[279]

Did you catch that? The "felt necessities of the time" and "prevalent moral and political theories" should be the basis of the rules by which men are governed. Using the "felt necessities" and "prevalent theories" model, judges can allow just about anything to be legal, depending on whose feelings, morals, and political theories are chosen for reference.

Guided by this dangerous thinking, we have seen countless abortions performed in America. Even the grisly partial-birth abortion procedure has passed legal muster—a practice the late Senator Daniel Patrick Moynahan called "near infanticide."

Decency Derailed

Along with millions of babies, matters of decency have also been aborted. U.S. Supreme Court Justice Ruth Bader Ginsburg, while serving as an attorney for the ACLU in 1977, wrote a paper, entitled "Sex Bias in the U.S. Code," for the U.S. Commission on Civil Rights. In it, she argues that the legal age for sexual activity should be lowered to 12 years old.[280] If enough judges agree the age change "is a necessity" based on the perverted "moral and political theories" of Alfred Kinsey, for instance, Americans would have to accept that it would be legal for an adult to have sex with a 12-year-old child. Lest you think that too crazy to happen, bear in mind that Kinsey actually promoted the idea of adults having sex with children, triggering other forces that now push in similar directions. A University of Minnesota publisher produced a book that outlines the "benefits" of children having sex with adults, and the North American Man/Boy Love Association has promoted this idea for years. These kinds of philosophical foundations are now in play with relativistic judges.

Consider the 2003 U.S. Supreme Court ruling in *Lawrence vs. Texas*. The court struck down the Texas sodomy law and, via the precedent, similar laws in several other states. The effect of the ruling instantly made homosexual sex legal. To arrive at such a ruling, the justices not only ignored the Constitution and the Founders' intent, but even went so far as to cite the law of another country in support of its decision! Justice Anthony M. Kennedy's majority opinion cited a 1967 British Parliament vote repealing laws against homosexual acts and a 1981 European Court of Human Rights decision that such laws violated the European Convention on Human Rights.[281]

Ignoring the Constitution and looking to case law—including that of other countries—to justify what our laws don't permit is the motive behind the case-law philosophy. Not surprisingly, Langdell also pioneered the case-law philosophy.

John Dewey similarly believed a strict adherence to the Constitution was an obstacle to the liberal, humanistic, and socialist changes he and many like him desired to accomplish: "The belief in political fixity, of the sanctity of some form of state consecrated by the efforts of our fathers and hallowed by tradition, is one of the stumbling-blocks in the way of orderly and directed change."[282]

Breaking the Law to Make the Law

Although judges and legal scholars now refer to judges as "making law," Founding Father and architect of much of early U. S. legal philosophy William Blackstone never believed judges "made law" but that they were to study the U.S. Constitution to "discover" or "apply" the law.

Although introduced in the nineteenth century, legal positivism began to make real headway when Earl Warren became chief justice of the U.S. Supreme Court. In the 1958 case, *Trop vs. Dulles*, Warren declared the Eighth Amendment of the U.S. Constitution could not have the same meaning now as it did at the time written. (The amendment reads as follows: "Excessive bail shall not be required, nor excessive fines imposed, nor cruel and unusual punishment inflicted.") In *Trop vs. Dulles*, the U.S. State Department had attempted to strip a man of his U.S. citizenship because he deserted the armed forces during World War II. But Trop's attorneys argued it was "cruel and unusual punishment" to take away his citizenship. Chief Justice Warren agreed, stating "the Amendment must draw its meaning from the evolving standards of decency that mark the progress of a maturing society." Legal positivism has been racing through court decisions at an ever-increasing pace since the mid-1900s.

The clear implication of legal positivism? Since morals and standards change over time, so does the meaning of the Constitution. Strangely, the Constitution has supposedly become much harder to understand than it once was.

Joseph Story, professor of law at Harvard and associate justice of the U.S. Supreme Court, was a leading constitutional scholar of the nineteenth century. In *Commentaries on the Constitution* (1833), he advocated interpreting the Constitution according to its plain meaning and the intent of its authors. Story emphasized that the Constitution was deliberately written so as to be understood by the common man:

> I have not the ambition to be the author of any new plan of interpreting the theory of the Constitution, or of enlarging or narrowing its powers, by ingenious subtleties and learned doubts. . . . Upon subjects of government; it has always appeared to me that metaphysical refinements are out of place. A constitution of government is addressed to the common sense of the people, and never was designed for trials of logical skill, or visionary speculation.[283]

Compare Story's eloquent yet humble thinking with the aggressive positivism of Charles Hughes, New York governor and chief justice of the U.S. Supreme Court: "We are under a Constitution, but the Constitution is what the judges say it is."[284]

Legal Reality

In 1985, to illuminate the destructiveness of this view, Edwin Meese, attorney general under then-president Ronald Reagan, delivered a speech to the American Bar Association in which he declared:

> It was not long ago when constitutional interpretation was understood to move between the poles of "strict construction" and "loose construction." Today, it is argued that constitutional interpretation moves between "interpretive review" and "non-interpretive review." As one observer has pointed out, under the old system the question was how to read the Constitution; under the new approach, the question is whether to read the Constitution. . . . The result is that some judges and academics feel free (to borrow the language of the great New York jurist, Chancellor James Kent) to "roam at large in the trackless fields of their own imaginations."[285]

In the 1992 U.S. Supreme Court ruling in *Planned Parenthood of Southeastern Pennsylvania vs. Casey, Governor of Pennsylvania,* Justices Sandra Day O'Connor, Souter, and Kennedy stated in the majority opinion, "At the heart of liberty is the right to define one's own concept of existence, of meaning of the universe and the mystery of human life."

Columnist John Leo has written:

> This "mystery passage" [as it has become known] can be cited easily next time to justify suicide clinics, gay marriage, polygamy, inter-species marriage [such as marrying one's

dog or cat] or whatever new individual right the court feels like inventing. We are moving firmly into the court's post-constitutional phase.[286]

The seismic shift represented in the *Casey* decision is how we define reality. The new definition flows from a postmodern philosophy that refuses to acknowledge any absolutes—nothing right, nothing wrong, nothing moral, nothing immoral. Truth does not exist, and there are no absolutes that transcend time or situation. Everything is subject to individual interpretation.

For the U.S. Supreme Court to descend into the abyss of moral relativism is disastrous. The Constitution has been the shield and defender of essential liberties for well over 200 years, based on "The Law of Nature and of Nature's God." Now, according to Justice Kennedy and five of his colleagues, its meaning has become no more predictable than the shifting sand of personal opinion.

Liberal elitists attempt to intimidate the American people by telling them they're not allowed to question the rulings of judges or have an opinion on legal rulings—particularly if they don't have a law degree. But book sense is not a substitute for common sense. As Vance Havner said, "You don't have to be listed in 'Who's Who' to know what's what." The real bottom line is that liberals don't want to be held to any standard other than their own mushy amalgamation of sound-bite thinking on issues of epic significance. They don't want to be accountable to the rule of law—they want to *be* the law.

Americans should not be silent concerning the laws and court rulings that impact their lives. While judges may wish it, we are not slaves of the black-robed usurpers. Perhaps it is because judges are lawyers—and most lawyers are liberal—that they seem to be so readily capable of ignoring truth, distorting reality, and quickly accepting the fallacies of a postmodern worldview.

The rejection of a fixed moral standard as the basis for law means there is no longer a benchmark by which a society judges good and bad behavior. After the 1962 and 1963 U.S. Supreme Court rulings that outlawed prayer and the Bible in America's public schools, cheating, stealing, rape, murder, and assault increased dramatically throughout the culture. After the 1980 U.S. Supreme Court ruling outlawing the posting of the Ten Commandments in our nation's public schools, the increase in deviant behavior rose higher still, and that trend continues to this day.

What's more, without a fixed moral standard as the basis for law, government has no moral purpose for its existence. According to Romans 13, the God-given purpose of civil government is to protect the righteous and punish the wicked; but without a moral foundation to uphold, defend, and use as the standard by which to judge and punish evil doers, government has nothing to enforce.

The lack of a fixed moral standard as the basis for law means our rights are not God-given but only granted to us by the government. These days, people are dangerously close to accepting the idea that the State grants rights to American citizens. This thinking will lead to calamity. Government is not the god who creates rights. It is merely God's minister to protect the rights God has given mankind.

Absent a fixed moral standard as the basis for law, "might makes right." Thus the groundwork is laid for one of two (and possibly both) disastrous ends. Anarchy is one. And that would most likely lead to the second, which is for our nation to be subjected to the feelings, opinions, agenda, and worldview of a small group of immoral, elitist judges who rule from behind the bench or a dictator who rules from behind a gun. Attorney John Whitehead puts it this way:

Those who do not favor taking God's law as the ultimate standard for civil morality and public justice will be forced to substitute some other criterion of good and evil for it. The civil magistrate cannot function without some ethical guidance, without some standard of good and evil. If that standard is not to be the revealed law of God (which, we must note, was addressed specifically to perennial problems in political morality), then what will it be? In some form or expression it will have to be a law of man (or men)—the standard of self-law or autonomy. And when autonomous laws come to govern a commonwealth, the sword is certainly wielded in vain, for it represents simply the brute force of some men's will against the will of other men. "Justice" then indeed becomes a verbal cloak for whatever serves the interests of the strongmen in society (whether their strength be that of physical might or of media manipulation). Men will either choose to be governed by God or to be ruled by tyrants.[287]

The loss of a fixed moral standard means Lady Justice is no longer blind, and those who have money and influence have a greater chance of getting what they want—to the detriment and harm of the middle class and the poor. Lacking moral law, man will not be restrained from within, so he must be restrained from without. More intrusive and larger government presence in our lives will be required.

Finally, the loss of a fixed moral standard means injustice will naturally follow, resulting in the unjust suffering and death of many. One Christian author outlines the destructive consequences when evolutionary thinking is applied to law and morality:

Darwinian evolution has placed law in the arena with evolving man. If man has evolved, then the standards primitive man once held must change along with him. When the higher law is abandoned, another law takes its place. The humanistic doctrine of evolution allows man to create for himself the law he believes will most benefit evolving man. Law then is what men or the courts say it is. Wrongs are defined in terms of what hurts man. There is no appeal to a law-order outside man. For example, abortion is made legal because it is convenient for the mother. For some women, having a baby is "harmful" because it restricts their freedom. These women are "wrongfully" curtailed in their desire to live as they wish. Laws are then passed to alleviate the "problem." The developmental fetus is termed a "non-person" without protection from the more powerful. There is no consideration that God has defined the nature of life, or that freedom should be defined in terms of submission to the commandments of God. Nor are the necessarily destructive and suicidal long-term consequences of such legal thought and practice seriously considered.[288]

The True Purpose of Law

There are tens of thousands of federal and state laws, many of which lead down the path of socialism and redistribution of wealth. The reason we have so many laws is that we have politicians who don't understand the purpose of the law.

Frederic Bastiat wrote *The Law*, first published in 1850, when France was going through one of its many transitions in government. Bastiat proclaims the purpose of the law is to make justice reign or, more precisely, to eliminate injustice. The law is simply the organization of justice, a collection of people coming together to do as a group what they cannot do as individuals: protect our life, liberty, and property.

God is the giver of liberties, and the law its protector. If, on the other hand, government is considered the giver of liberties, the obvious peril is that what the government gives, the government can take away.

For justice to fully reign we must stop the politicians from making an unjust living for themselves or their special interests through the work of the taxpayers. We must stop politicians from plundering us, as Bastiat describes:

> When a portion of wealth is transferred from the person who owns it—without his consent and without compensation, and whether by force or by fraud—to anyone who does not own it, then I say that property is violated; that an act of plunder is committed.[289]

Bastiat explains two reasons—greed and philanthropy—politicians use law to plunder:

> You say: "There are persons who have no money," and you turn to the law. But the law is not a breast that fills itself with milk. Nor are the lacteal veins of the law supplied with milk from a source outside the society. Nothing can enter the public treasury for the benefit of one citizen or one class unless other citizens and other classes have been forced to send it in. If every person draws from the treasury the amount that he has put in it, it is true that the law then plunders nobody. But this procedure does nothing for the persons who have no money. It does not promote equality of

income. The law can be an instrument of equalization only as it takes from some persons and gives to other persons. When the law does this, it is an instrument of plunder." [290]

When the law is used to take from one and give to another, this is nothing less than socialism. So, these "do-gooders" use the force of law to steal from one citizen the fruit of his labor in order to give it to others.

Some may argue that if we leave people to themselves some will starve, some will not have clothes, and some will not have adequate healthcare. In reality, however, if the government would get out of the way and fulfill simply its limited purpose, prosperity would be distributed to far more people because the choice would be to either work and eat or not to work and not to eat. Socialistic laws reward laziness and irresponsibility through our growing welfare state. Bastiat upholds the rightness of keeping government out of wealth control:

> Under such a regime, there would be the most prosperity—and it would be the most equally distributed. As for the sufferings that are inseparable from humanity, no one would even think of accusing the government for them. This is true because, if the force of government were limited to suppressing injustice, then government would be as innocent of these sufferings as it is now innocent of changes in the temperature. [291]

Neither Bastiat nor I argue against generosity, compassion, and charity. Our point is that charity is not the purpose of the law is not charity. Charity is the role of individuals, non-profits, ministries, and churches. Were government to stay in its rightful place, the level of prosperity would be so great that charitable organizations would be flush with the resources needed to do necessary good works.

The true purpose of the law and civil government is to reward those who live rightly and to punish the wicked. In recent years, the purpose of the law has been turned on its head in America as those who are involved in right living are punished through a punitive tax system that rewards with a monthly welfare check, not the workers but those involved in all sorts of irresponsible, destructive, immoral, and often illegal behavior.

So what would a nation look like that rejected socialism, plunder, and big government for freedom, liberty, and the proper use of the law? Bastiat tells us:

> If a nation were founded on this basis, it seems to me that order would prevail among the people, in thought as well as in deed. It seems to me that such a nation would have the most simple, easy to accept, economical, limited, nonoppressive, just, and enduring government imaginable.[292]

America is the longest standing constitutional republic in the history of the world. Unless we return to the proper, limited, and fundamental purpose of the law, our freedoms will not be secure much longer. Today the law is being used to infringe on our God-given rights and to establish Statism, which the *American Heritage Dictionary* describes as "the practice or doctrine of giving a centralized government control over economic planning and policy."

America has embraced what Alexis de Tocqueville called "soft despotism," which gives people the illusion that they have control over their government when in reality they have very little. Samuel Gregg explains:

De Tocqueville's vision of "soft-despotism" is thus one of the arrangements that mutually corrupt citizens and the democratic state. Citizens vote for those politicians who promise to use the state to give them whatever they want. The political-class delivers, so long as citizens do whatever it says is necessary to provide for everyone's desires. The "softness" of this despotism consists of people's voluntary surrender of their liberty and their tendency to look habitually to the state for their needs.[293]

De Tocqueville described the concept this way:

After having thus successively taken each member of the community in its powerful grasp and fashioned him at will, the supreme power then extends its arm over the whole community. It covers the surface of society with a network of small complicated rules, minute and uniform, through which the most original minds and the most energetic characters cannot penetrate, to rise above the crowd. The will of man is not shattered, but softened, bent, and guided; men are seldom forced by it to act, but they are constantly restrained from acting. Such a power does not destroy, but it prevents existence; it does not tyrannize, but it compresses, enervates, extinguishes, and stupefies a people, till each nation is reduced to nothing better than a flock of timid and industrious animals, of which the government is the shepherd.[294]

Soft despotism occurs because the people have forgotten—or never were educated—about the true purpose and intent of the law. When a people have become sufficiently ignorant and selfish, they vote for politicians who promise to offer them the government trough. Politicians gladly plunder some for the benefit of their special interest groups and voting blocs, all while taking advantage of constituents' ignorance and selfishness in order to garner still more power and control by making people more and more dependent upon them and the government.

Soft despotism is furthered through an incestuous and mutually beneficial relationship between judges and politicians to the detriment of freedom-loving people and their liberty and property. The welfare state in America has gone a long way toward encouraging people to vote themselves a raise by voting for politicians who promise the most government handouts.

Though never an economist by trade, Langdell and his legal positivism have reached deep into the pockets of most Americans. And we're all worse off for it.

20

SAUL ALINSKY
(1909-1972)

A young Italian Marxist by the name of Antonio Gramsci advised World War II dictator Mussolini that violence was not the way to bring about a lasting revolution people would embrace and maintain. Gramsci wrote eloquently of a "quiet" revolution—one that would transform a culture from within by changing the basic worldview of each and every institution in society. He also cautioned that this revolution would be "a long march through the institutions," not a blitzkrieg of change. So clear was his strategic thinking that Gramsci targeted Christianity specifically as the greatest philosophical adversary along the way.

Later in the twentieth century, Gramsci's vision captivated another rising neo-Marxist who codified the Gramsci dream in a 1971 book, *Rules for Radicals: A Pragmatic Primer for Realistic Radicals*. There, Saul Alinsky detailed the need to penetrate the middle class and re-organize from within. Alinksy articulated tactics for infiltrating every conceivable social institution—including churches.

Phyllis Schlafly connected current events to the Alinsky program in her timely and insightful February 2, 2009 *Investor's Business Daily* article, "Alinski's Rules: Must Reading in Obama Era":

> Alinsky's worldview was that mankind is divided into three parts: "the haves, the have-nots and the have-a-little, want mores." His purpose was to teach the have-nots how to take power and money away from the haves by creating mass

organizations to seize power, and he admitted "this means revolution."

He wanted a radical change of America's social and economic structure, and he planned to achieve that through creating public discontent and moral confusion. Alinsky developed strategies to achieve power through mass organization, and organizing was his word for revolution.

He wanted to move the U.S. from capitalism to socialism, where the means of production would be owned by all the people (i.e., the government). A believer in economic determinism, he viewed unemployment, disease, crime and bigotry as by-products of capitalism. "Change" was Alinsky's favorite word, used on page after page. "I will argue," he wrote, "that man's hopes lie in the acceptance of the great law of change."

Class envy, race-baiting, anti-Christian bigotry, and redistribution of wealth describe the change for which Alinksy was calling. It would not be a stretch—and in fact it is Schlafly's point—to suggest that Alinsky was the source for candidate Obama's 2008 campaign slogan. Yet Scripture warns of the wrong kinds of change: "He shall speak pompous words against the Most High, shall persecute the saints of the Most High, and shall intend to change times and law" (Daniel 9:25, NJKV).

Saul Alinsky has no compunction about speaking "against the Most High" because his allegiance lay elsewhere. The depth of Alinsky's evil intent is clear from the dedication page of his book:

> Lest we forget at least an over-the-shoulder acknowledgement to the very first radical; from all our legends, mythology,

and history…the first radical known to man who rebelled against the establishment and did it so effectively that he at least won his own kingdom—Lucifer.[295]

Here you see a rare, forthright declaration of the basic force behind all the thinkers described in this book. Alinsky betrays the secret that the globalist vision is threaded through a diverse assembly of influencers thanks to a strategy created by the Devil himself. It explains succinctly the hatred of Christians and the Biblical worldview. It also reaffirms the point I've made from the beginning of this book: we are in a spiritual battle, and the prize is hearts and minds.

The Underlying, Undermining Strategy

Before we look at the many national leaders who have adopted Alinky's worldview, I want to make crystal clear exactly what Alinksy's worldview was all about. Here are a few excerpts from *Rules for Radicals*:

> A Marxist begins with his prime truth that all evils are caused by the exploitation of the proletariat by the capitalists. From this he logically proceeds to the revolution to end capitalism, then into the third stage of reorganization into a new social order of the dictatorship of the proletariat, and finally the last stage…the political paradise of communism. (p. 10)

> An organizer working in and for an open society is in an ideological dilemma to begin with, he does not have a fixed truth…truth to him is relative and changing; everything to him is relative and changing.…To the extent that he is free from the shackles of dogma, he can respond to the realities of the widely different situations… (pp. 10-11)

From the moment the organizer enters a community he lives, dreams...only one thing and that is to build the mass power base of what he calls the army. Until he has developed that mass power base, he confronts no major issues....Until he has those means and power instruments, his "tactics" are very different from power tactics. Therefore, every move revolves around one central point: how many recruits will this bring into the organization, whether by means of local organizations, churches, service groups, labor Unions, corner gangs, or as individuals....Change comes from power, and power comes from organization. (p.113)

The first step in community organization is community disorganization. The disruption of the present organization is the first step toward community organization. Present arrangements must be disorganized if they are to be displaced by new patterns....All change means disorganization of the old and organization of the new. (p.116)

An organizer must stir up dissatisfaction and discontent....He must create a mechanism that can drain off the underlying guilt for having accepted the previous situation for so long a time. Out of this mechanism, a new community organization arises....The job then is getting the people to move, to act, to participate; in short, to develop and harness the necessary power to effectively conflict with the prevailing patterns and change them. When those prominent in the status quo turn and label you an "agitator" they are completely correct, for that is, in one word, your function—to agitate to the point of conflict. (p.117)

Alinsky has influenced many of our nation's leaders, and now you can see where they desire to take our nation—to becoming a socialist state. Hillary Clinton wrote her senior thesis at Wellesley College on Alinsky's strategies. President Obama, while at Harvard, attended the Industrial Areas Foundation, a group founded by Alinsky, and when he returned to Chicago, Obama taught Saul Alinsky's worldview and strategies.

Alinksky's influence extends beyond elected officials to radical activists and college professors. After studying Alinsky, for instance, Professor Richard Andrew Cloward and Frances Fox Piven wrote an article in the May 2, 1966, far-left magazine, *The Nation*. This husband-and-wife pair of radical socialists from Columbia University developed the Cloward-Piven Strategy, which advocates implementing socialism by swamping the welfare system of states as well as the federal government with new recipients.

Cloward and Piven also called for a protest movement, marches, and rallies to put extreme pressure on politicians to create new benefits. Once the resulting financial crisis becomes reality, the collapse of state and federal budgets would spawn a socialist state and the nationalizing of failed financial institutions such as mortgage lenders.

Among their many accomplishments, Cloward and Piven inspired an activist named George Wiley to found a liberal organization that set in motion a startling chain reaction. Wiley's work influenced Wade Rathke who, along with Bill Ayers, was a member of the Radical Students for a Democratic Society. Rathke, in turn, started Arkansas Community Organizations for Reform Now to employ the Cloward-Piven strategy.

He was so successful in Arkansas that the organization expanded and changed the "A" in its name from Arkansas to Association, and it became known as the Association of Community Organizers for Reform—the now infamous ACORN.

James Simpson, writing for worldviewtimes.com, noted:

> As a young attorney in the 1990s, Barack Obama represented ACORN in Washington in their successful efforts to expand Community Reinvestment Act authority. In addition to making it easier for ACORN groups to force banks into making risky loans, this also paved the way for banks like Superior to package mortgages as investments, and for the government-sponsored enterprise Fannie Mae and Freddie Mac to underwrite them.[296]

The financial housing crisis that made headlines in 2007 was brought on through Saul Alinksy's ideas, via the Cloward-Piven Strategy of implementing socialism through big government destruction of contract law and free market principles. This "economic sabotage" was first tried in New York City, and by 1975, the city was on verge of financial devastation. Although New York had a manageable 150,000 welfare cases in 1960, a decade later the number had soared past the 1.5 million mark.

Barack Obama was a community organizer with Project Vote, an affiliate of the ACORN, before he entered public service. His "organizing" was built on the model of Saul Alinsky.[297]

Obama's activities come right from the Alinsky playbook. In *Rules for Radicals*, Alinsky describes his purpose:

> In this book we are concerned with how to create mass organizations to seize power and give it to the people; to realize the democratic dream of equality, justice, peace.... "Better to die on your feet than to live on your knees." This means revolution.[298]

In an obvious plug for socialism, Alinksy said radicals "hope for a future…where the means of production will be owned by all of the people instead of just a comparative handful."[299] In *Rules for Radicals*, Alinksy admitted that his goal was to "present an arrangement of certain facts and general concepts of change, a step toward a science of revolution."[300] He also reflected on the book *The Prince* which he said "was written by Machiavelli for the Haves on how to hold onto power. *Rules for Radicals* is written for the Have-Nots on how to take it away."[301]

Many conservatives have joked that President Obama thinks himself to be God. Alinsky probably wouldn't argue since he thinks that of any community organizer. According to Alinsky, an organizer "is in a true sense reaching for the highest level for which man can reach—to create, to be a 'great creator,' to play God."[302]

Hegelian Organization

One of the rules that distinguishes an Alinsky radical from a run-of-the-mill liberal is action. Alinsky tells us:

> Liberals protest; radicals rebel. Liberals become indignant; radicals become fighting mad and go into action. Liberals do not modify their personal lives[,] and what they give to a cause is a small part of their lives; radicals give themselves to the cause. Liberals give and take oral arguments; radicals give and take the hard, dirty, bitter way of life.[303]

It is the radicals that will bring about the ultimate goal. For Saul Alinsky, that goal is communism:

> A Marxist begins with his prime truth that all evils are caused by the exploitation of the proletariat by the capitalists. From

this he logically proceeds to the revolution to end capitalism, then into the third stage of reorganization into a new social order of the dictatorship of the proletariat, and finally the last stage—the political paradise of communism.[305]

Alinsky and his ilk buy into moral relativism, the end-justifies-the-means thinking, and thus do not eschew even lying to accomplish their goals:

> An organizer working in and for an open society is in an ideological dilemma to begin with, he does not have a fixed truth—truth to him is relative and changing; *everything* to him is relative and changing.... To the extent that he is free from the shackles of dogma, he can respond to the realities of the widely different situations.... [305]

> *The third rule of ethics of means and ends is that in war the end justifies almost any means....*[306]

As did Marx, Alinsky understood the techniques of Hegel's dialectic for community organizing. Alinsky's version is to create conflict and become an agitator:

- "...the organizer is constantly creating new out of the old. He knows that all new ideas arise from conflict; that every time man as had a new idea it has been a challenge to the sacred ideas of the past and the present and inevitably a conflict has raged."[307]

- "An organizer must stir up dissatisfaction and discontent....He must create a mechanism that can drain off the underlying guilt for having accepted the previous situation for so long a time. Out of this mechanism, a new community organization arises....[308]

• "The job then is getting the people to move, to act, to participate; in short, to develop and harness the necessary power to effectively conflict with the prevailing patterns and change them. When those prominent in the status quo turn and label you an 'agitator' they are completely correct, for that is, in one word, your function—to agitate to the point of conflict." p.117

In case anyone misses the point, Alinsky is clear that he and his kind must "crush the opposition, bit by bit."[309]

And now, thanks to President Obama, America has agitators in some very high places. Consider, for example, the background of President Obama's former green jobs czar, Van Jones. Trevor Louden, a columnist and researcher at worldviewtimes.com, is credited with breaking the news story about Van Jones's controversial background. Louden writes:

Van Jones first moved to San Francisco in the spring of 1992, while studying law at Yale, when the leftist Lawyers Committee for Human Rights hired several law students to act as legal observers during the trial of policemen charged with assaulting Rodney King. Not guilty verdicts in the King case led to mass rioting—which Jones joined in. Arrested and jailed, Van Jones met a whole new circle of friends.[310]

Years after the Rodney King event, the *East Bay Express* newspaper featured an interview with Jones on November 2, 2005, in which Jones describes these new friends:

I met all these young radical people of color—I mean really radical, communists and anarchists. And it was, like, "This is what I need to be a part of...." I spent the next ten years of my life working with a lot of those people I met in jail, trying to be a revolutionary....I was a rowdy nationalist on April 28th, and then the verdicts came down on April 29th....By August, I was a communist.[311]

Jones went on to lead an organization called Standing Together to Organize a Revolutionary Movement (STORM). Then in March 2009 President Obama took him off the streets to become our country's Green Jobs Czar until his controversial past came to light, and he was forced to resign in September 2009.

President Obama, Senator Hillary Clinton, and other socialist radicals have spent their elected years pushing legislation that uses government money to hire militant people who will swell the welfare rolls, register illegals to vote, and carry out the Cloward-Piven/Alinsky strategy at taxpayer expense. But Clinton and Obama are not the first national leaders to embrace Alinsky. In his November 2007 article "Hillary, Obama, and the Cult of Alinsky," Richard Lawrence Poe shows the impact of Alinsky's worldview on President Truman and Senator Robert Kennedy as well:

One Alinsky benefactor was Wall Street investment banker Eugene Meyer, who served as Chairman of the Federal Reserve from 1930 to 1933. Meyer and his wife Agnes co-owned *The Washington Post*. They used their newspaper to promote Alinsky.

Agnes Meyer personally wrote a six-part series in 1945, praising Alinsky's work in Chicago slums. Her series, called

"The Orderly Revolution," made Alinsky famous. President Truman ordered 100 reprints of it.

During the Sixties, Alinsky wielded tremendous power behind the scenes.

When President Johnson launched his War on Poverty in 1964, Alinsky allies infiltrated the program, steering federal money into Alinsky projects.

In 1966, Senator Robert Kennedy allied himself with union leader Cesar Chavez, an Alinsky disciple. Chavez had worked ten years for Alinsky, beginning in 1952. Kennedy soon drifted into Alinsky's circle.

Many leftists view Hillary as a sell-out because she claims to hold moderate views on some issues. However, Hillary is simply following Alinsky's counsel to do and say whatever it takes to gain power.

Barack Obama is also an Alinskyite. Trained by Alinsky's Industrial Areas Foundation, Obama spent years teaching workshops on the Alinsky method. In 1985 he began a four-year stint as a community organizer in Chicago, working for an Alinskyite group called the Developing Communities Project. Later, he worked with ACORN and its offshoot Project Vote, both creations of the Alinsky network.

Camouflage is key to Alinsky-style organizing. While trying to build coalitions of black churches in Chicago, Obama caught flak for not attending church himself. He became an instant churchgoer.

That Hillary Clinton and Barack Obama share an Alinskyite background tells us two things. First, they are leftists, dedicated to overthrowing our Constitutional system. Second, they will go to any length to conceal their radicalism from the public.[312]

The connection is no secret. In the *Boston Globe*, Alinsky's son praised the impact of his father's worldview on President Obama and his campaign:

All the elements were present: the individual stories told by real people of their situations and hardships, the packed-to-the rafters crowd, the crowd's chanting of key phrases and names, the action on the spot of texting and phoning to show instant support and commitment to jump into the political battle, the rallying selections of music, the setting of the agenda by the power people. The Democratic National Convention had all the elements of the perfectly organized event, Saul Alinsky style.

Barack Obama's training in Chicago by the great community organizers is showing its effectiveness. It is an amazingly powerful format, and the method of my late father always works to get the message out and get the supporters on board. When executed meticulously and thoughtfully, it is a powerful strategy for initiating change and making it really happen. Obama learned his lesson well.

I am proud to see that my father's model for organizing is being applied successfully beyond local community organizing to affect the Democratic campaign in 2008. It is a fine tribute to Saul Alinsky as we approach his 100th birthday.[313]

Alinsky Now

Some experts believe America is experiencing the revolution called for by Saul Alinksy. Herbert E. Meyer served during the Reagan Administration as special assistant to the director of Central Intelligence and vice chairman of the CIA's National Intelligence Council. He holds the U.S. National Intelligence Distinguished Service Medal, the intelligence community's highest honor. In a May 20, 2009 article, Mr. Meyer wrote that America is experiencing a revolution, even if most Americans don't recognize what is happening. Even though there's no civil war in progress, Mr. Meyer explains that a revolution occurs when leaders change the laws to suit themselves and garner power otherwise not allowed by the U.S. Constitution:

> …you cannot claim to have the rule of law if the government can set aside the rule of law when it decides that "special circumstances" have arisen that warrant illegality. When the President and his aides handed ownership of Chrysler Corp. to the United Auto Workers union, they tried to avoid sending that beleaguered company into bankruptcy by muscling its bondholders into accepting less money for their assets than the law entitled them to collect. These contracts, and the law under which they were signed, were mere obstacles to a thuggish President bent on paying off his political supporters.[314]

Mr. Meyer supports a point I've made numerous times that the Democrats have not destroyed our nation alone. Many Republican have helped simply by "going along" or by not standing up for truth. You can have either socialist party R or socialist party D. They're moving at different speeds, but the destination is the same. The worst, of course, are Republicans like Arlen Specter "the defector" who wore a Republican uniform for years before switching jerseys and joining the Democrats. President George W. Bush and his team had supported Specter for re-election in his last campaign as a Republican primary in 2004—despite the fact that the alternative appeared to be a genuine conservative who was gaining fast in the polls. The Bush support helped Specter edge out his rival with a 51% majority in the primary contest.

Meyer explains exactly how Republicans facilitate the revolution:

> This revolution won't be stopped, and our country won't be rescued, by the Republicans in Washington. This isn't because they lack the votes. It's because most of them are careerist hacks who've been playing footsie with the Democrats for too long; with very few exceptions they lack the intellectual firepower to articulate the present danger, and the political courage to stand up to this Administration and really fight. But for the absence of frock coats and pince-nez glasses, these Republicans in Washington remind me of those bumbling Weimar Republic politicians in Berlin who never grasped where Hitler and the Nazis were going until it was too late to stop them, or of those hapless Mensheviks in Moscow's *Duma* who let themselves be tossed into history's dustbin by Lenin and his Bolsheviks. (Yes, of course I

realize it's explosive to keep bringing up the Nazis and the Bolsheviks in an essay about the Democrats. I'm not doing this to be incendiary; I'm doing this to be accurate.)...It was only *after* the Nazis had secured their grip on power in Germany, and only *after* the Bolsheviks had seized control of Russia, that they set out to disarm and destroy the vast numbers of ordinary citizens who—to the astonishment and fury of the revolutionaries—just wouldn't go along.[315]

Not everyone goes along with the Alinsky revolution, and the result is revolutionary thinking in the other direction. Ellis Goodwin reported in *The Express-Star* on the August, 2009 town hall meeting with Oklahoma Senator Jim Inhofe:

In late August of 2009, U.S. Senator from Oklahoma Jim Inhofe, speaking at a town hall meeting on the actions of the Obama Administration, said that, "People are not buying these concepts that are completely foreign to America," Inhofe said. "We're almost reaching a revolution in this country."[316]

The reality of an Alinsky-inspired revolution, though, is that it does not end pretty for dissenters. The few true conservatives in the Republican Party or elsewhere are often characterized and marginalized by their own party. And it could get much worse.

In one respect, I have to tip my hat to Saul Alinksy. He knew what he believed, and why he believed it, and he made disciples. As Alinsky demonstrates, the radical, godless left is often more committed to making disciples than are we Christians. And regrettably, his disciples have ended up in some very high places.

21

SIGMUND FREUD
(1856-1939)

"To demolish religion with psychoanalytic weapons," Freud biographer Peter Gay reported, "had been on Freud's agenda for many years."[317] Sigmund Freud, like Friedrich Nietzsche who strongly influenced him, hated God and Christianity. In his own book, *The Future of an Illusion,* Freud describes his "absolutely negative attitude toward religion, in every form and dilution."[318]

As Dr. Benjamin Wiker points out in *Ten Books That Screwed up the World*:

> We cannot forget Nietzsche's assumption that religion was an entirely human creation. Since Freud read Nietzsche, this may have done as much as anything to help form his presentation of religion in *The Future of an Illusion.*[319]

With that viewpoint at the core of Freud's thinking, Wiker goes on to describe the psychoanalyst's resultant, perverted worldview:

> His rebellion took the form of baptizing as natural the most hideously unnatural sins, sins condemned by every society as the most unholy and unthinkable….Freud damned as unnatural the Christian-based morality of Western society.[320]

Freud himself points out several of these "unholy and unthinkable" inclinations: "Among these instinctual wishes are those of incest, cannibalism, and lust for killing."[321]

Freud believed that it is the people who reject a Biblical worldview and follow their "natural" desires that are truly sane. As Dr. Wicker explains:

> He [Freud] claimed that psychological disorders were the result of the unnatural repression of our naturally unholy and anti-social desires, and that some people just couldn't handle the repression....Therefore, neurotics are the only sane people because they react to unnatural frustration by training to reclaim their original, natural, asocial and amoral state. The result: the anti-social psychopath who kills without conscience is the most natural of all. The interesting effect of Freud's proclamation that evil is natural was the seemingly unintended consequence of making psychopathic insanity natural. [322]

The Soul of a Soul-less Discipline

The word "psychology" derives from the Greek word "psyche," the study of the soul—which, ironically, should be impossible for Secular Humanistic psychologists who deny the spiritual world and the soul. Author Alan Bloom notes that for Secular Humanists "the self is the modern substitute for the soul."[323] And when humanists refer to the mind, they really mean the brain.

Contrast the significance the Christian worldview places on this realm which Freud insists doesn't even exist. The Biblical worldview, of course, acknowledges both the spiritual and natural worlds. The brain is part of the natural world, but the mind and heart, as described in the Bible, are connected to the soul—the spiritual side of man.

Scripture mentions the heart 826 times, where "heart" refers to the core of a person's being. Proverbs 4:23 says the heart is "the source of life." From the heart proceed our good and bad thoughts, emotions, and behavior. The Bible admonishes us to love the Lord our God with all our *heart*, soul, strength, and *mind*.

In Scripture, the words "heart" and "mind" are often interchangeable, and other times they complement one another. Jeremiah 17:9, for instance, describes the heart as "more deceitful than anything else and desperately sick," so the mind must moderate the heart. The Bible also describes the nature of those who ignore God as it tells us how to practice godliness:

- Psalm 14:1—"The fool has said in his heart, 'There is no God'."

- Proverbs 23:19—"Hear, my son, and be wise; And guide your heart in the way."

- Proverbs 23:7—"For as he thinks in his heart, so he is."

Your heart and mind are part of your soul, the core of who you are that will still be after you die. They will live forever and be judged by God (Romans 2:5; Revelation 2:23). The person who repents of sin and surrenders his or her will to the Lordship of Jesus Christ is the person who has received mercy and grace. That person has been saved by God on the basis of Christ's complete payment for sin at Calvary.

According to Romans, the moral law is written on the heart and mind of every person—thus the conscience. "Con" means with and "science" means knowledge. So, every time people sin or rebel against God, they know it is wrong.

We come to understand that we don't murder fellow human beings because murder goes against the character of God. We are not to lie, steal, or break any of the other Ten Commandments because doing so would go against who God is. Romans 1:21 reminds us, "although they knew God, they did not glorify Him as God, nor were thankful, but became futile in their thoughts, and their foolish hearts were darkened." And Romans 2:15 points out that people "show the work of the law written in their hearts, their conscience also bearing witness, and between themselves their thoughts accusing or else excusing them."

The Bondage of Being Guilt-Free

People can either accept the guilty feeling of the law that accuses them of their transgression when they sin, or they can excuse the guilty feeling and learn to ignore it. If they ignore the guilt long enough or often enough, they will become people "speaking lies in hypocrisy, having their own conscience seared with a hot iron" (1 Timothy 4:2).

You can see, then, that people who listen to Freud and his devotees—believing that sinful thoughts and impulses are natural instead of understanding that their guilt is a sign they have violated the character and nature of God—are headed in a seriously wrong direction. The end result can be true insanity if their rebellion against God goes too far. Norm Geisler explains how this works out in a person's life:

> [T]he root cause of the character disorders (moral corruption)…is directly associated with a person's refusal to acknowledge and act upon what is morally right and reject what is morally wrong. It becomes harder and harder for the individual to get help with his character disorder because of the increased moral depravity. This increase is associated with greater levels of insensitivity in that person's conscience. For example, during the progressive moral deterioration in the life of the person who uses pornography,

his sequence of feeling-to-thought-to-deed proceeds with less and less intervention of the inhibitory mechanism of conscience and guilt.[324]

This is the effect of having a "seared" conscience, yet no one will have an excuse at Judgment for rejecting God. Romans 3:19–20 warns:

Now we know that whatever the law says, it says to those who are under the law, that every mouth may be stopped, and all the world may become guilty before God. Therefore by the deeds of the law no flesh will be justified in His sight, for by the law is the knowledge of sin.

Everyone has broken the law. No one can justify their entry into heaven by claiming they have "lived a good enough life" because God's standard is to keep the complete moral law, and no one has done that.

To further underscore that committing sin is breaking the moral law, 1 John 3:4 says, "Everyone who commits sin also breaks the law; sin is the breaking of law." And Romans 3:10 explains, "There is none righteous, no, not one." Finally, Romans 3:23 concludes: "…all have sinned and fall short of the glory of God."

Becoming a Real You

Throughout this book we have seen how one's worldview impacts not only a person's public life but also his or her personal life. Freud's impact as "the father of psychoanalytic theory" has rippled through psychological thinking and into the general population, leaving bizarre thoughts and actions in its wake. David Noebel cites the book, *The Road to Malpsychia: Humanistic Psychology and Our Discontent,* which reports:

Milton reveals that Harvard's Timothy Leary routinely had sex with his patients, took psilocybin and LSD, pushed drugs on his own students, and entertained the goal of having four million Americans turned on to LSD.[325]

Humanist, psychologist, and member of the Frankfurt School Erich Fromm greatly respected Freud. And while disagreeing in some areas, Fromm and Freud were united in their attack on Christianity. Fromm declared, "man challenges the supreme power of God, and he is able to challenge it because he is potentially God."[326]

Psychologist Abraham Maslow developed the idea of self-actualization—which means a person's innate goodness has evolved. As David Noebel describes:

> Abraham Maslow refers to those in touch with their inherent goodness as self-actualized. He categorizes this drive to get in touch with our inherent goodness as a need that can be attended to only after we have satisfied our lower needs—namely, physiological, safety, social, and ego needs. We must satisfy these needs as well as our need for self-actualization before we can truly be declared mentally healthy.[327]

Maslow claimed that very few people ever reach the state of being self-actualized. Among those that he said had reached this state include two individuals discussed in this book: William James (Chapter 11) and Aldous Huxley (Chapter 13).

Dr. Noebel explains why self-actualized people are the ones humanists look to as leaders:

> Humanists embrace self-centeredness in an effort to create a better world. The call for individuals to be true to their feelings and innermost nature allows for experimentation. If we feel our innermost nature is calling us to act in a certain

way, who has the authority to tell us we are misinterpreting our feelings? Humanism affirms our freedom to experiment with values and to test the aspects of morality that truly mesh with our inner nature. Self-actualized people are the final authority for Humanist ethics, regardless of the amount of scientific experimentation required to discover *the good*. However, the good discovered by one person is the good only for that person. Another person may decide something else is the good or that neither good nor rules exist. Humanist psychologists discourage this line of thinking, however, by arguing that few people are self-actualized and the non-self-actualized must turn to the self-actualized for guidance. According to Maslow, people not yet self-actualized can learn what is right by watching those who are. Thus, Humanists must look to mentally healthy (self-actualized) people to determine scientifically, for example, if pedophilia (man/boy sex) is moral or not.[328]

Maslow evidences this propensity when he suggests, "I propose that we explore the consequences of observing whatever our best specimens choose, and then assuming that these are the highest values for all mankind."[329]

Does this mean that when U.S. Supreme Court Justice Ruth Bader Ginsburg was an attorney for the ACLU in 1977 and argued for lowering the sex age limit to twelve she was following the leadership of someone that was self-actualized? I suggest that the reality is humanists look to perverts to set the standards because they're the ones who do not reject their "natural instincts" and are humanistically the "truly sane."

Humanistic psychologists deny our sinful nature that results from the original sin of Adam and Eve. Thus they believe man is simply a product of his environment. When they apply Darwinian evolution to their worldview, they contend that society is evolving along with nature and that things will get better and better as we become more enlightened—or as Maslow claimed, self-actualized. In truth, the twentieth century was the bloodiest of all centuries; things are not getting better.

The Bible declares that all have sinned and fallen short of the glory of God. It also holds that the days will become increasingly wicked, with people doing what is right in their own eyes, calling evil good and good evil. Indeed Freud, Maslow, Fromm, and others in their line of psychologists prove that this has come true. Calling "evil good and good evil," they declare Christians insane and those who act out compulsions such as child-molestation and murder sane.

David Noebel summarizes the contrast between the Biblical worldview and humanistic psychology:

> Secular Humanists make three assumptions about the self, mind, and mental processes: 1) we are good by nature and are therefore perfectible; 2) society and its social institutions are responsible for the evil we do; and 3) mental health can be restored to those who get in touch with their inner (good) self. While other worldviews may agree with some or all of these premises, Christians disagree with all three. Christians insist that we must admit our own sinful nature and take responsibility for our immoral acts instead of blaming someone or something else. Humanist psychology, however, allows us to intellectually deny responsibility for our behavior and moral choices.[330]

As Benjamin Wiker points out, "the greatest crimes in the history of mankind came not from those in thrall to the 'illusion' [as Freud called Christianity] of Judaism and Christianity, but from those who claimed to be atheistic, scientific socialists."[331]

Tyrannical, atheistic, socialist governments down through the ages have waged war against the Christians within their own countries because Bible-minded Christians stand directly opposed to their evil schemes against life and liberty. Thus humanistic governments join Freud in labeling Christians as mentally unstable. In *Modern Times*, Paul Johnson explains that "...the notion of regarding dissent as a form of mental sickness, suitable for compulsory hospitalization, was to blossom in the Soviet Union into a new form of political repression."[332]

The Descent of Dissent

These techniques are disturbingly present in America today. In early 2009, the U.S. Department of Homeland Security released a report that labeled as "extremists" those opposed to abortion, the unconstitutional increase in the size and scope of the federal government, the weakening of America's national sovereignty, infringement of the Second Amendment of the U.S. Constitution (right to keep and bear arms), and even those who simply show interest in "end times prophecies."

It is not a great leap for a government to go from labeling opposition as "extremists" to labeling them "terrorists" and taking punitive action against them. In June 2009, Rep. Steven LaTourette (R-OH) cited e-mails in which an attorney with President Obama's auto task force called an attorney representing the senior bondholders of Chrysler a "terrorist."[333]

That same month, the Speaker of the California State Assembly referred to conservative talk show hosts as terrorists when asked, "How do you think conservative talk radio has affected the Legislature's work?" Her answer:

> The Republicans were essentially threatened and terrorized against voting for revenue. Now [some] are facing recalls. They operate under a terrorist threat: "You vote for revenue and your career is over." I don't know why we allow that kind of terrorism to exist. I guess it's about free speech, but it's extremely unfair.[334]

Even now members of the U.S. Congress and high-ranking federal government officials are calling for some sort of "fairness doctrine" or "diversity doctrine" that would eliminate most conservative radio programs from the airwaves—or at the very least require equal time to be given to opposing views. Such a federal law would require even Christian radio programs to give equal time to groups in favor of homosexuality.

The Government's Solution for the Mentally Disturbed

On June 17, 2009, Foxnews.com reported that the Pentagon uses a personnel exam that asks:

> Which of the following is an example of low-level terrorism?
>
> — Attacking the Pentagon
>
> — IEDs
>
> — Hate crimes against racial groups
>
> — Protests

According to the report, the correct answer is "Protests."[335] After this exam was made public, the Pentagon claims to have discontinued its use.

In August 2009, Americans that dared to publicly dissent at town hall meetings regarding President Obama's socialized healthcare bill were marginalized as not being mentally stable. U. S. Speaker of the House of Representatives Nancy Pelosi went so far as to say that those who expressed their disapproval were essentially "carrying swastikas and symbols like that to a town meeting on health care."

As you've seen, one of the 21 people we looked at in this book, William James, is the man behind the idea of mandatory national service for America's youth and founder of the first American psychological laboratory. What better way to "cure" America's young people from their mental illness derived from the influence of parents and churches than to be subjected to the social justice curriculum written by the likes of Bill Ayers?

If you harbor any doubt that there are psychologists, educational elite, elected and government officials who see America's parents as the threat to their worldview, then consider the following:

Dr. Pierce, professor of Education and Psychology at Harvard University, has said, "Every child who enters school at the age of five is mentally ill because he enters school with an allegiance toward our elected officials, our founding fathers, our institutions, the preservation of this form of government that we have, patriotism, nationalism, sovereignty. All this proves that the children are sick, because a truly well individual is one who has rejected all of those things, and is what I would call the true international child of the future."[336]

In concert with Pierce's notion, Hillary Clinton has for years been advocating for the U. N. Convention on the Rights of the Child. If ever ratified by the U.S. Senate, parental authority will be put in the place Pierce and other such Freudians would have it: nowhere. It would be eliminated. Several years ago, *Harper's* magazine revealed Clinton's radical, anti-family agenda in "Child Saver: What She Values Will Not Help the Family":

> The traditional family is, for the most part, an institution in need of therapy, an institution that stands in the way of children's rights—an obstacle to *enlightened adults*.... She condemns the State's assumption of parental responsibilities, not because she has any faith in parents themselves but because she is opposed to the principle of parental authority in any form....Her writings leave the unmistakable impression that it is the family that holds children back; *it is the state that sets them free.*[337] [Emphases mine]

Freud's hatred of Christianity and the Christian philosophy of family, parental authority, and freedom of religion lives on.

22

MARGARET SANGER
(1879-1966)

If you were to ask anyone to name the people who have directly or indirectly caused the most deaths in the twentieth century, names such as Hitler, Stalin, and Ho Chi Minh would likely top the lists. I submit, though, that there is one person whose track record in blood leaves any one of the others in a distant second place.

As of this writing, some 50 million babies have been murdered in America alone through abortion, and in many ways each death can be traced to the work of the woman who is the subject of this chapter. Founded by Margaret Sanger, Planned Parenthood has for decades led the way in providing abortions to America's women. It now generates an estimated $1 billion per year in its despicable industry soaked with the blood of America's infants.

I've studied the lives of many people, and Margaret Sanger is one of the most vile, mean, and racist of all. Liberal professors and media outlets that say anything positive about Planned Parenthood or Margaret Sanger show themselves to be ignorant, racist, or both.

Rooted in Dirt

After divorcing her first husband and the father of her three children, Sanger became the publisher of a liberal newspaper called *The Woman Rebel* which boasted the slogan "No Gods! No Masters!" And indeed, as a member of the Socialist Party, she was a rebel in more ways than one could count.

The premiere issue of *The Woman Rebel*, denounced marriage as a "degenerate institution," capitalism as "indecent exploitation," and sexual modesty as "obscene prudery." In the next issue, an article entitled "A Woman's Duty" stated that "rebel women" were to "look the whole world in the face with a go-to-hell look in their eyes." In issues to follow, she published articles on sexual liberation, social revolution, contraception, and two articles that defended political assassinations. As a just reward for her work, Sanger was served a subpoena indicting her on three counts of publishing lewd and indecent articles. To avoid prosecution, she fled to England, where she became acquainted with the eugenics movement. She spent a year there before returning to the U.S. to promote the new and even more horrendous ideas she had learned in Europe.

Once back in the States, Sanger organized a public relations campaign to have all charges against her dropped. To put her eugenics worldview into practice she opened a birth control clinic in Brownsville, New York, an area inhabited by Slavic, Latino, Italian, and Jewish immigrants. Sanger stated that these ethnic groups were "dysgenic and diseased races" that needed to have their "reckless breeding" curbed. Barely two weeks after the clinic opened, it was shut down, and Sanger and her sister were sentenced to 30 days in a workhouse for distributing obscene material and prescribing dangerous medical procedures.

Not the least discouraged, Sanger became acquainted with the doctors and scientists who had worked with Nazi Germany's "race purification" program and who had no compunction about the euthanasia, sterilization, abortion, and infanticide programs of the early Reich. Sanger even published several articles in *Birth Control Review* that reflected Hitler's White Supremacist worldview.

During the next few years, Sanger authored several best-selling books and spoke regularly to large and receptive audiences, not only in America but throughout the world. In *The Pivot of Civilization*, she praised the cause of eugenics, openly calling for the eradication of "human weeds," for the "cessation of charity," for the segregation of "morons, misfits, and the maladjusted," and for the coercive sterilization of "genetically inferior races." Sanger became a celebrity with a following.

As her popularity soared, Sanger married a multimillionaire, who eagerly funded her cause. To avoid further legal trouble, she opened a new clinic but called it a "Research Bureau." The new strategy of creating benign-sounding terminology for her work and ideas rocketed her to a new level of success. In addition to her husband's money, she received large grants from foundations such as Rockefeller, Ford, and Mellon.

Reinventing Her Plans

When the horrors of Hitler's Nazi doctors and scientists came to light after World War II, Sanger once again had to remake her image and distance herself from the disgraced Europeans. She founded a new organization with a new name: Planned Parenthood, successfully hiding her racism and bigotry behind family-friendly terms like "family planning." But family planning means today what it meant in Sanger's day—abortion on demand.

You might be tempted to think Planned Parenthood has by now rejected its racist roots, but you would be mistaken. Dr. Alan Guttmacher, the man who succeeded Sanger as president of Planned Parenthood, made it clear that "we are merely walking down the path that Mrs. Sanger carved out for us." Similarly, Faye Wattleton, president of the organization during the 1980s, said she was proud to be "walking in the footsteps" of Sanger. And in 1994 then-president of Planned Parenthood Pamela Maraldo continued the tradition of extolling the organization's tradition: "Today, Planned Parenthood proudly carries on the courageous tradition of Margaret Sanger." Bear in mind, too, that the organization carries on this "proud heritage" with massive amounts of taxpayer funds. If America socializes healthcare, government-funded abortions will probably increase drastically. They will eventually be provided to any woman who wants to murder her unborn child.

There are some frightening historical precedents for this kind of moral slippage. We typically lay the blame for German atrocities in World War II primarily at the feet of the country's leaders. But I contend that the worldview, values, and conduct of a vast number of Germany's populace are to blame, as much as Hitler's Nazi Party. And make no mistake, if our government begins to euthanize millions of senior citizens and the disabled through the rationing of healthcare, most of the American people will be as responsible as any doctors and politicians because we allowed the foundation to be laid with the desire for abortion on demand and the right to die. We allowed our children to be imbued with postmodernism, moral relativism, situational ethics, and the end-justifies-the-means rationalization.

Deadly Consequences

History may not repeat itself precisely, but it does rhyme. What happened in Germany is now possible in America as the barrier of a Christian worldview has largely been removed from the American conscience. Just before he died, Dr. Leo Alexander, chief medical assistant to the prosecution at the Nuremberg trials, observed about the U. S., "It is much like Germany in the Twenties and Thirties. The barriers against killing are coming down."[338]

The foundation was laid for the slaughter of five million Jews and six million non-Jews not by the Nazi Party, but by the parents of disabled children and family members of the mentally ill and disturbed. In the 1930s and 40s Germany:

> the lives of hundreds of thousands of terminally ill, incurably sick and mentally incompetent patients were terminated, not by sadistic monsters but by Europe's medical elite. The history of that era is all too similar to the present to be ignored.[339]

Hugh Gallagher confirms it "would be a mistake to call [the German euthanasia experience] a Nazi program. It was not. The program was conceived by physicians and operated by them. They did the killing."[340]

To date, millions of Americans have chosen to abort their children, and millions have voted for candidates who promise to uphold a woman's legal right to kill her unborn child. The German people learned that selfishness and moral relativism laid the foundation for the slaughter of more than 11 million people. What has America's slaughter of 50 million unborn babies laid the foundation for? Will Christians speak up or be silent? Or will they ignore Abraham Lincoln's somber warning, "Silence makes cowards out of the best of men."

In 1996, Mark Rothe and Dr. Timothy Quill drafted an amicus brief that they submitted to the U.S. Supreme Court in which they argued against the legalization of physician-assisted death. They argued:

> First, child euthanasia was permitted for disabled and "defective" infants and children. Soon thereafter, an adult

program for an "easy death" of mentally ill and incurably sick Germans was instituted on grounds of compassion. Later, Jews and other "undesirables" were included, this time for racial and eugenic reasons. Ultimately, the genocide that was the Final Solution grew out of these programs of medicalized killing.[341] The practice of physician aid-in-dying had small beginnings. In March 1937, a child was killed by his father because he was significantly mentally ill. When put on trial for murder, the local health office came to the father's defense, influencing the court to grant him a nominal prison sentence instead of the death penalty asked for by the prosecutor.[342] The next year, a man named Knauer wrote the German government, asking that his blind and mentally retarded daughter, born without an arm and leg be granted Gnadentod (mercy death). The chancellor instructed Dr. Karl Brandt to investigate and, if the letter were true, to grant the request. [343]

And these are not isolated cases. There are more:

Many parents were eager to obtain the Wohltat of physician-assisted death for their ill, deformed, or disabled children and many "wrote to hospitals to ask if their child could be relieved of his or her misery and be granted euthanasia."[344] In May 1939, an advisory group, the *Committee for the Scientific Treatment of Severe and Genetically Determined Illness*, was formed to determine if and how a euthanasia program for children and adults would operate.[345] The adult project was housed in Berlin at number 4 Tiergartenstrasse. It was thus code-named "T-4" and in the beginning there appeared to be a broad level of support for this throughout the country.[346]

Within a few years, there were up to 30 killing centers in Germany. "The German experience in physician-assisted death was the direct result of utilitarian, cost-benefit analysis and the view within the medical community that the value of human life is relative, that some persons are better off dead. It was not the result of jack-booted thugs in brown shirts."[347]

Keep in mind that this is German people killing German people through what they believed were "mercy killings." The practice also served as a cost-benefit analysis not unlike what the U.S. government established through the 2009 stimulus bill. "The Federal Council is modeled after a U.K board....This board approves or rejects treatments using a formula that divides the cost of treatment by the number of years the patient is likely to benefit. Treatments for young patients are more often approved than treatments for diseases that affect the elderly...."[348]

"The T-4 program was not a part of the Holocaust, rather, it was T-4 and the child euthanasia programs which preceded and served as models for the genocide of the Final Solution."[349] "In fact, even the idea of the infamous shower room gas chambers originated in the T-4 program with the killing of German Gentile patients."[350] "No Jews were among them; most Jews had already been sent to the concentration camps. The Nazis considered euthanasia a quasi-ethical sort of murder, and reserved it for members of their own kind."[351] "Neither racism nor anti-Semitism were a factor in these developments in Germany. T-4 doctors occasionally even gave lethal injections to severely injured German soldiers."[352] Euthanasia was thought to be a blessing and a merciful act that was reserved for "true" Germans.

That is until a few years after the German euthanasia program was established. World War II had begun and all needed resources were needed to fund the war. Jews who had been denied a "mercy death" were now going to be exterminated by what the German people and doctors had created.

"Jews and other selected undesirables would be transported from the concentration camps to the same killing centers used by the T-4 program."[353] This new program was named 14f13. "After the success of T-4 and 14f13, the hospital gassing equipment and procedures were adopted by Adolf Eichmann for use in the Final Solution."[354] "The final solution to the 'Jewish problem' that was finally decided upon in early 1942, and implemented later, was chosen largely because the means to that solution already existed in the euthanasia program, killing centers, and gas chambers. Indeed, the same gassing equipment used in the T-4 and 14f13 hospital operations were dismantled, transported, and re-installed at Auschwitz, Treblinka, and Sobibor.[355] "The T-4 physicians and other personnel were also put to work in the camps."[356]

Dr. Andrew Ivy, another Nuremberg prosecutor's medical assistant, has stated that if it were not for the already established, physician-assisted death programs, "it is conceivable that the entire idea and technique of death factories for genocide would not have materialized."[357] Many experts believe if it were not for the already established death centers, the Jews might possibly have just been deported because many German soldiers that took part in firing squads either had mental breakdowns or committed suicide. The gas chambers of the T-4 program solved this "problem" of psychological casualties among the German army.

A nation's leaders usually mirror its people. President James Garfield cautioned Americans about this:

The people are responsible for the character of their Congress, [and other elected officials]. If that body be ignorant, reckless and corrupt, it is because the people tolerate ignorance, recklessness and corruption. If it be intelligent, brave and pure, it is because the people demand these high qualities to represent them…

Ideas have consequences, and once a nation becomes willing to murder its own children, the people will eventually murder each other. Fully nationalized healthcare in America will ultimately bring with it the euthanization of seniors who supported abortion on demand or the right to die. The right to die is becoming the *duty* to die, promoted by many humanist liberals. John Hardwig from the Department of Philosophy at the University of Tennessee wrote a 13-page paper entitled, *Is There a Duty to Die?* In his short but dangerous work, the good professor makes the case that indeed there is a duty to die under wide-ranging conditions such as:

> …when continuing to live will impose significant burdens— emotional burdens, extensive care giving, destruction of life plans, and, yes, financial hardship—on your family and loved ones. This is the fundamental insight underlying a duty to die.[358]

Fabian Socialist Julian Huxley became the first director general of the United Nations Educational, Science, and Cultural Organization and authored *UNESCO: Its Purpose and Its Philosophy* (1948) in which he declared:

> …even though it is quite true that any radical eugenic policy will be for many years politically and psychologically impossible, it will be important for UNESCO to see that the

eugenic problem is examined with the greatest care, and that the public mind is informed of the issues at stake so that much that is now unthinkable may at least become thinkable.

Even if we know abortion will continue and that active euthanasia will increase, we, as Christians, must speak out and oppose the satanic origin of these practices. To do less is to agree they are acceptable, and I, for one, will not agree because God has declared "thou shall not murder." I challenge Christians to give generously to pro-life groups and adoption agencies.

Churches must also plan now for ministries to seniors and the disabled who will otherwise be denied medical treatment through healthcare rationing. Many church members are doctors, nurses, and other medical professionals in position for "such a time as this." Christians in the medical community may soon be the only ones who will offer care to those the government would otherwise terminate. Jesus said, "Assuredly, I say to you, inasmuch as you did it to one of the least of these brethren, you did it to Me." Our elderly and infirm are fast becoming some of "the least of these."

It is not out of the question that a government which has already allowed the murder of 50 million babies and which now drafts legislation to permit euthanizing the disabled and senior citizens through the rationing of healthcare is also a government that would deny medical care and treatment to those deemed undesirable, unfit, and a nuisance because of their Biblical worldview.

Margaret Sanger's standing as the greatest death-monger of all time is unlikely to be challenged. In fact, her numbers seem destined only to grow.

23

ROGER BALDWIN
(1884-1981)

"The most effective humanist organization for destroying the laws, morals, and traditional rights of Americans has been the ACLU. Founded in 1920, it is the legal arm of the humanist movement, established and nurtured by the Ethical Cultural Movement."[359]

I didn't make that up. David Noebel and Tim LaHaye, two of America's most perceptive observers of contemporary culture, demonstrate it clearly in their excellent book, *Mind Siege.* The history and practices of the American Civil Liberties Union substantiates the conclusion that the organization has been a leader in undermining our constitutional liberties.

But what motive would inspire anyone to want to destroy America's free society? One hint is the founder's choice of office location. On January 20, 1920, Roger Baldwin established the ACLU's first office, set up in New York City in space shared with the American Communist Party's tabloid, *New Masses.*

Other hints are discovered among Baldwin's co-horts. John Dewey—Chapter 8's "father of modern education" in America— signed the *Humanist Manifesto I,* was a board member of the American Humanist Association, helped establish the League for Industrial Democracy, and assisted Baldwin in founding the American Civil Liberties Union. Another co-founder, William Z. Foster, had previously served as the head of the United States Communist Party. Baldwin, Dewey, and Foster set the tone for what the ACLU would become, and today, where there is an attack on religious liberty, you can bet the ACLU is involved either directly or indirectly.

Sneak Attacks

As with most things communist, Baldwin's organizing began like the proverbial wolf in sheep's clothing. Historian George Grant reports in *The Family Under Siege*:

> In 1920 he [Baldwin] also launched the Mutual Aid Society to offer financial help to leftist intellectuals, trade unionists, and the radical fringe.[360]

> Baldwin also started the International Committee for Political Prisoners to provide counsel and support to anarchist and communist subversives who had been deported for their criminal activities. He helped to establish the American Fund for Public Service—with two million dollars donated by Charles Garland, a rich young revolutionary from Boston—in order to pour vast sums of money into revolutionary causes. And finally, he developed close institutional ties with the Communist movement and the Socialists International.[361]

The mainstay of the organization's activities, eradicating religious freedom is only part of the ACLU agenda. Here is a list of "liberties" the ACLU strives to legitimize in America:

- Child pornography

- Abortion on demand

- Tax exemptions for Satanists

- Totally legalized drug use

- Mandatory sex education for all grades

- Prostitution

- Gambling

- Giving gays and lesbians the same legal benefits married people have

- Letting homosexuals become adoptive and foster parents

- Unconditional legal protection for flag-burners

- Greater benefits for illegal aliens and homosexuals who want to enter the U.S.

And the list of liberties the ACLU opposes? Pretty much everything conservatives support:

- Prayer in public school classrooms (as well as in locker rooms, sports arenas, graduation exercises, courtrooms, and legislative assemblies)

- Nativity scenes, crosses, and other Christian symbols on public property

- Voluntary Bible reading in public schools, even during free time and after class

- Imprinting "in God we trust" on our coins

- Access for students in Christian schools to any publicly funded services

- Accreditation for science departments at Bible-believing Christian universities

- The posting of the Ten Commandments in classrooms or courtrooms

- The words "under God" in the Pledge of Allegiance

- School officials searching students' lockers for drugs or guns

- Requiring people on welfare to work in exchange for their government aid

- Tax exemptions for Christian churches, ministries, and other charities

- Rating movies to alert parents about sex or violence

- Home-schooling

- Medical safety regulations and reporting of AIDS cases

- Public pro-life demonstrations

- Laws banning polygamy.[362]

Lest you think there is even the slightest undue conservative bias in my assertion that the ACLU has been one of America's most liberal and dangerous organizations from the get-go, consider the results of an investigation by the U.S. House of Representatives Special Committee on Communist Activities in the United States within the first dozen years of the ACLU's existence. On January 17, 1931, the committee reported:

> The American Civil Liberties Union is closely affiliated with the communist movement in the United States, and fully 90 percent of its efforts are on behalf of communists who have come into conflict with the law. It claims to stand for free speech, free press, and free assembly, but it is quite apparent that the main function of the ACLU is to attempt to protect the communists in their advocacy of force and violence to overthrow the Government, replacing the American flag by a red flag and erecting a Soviet Government in place of the republican form of government guaranteed to each state by the Federal Constitution.

Nearly four decades later, investigators from yet another source were still coming to the same conclusion. A police undercover agent, David D. Gumaer, revealed in 1969 that "206 past leading members of the ACLU had a combined record of 1,754 officially cited Communist front affiliations. . . . The present ACLU Board consists of sixty-eight members, thirty-one of whom have succeeded in amassing a total of at least 355 Communist front affiliations. That total does not include the citations of these individuals which appear in reports from the Senate International Security Subcommittee."[363]

A CLUe to Communist Influence

Despite the clever name of the organization, "civil liberties" was never Roger Baldwin's real goal. In fact, Baldwin was so committed to his radical liberalism that he was willing to use the power of governmental tyranny to "suppress" the masses and bring his worldview to bear:

> When the power of the working class is once achieved, as it has been only in the Soviet Union, I am for maintaining it by any means whatever. No champion of a socialist society could fail to see that some suppression was necessary to achieve it.[364]

As for his atheistic, communist worldview, Baldwin, by his own admission, was no "innocent liberal." His strategy was precise:

> I joined. I don't regret being a part of the Communist tactic, which increased the effectiveness of a good cause. I knew what I was doing. I was not an innocent liberal. I wanted what the Communists wanted and I traveled the United Front road to get it.[365]

So there you go. Roger Baldwin—the father of the ACLU and acclaimed liberal—admits he is a communist, and a communist by definition is an atheist and humanist. The American Civil Liberties Union is not about liberties. It's about communism, revolution, and oppression!

To accomplish his communist revolution in America, Baldwin's tactics are as true to communism as his underlying philosophy. It is a frighteningly effective way liberals in general have adopted as the means to achieve their goals—by using lies, deception, and lots of smoke and mirrors:

> We want to look like patriots in everything we do. We want to get a lot of flags, talk a great deal about the Constitution and what our forefathers wanted to make of this country

and how that we are the fellows that really stand for the spirit of our institutions.[366]

While appealing to the Constitution and waving the American flag, Baldwin and company trash the Constitution, defend the right to burn the flag, and persecute genuine patriots in order to achieve their goals. Baldwin outlines his plans:

> I am for socialism, disarmament, and ultimately for abolishing the state itself as an instrument of violence and compulsion. I seek social ownership of property, the abolition of the propertied class, and sole control by those who produce wealth. Communism is the goal. It all sums up into one single purpose—the abolition of dog-eat-dog under which we live.[367]

The approach has been stunningly successful. Despite Baldwin's hatred for the U.S. Constitution, America, God, private property, the free enterprise system, and freedom of religion, in 1981, then-President Jimmy Carter (a Democrat, in case you've forgotten) gave Baldwin the Medal of Freedom—our nation's highest civilian honor!

Fortunately, not everyone is blind to the ACLU's true intent. Mark Campisano, former Supreme Court clerk for Justice William Brennan, asserts:

> An accounting of the ACLU's case load suggests that the organization is an ideological chameleon—that beneath the protective coloration of civil liberties, the ACLU is pursuing a very different agenda—a very liberal agenda.[368]

According to William Donohue, the ACLU is the very incarnation of liberalism:

Social reform, in a liberal direction, is the sine qua non of the ACLU. Its record, far from showing a momentary wavering from impartiality, is replete with attempts to reform American society according to the wisdom of liberalism. The truth of the matter is that the ACLU has always been a highly politicized organization.[369]

In concluding this review of the Roger Baldwin legacy, I'll add that—besides fronting for communism, undermining American ideals, and crusading relentlessly against the freedoms we hold dear—the ACLU also shows a vile level of bad taste in the causes it celebrates. In 1978, it rabidly defended "the right of American Nazis to march through a predominantly Jewish suburb of Chicago."[370]

So may I submit to you my suggestion for an alternate name to go with the initials ACLU? It may help you remember the organization's real agenda: American Communist and Leftist Union.

Conclusion

Why This Can Be Our Finest Hour

As frequently as I am asked "How did America find herself where she is today?," I am asked by Bible-minded and committed Christians throughout America, "What can we do in response to what is happening to America?" This book—and more specifically, this chapter—is my answer.

Our resurrected Lord Jesus in Matthew 28:19-20 commands all of His converts to make disciples who will follow Him. Many in the Church think the Great Commission is a call to evangelism, but it is not—it is to make disciples. Evangelism is the first of a four-step process.

First, we must evangelize or proclaim the reason for the death, burial, and resurrection of Jesus Christ and call people to faith and repentance in Him. Jesus tells us in verse 20 that we are to teach converts to observe all things that He commanded or taught His disciples.

Jesus spoke on many issues, including creation, family, civil government, servant leadership, marriage, economics, law, history, education, social issues, doctrine (the will of God for our lives), theology (the character and nature of God), and much more. Yet countless studies reveal that many Christians are still drinking milk instead of eating meat. They need teachers when they should be teaching others.

They don't even know how to defend essential Christian doctrines and cannot readily discern right from wrong. Hebrews 5:12-14 speaks of this and says those who have been Christians for a long time and yet still find themselves unskilled in teaching others need to get their act together and be obedient to what Christians are commanded to do.

Hebrews 5:14 indicates that those who are spiritually mature *can* discern good from evil, but one of the biggest problems in the Church today is lack of discernment. Ephesians 4:14 warns that spiritually immature believers are like children who lack discernment and will be blown here and there by every wind of doctrine and by the cunning and craftiness of men in their deceitful scheming. Matthew 7:15 says many will appear to be Christians—some will even be pastors—but they will be wolves in sheep's clothing.

The Church in America has been greatly weakened and in some cases completely compromised by false teaching and a false gospel. As a result, the Church is more a reflection of the culture rather than a reflection of Jesus Christ.

We are called to be *in* the world but not *of* the world, and there is a great need for Christians to mature and carry out the responsibilities of a disciple:

- Proclaim truth to the unbeliever—evangelism;
- Live the truth—be a disciple and make disciples;
- Defend the truth—apologetics;
- Instruct in the truth—worldview training.

We have already discussed evangelism and discipleship, but what about apologetics and worldview training? Apologetics is the defense of foundational Christian doctrines such as original sin, the death, burial, and resurrection of Jesus Christ, how we know Jesus is God, and how we know the Bible is true. Engaging in apologetics fulfills the Biblical mandate to contend earnestly for the faith (Jude 3), to be ready at any moment to give a reason for the hope we profess (1 Peter 3:15).

Worldview training involves teaching yourself or others specific Biblical principles for how Christians are to live in this world. Second Timothy 3:16 tells us the Bible was written by God and is profitable for doctrine, for reproof, for correction, and for instruction in righteousness. Righteousness means "right living" or "how to live right" according to God or in a manner consistent with God's character and nature. The Bible reveals God's character and nature. So, by studying God's Word, we develop a comprehensive, Biblical worldview. Scripture is the lens through which we see the world. Regardless of whether the subject is law, science, economics, history, family, social issues, education, doctrine, or theology, we will know how to think and, therefore, how to live.

Once a person surrenders his or her life to the lordship of Christ, we are to teach the essential Christian doctrines and how to defend them. Then we are to teach specific Biblical principles for living the Christian life (worldview training). Once a Christian is mature in faith, we are to encourage the believer to go out and make disciples of Jesus Christ.

So why is this perhaps the greatest hour for the true American Church? Let me give you six reasons.

(1) The emptiness of materialism

The late Francis Schaeffer said that when the dull ache of the human soul could no longer be filled with material prosperity people would begin to look for a substitute. America is quickly losing its world status as a superpower, and one major reason is our nation's financial crisis. As more people can no longer buy "dream" homes, big screen TVs, cars, or take lavish trips, many are turning to spiritualism. Children of the 1980s and 90s, they watched as the materialism of their parents did not guarantee happy homes or prevent the breakup of their marriages. Having experienced firsthand the reality that money does not buy happiness, many turn to spiritualism over materialism.

Today's financial crisis will bring many to the end of themselves. Their value can no longer be measured by possessions or income. When many go looking for peace, we can introduce them to the Prince of Peace.

(2) The vanity of pleasure

Hedonism, the pursuit of pleasure, has left millions, and will leave millions more, empty and numb. G. K. Chesterton put it this way: "Despair does not lie in being weary of suffering, but in being weary of joy." And Dr. Ravi Zacharias offers this perspective:

> When the pleasure button is repeatedly pressed and can no longer deliver or sustain, the emptiness that results is terrifying. Surely, the loneliest moment in life is when you have just experienced what you thought would deliver the ultimate, and it has let you down. Several have expressed this, either in its impassioned form or in an honest confession of the pursuit of meaning.

King Solomon was the richest man in history. Yet after serving God, he was led away from God and sought meaning and happiness in the pursuit of pleasure. The description of his homes, wives, concubines, horses, stables, barns, business, hobbies, servants, and employees makes Bill Gates or Donald Trump look like paupers. But in the end, Solomon declared it all to be vanity and that only serving God would bring true and lasting peace, contentment, and meaning.

Many frantically push the pleasure button each day but find it no longer works. Christians have the answer, and Jesus Himself said He had come so that people would have life and have it more abundantly. He means that Christians can have a life deep in meaning, purpose, and spiritual security.

(3) The desire to be spiritual

Secular Humanism has failed. It proclaimed that truth could be found through human reason alone, but this did not work out so well inasmuch as atheism led to two world wars and the deaths of more than 100 million people. The bloodiest of all centuries happened because of atheism.[371]

In denying the spiritual world and man as a spiritual being, Secular Humanism shows itself bankrupt of satisfaction for a generation desiring a spiritual experience. People today hope at least to find some kind of spiritual salve for a guilty conscience. They are seeking truth, but the postmodern world tries to tell them truth is subjective. While they may not be seeking *the* truth, they do want *some* truth.

Christians should explain why the seekers feel guilty: Tell them Who created the conscience, how it is stamped with the moral law, and that it is a reflection of God's character and nature. We must give them hope in that their guilt reveals their sinfulness and the need to repent. We can introduce them to *the* Truth, the Person Jesus Christ Who is the only Way, Truth, and Life.

(4) The personal God

Many who have been following a cult or a false religion find Christianity very compelling when they learn about our personal Savior. Muslims are coming to salvation in Jesus Christ, for instance, because He is a personal God Who became a man while yet being fully God. He laid down His life as a ransom for the sins of the world. This is very impressive to Muslims, for they've known only a god who is impersonal—one who may ask them to lay down their lives for him, but certainly not the other way around.

(5) The answer to evil

The unbeliever cannot understand or explain why there is so much evil and injustice in our world. This is one of the main criticisms skeptics and critics offer for their lack of belief in God. They cannot understand why a loving God would allow so much evil, suffering, and injustice. But for Christians skilled in defense of the faith, this issue is our opportunity to explain God's original plan, man's sin, and God's ultimate answer to this universal problem of evil. Sin is what it is because God is Who He is. John Newton, the slave trader turned crusader for Christ, proclaimed that he was a great sinner, but Christ is a greater Savior.

(6) The offer of mercy from judgment

America is indeed being judged by God, and as this judgment is likely to increase drastically, we have an opportunity to take what is happening and explain the consequences of sin and of rejecting God. We can use God's judgment of our national sins as an opportunity to explain to the unbeliever what sin is, why God must judge sin, and that the judgment nations experience in this life is nothing compared to the eternal judgment unrepentant individuals will receive in the next world. We can share with them that grace and mercy are extended only to those who repent, that Jesus has provided the way for us to pass from judgment into life.

Even Persecution Can Bring Our Finest Hour

Untold numbers have come to Jesus Christ though the faithful commitment of Christians who refused to deny their Lord even in the face of persecution. Perhaps the greatest example of this is the living testimony of the early disciples of Jesus Christ that continues to this day:

- Paul and Matthew were beheaded;
- Barnabas was burned;
- Mark was dragged to death;
- James, the less, was clubbed to death;
- Peter, Philip, and Andrew were crucified;
- Thomas was speared;
- Luke was hung by the neck until dead;
- Stephen was stoned.

Like our brothers and sisters in Cuba, China, the former Soviet Union, and many Muslim nations, we are not immune to persecution. Indeed, it is likely to increase here. I take encouragement from these Scriptures, and I pray you do, too:

> 2 Corinthians 4:8-9—We are hard-pressed on every side, yet not crushed; we are perplexed, but not in despair; persecuted, but not forsaken; struck down, but not destroyed.

> 2 Corinthians 4:16-18—Therefore we do not lose heart. Even though our outward man is perishing, yet the inward man is being renewed day by day. For our light affliction, which is but for a moment, is working for us a far more exceeding and eternal weight of glory, while we do not look at the things which are seen, but at the things which are not

seen. For the things which are seen are temporary, but the things which are not seen are eternal.

Philippians 1:12, 20-21—But I want you to know, brethren, that the things which happened to me have actually turned out for the furtherance of the gospel.... [A]ccording to my earnest expectation and hope that in nothing I shall be ashamed, but with all boldness, as always, so now also Christ will be magnified in my body, whether by life or by death. For to me, to live is Christ and to die is gain.

In his book, *The Great Evangelical Disaster*, Francis Schaeffer warned:

....Something has happened in the last sixty years [1920 to 1980s]. The freedom that once was founded on a Biblical consensus and a Christian ethos has now become autonomous freedom, cut loose from all constraints. Here we have the world spirit of our age—autonomous man setting himself up as God, in defiance of the knowledge and the moral and spiritual truth which God has given. Here is the reason why we have a moral breakdown in every area of life. The titanic freedoms which we once enjoyed have been cut loose from their Christian restraints and are becoming a force of destruction leading to chaos. And when this happens, there really are very few alternatives. All morality becomes relative, law becomes arbitrary, and society moves toward disintegration. In personal and social life, compassion is swallowed up by self-interest...when the memory of the Christian consensus which gave us freedom within the Biblical form is increasingly forgotten, a manipulating authoritarianism will tend to fill the vacuum. At this point the words "right" and "left" will make little difference. They are only two roads to the same end; the results are the same. An elite, an authoritarianism as such, will gradually force form on society so that it will not go into chaos—and most people would accept it.

The chaos is growing, and politicians will seek to make it worse so they can justify bigger government, fewer freedoms, and more power and wealth for the elite ruling class. Are Americans waking up too late? Are the numbers of Americans who understand the threat—or even care—too small? If the answer to these two questions is yes, then the only question left to ask is what will happen to those of us who refuse to accept it? If America's fate is sealed, then this one thing I know: future generations in America will ask the same questions that post-World War II generations asked about the Holocaust of Germany. Where were the people of the churches? Why did they let this happen? Why did they compromise?

Albert Einstein, who was exiled from Germany because he was a Jew, noticed the faithfulness of the remnant in Germany. Einstein reveals why the Church must respond when a government and its leaders become evil, promote injustice, and become tyrannical:

> Being a lover of freedom, when the [Nazi] revolution came I looked to the universities to defend it, knowing that they had always boasted of their devotion to the cause of truth; but no, the universities were immediately silenced. Then I looked to the great editors of the newspapers, whose flaming editorials in the days gone by had proclaimed their

love of freedom; but they, like the universities, were silenced in a few short weeks. Only the Church stood squarely across the path of Hitler's campaign for suppressing truth. I never had any special interest in the Church before, but now I feel a great affection and admiration for it because the Church alone had the courage and persistence to stand for intellectual and moral freedom. I am forced to confess that what I once despised I now praise unreservedly.[372]

In standing for what is just, righteous, and true, we are standing for Jesus Christ, because justice, righteousness, and truth are reflections of His character and nature. This is a powerful witness for the unsaved and unbelieving world. Even in the face of death, the world will see that we are so committed to the cause of Christ that we are willing to lay down our lives for Him.

Wise Fools? No, Just Fools

Romans 1:22 says that "professing to be wise, they became fools," which is to say they became vain, useless, and futile in their thinking. This clearly describes Karl Marx, John Dewey, John Maynard Keynes, Aldous Huxley, Charles Darwin, Friedrich Nietzsche, Alfred Kinsey, Margaret Sanger, and the other influencers we've discussed in this book. Among these "leading intellectuals" are child molesters, drug users, family deserters, and at least one who went insane, but the flood of their combined thinking overwhelms much of what we treasure in America. [373]

Pastor Martin Niemoller was one of some 800 pastors who tried to stop Adolf Hitler. After surviving a concentration camp, he said that if the 14,000 evangelical pastors in Germany had merely stood up to Hitler's ungodly regime, the numbers of dead might have been as little as 10,000 instead of 11,000,000. A few good men and women can make a very big difference. Yet I fear America's days are numbered because most do not understand—much less expose—the worldviews of those who control us from their graves.

People who share the worldviews of these enemies of our constitutional republic and Biblical worldview do not want their agenda and its consequences to be revealed. Above all, they do not want us to equip and train our children and grandchildren with a Biblical worldview by which to recognize, reject, and fight against their seductive and destructive lies. But enough courageous Christians can still make a difference. They have at many other times in history and in many other places today. Martyrs of the past have always inspired an expanding church, and persecuted Christians in countries such as modern-day China demonstrate how dramatically adverse social conditions can bring explosive church growth.

Our ultimate measure of success lies not in the legislation passed or in the character of representatives we elect. It consists, rather, in how well we fulfill the Great Commission. The culture war neither defines us, nor sets the standard for our success or failure. Through Christ we win, even if, in the eyes of the world, we are losers. So please join me in making this the finest hour for Christians in America.

BIBLIOGRAPHY

Aikman, David, *The Delusion of Disbelief*. Carol Stream, IL: Tyndale Publishers, Inc., 2008.

Anderson, Martin, *Imposters in the Temple: American Intellectuals Are Destroying Our Universities and Cheating Our Students of Their Future*. New York: Simon & Schuster, 1992.

Black, Jim Nelson, *Freefall of the American University: How Our Colleges Are Corrupting the Mind and Morals of the Next Generation*. Nashville, TN: Thomas Nelson, 2004.

Buchanan, Patrick J., *The Death of the West*. New York: St. Martin's Press, 2002.

Chandler, Robert, *Shadow World*. Washington, DC: Regnery Publishers, Inc., 2008.

Coulter, Ann, *Godless: The Church of Liberalism*. New York: Crown Forum, 2006.

Coulter, Ann, *Treason: Liberal Treachery*. New York: Crown Forum, 2003.

Courtois, Stephane, ed., *The Black Book of Communism*. Cambridge: Harvard University Press, 1999.

Dalrymple, Theodore, *Life at the Bottom: The Worldview That Makes the Underclass*. Chicago: Ivan R. Dee, 2001.

Dalrymple Theodore, *Our Culture, What's Left of It*. Chicago: Ivan R. Dee, 2005.

Day, Vox, *The Irrational Atheist*. Dallas, TX: Benbella Books, Inc., 2008.

Dobbs, Zygmund, *Keynes at Harvard*. West Sayville, NY: Veritas Foundation, 1962.

Dobbs, Zygmund, *The Great Deceit: Social Pseudo-Sciences*. West

Sayville, NY: Veritas Foundation, 1964.

Evans, M. Stanton, *Blacklisted by History: The Untold Story of Senator Joe McCarthy and His Fight Against America's Enemies*. New York: Crown Forum, 2007.

Flew, Antony, *There Is a God*. New York: HarperOne, 2007.

Gilder, George, *The Israel Test*. New York: Richard Vigilante Books, 2009.

Goldberg, Jonah, *Liberal Fascism*. New York: Doubleday, 2007.

Hart, David B., *Atheist Delusions: The Christian Revolution and Its Fashionable Enemies*. New Haven: Yale University Press, 2009.

Herman, Arthur, *The Idea of Decline in Western History*. New York: The Free Press, 1997.

Howse, Brannon, *Christian Worldview for Children*. Collierville, TN: Worldview Weekend Publishing, 2006.

Howse, Brannon, *Christian Worldview for Students*. Collierville, TN: Worldview Weekend Publishing, 2006.

Howse, Brannon, *Christian Worldview for Students, Vol. 2*. Collierville, TN: Worldview Weekend Publishing, 2006.

Howse, Brannon, *Put Your Beliefs to the Test*. Collierville, TN: Worldview Weekend Publishing, 2006.

Huntington, Samuel P., *The Clash of Civilizations*. New York: Simon & Schuster, 1996.

Jay, Martin, *The Dialectical Imagination: A History of the Frankfurt School and the Institute of Social Research 1923-1950*. Berkeley, CA: University of California Press, 1996.

Johnson, Paul, *Intellectuals: From Marx and Tolstoy to Sartre and Chomsky*. New York: Harper Perennial, 2007.

Lennox, John C., *God's Undertaker: Has Science Buried God?* Oxford, UK: Lion Books, 2007.

Meyer, Stephen C., *Signature in the Cell: DNA and the Evidence for Intelligent Design*. New York: HarperOne, 2009.

Nicholi, Armand M., *The Question of God*. New York: The Free Press, 2002.

Noebel, David A., *Understanding the Times: The Collision of Today's Competing Worldviews*, Revised 2nd Edition. Manitou Springs, CO: Summit Press, 2006.

Noebel, David A., *Clergy in the Classroom: The Religion of Secular Humanism*, Revised 3rd Edition. Manitou Springs, CO: Summit Press, 2007.

Pearcey, Nancy, *Total Truth: Liberating Christianity from Its Cultural Captivity*. Wheaton, IL: Crossway Books, 2004.

Rummel, R. J., *Death by Government*. New Brunswick, NJ: Transaction Publishers, 1994.

Wells, Jonathan, *Icons of Evolution: Science or Myth?* Washington, DC: Regnery Publishing, Inc., 2000.

Windchy, Eugene G., *The End of Darwinism*. Bloomington, IN: Xlibris Corporation, 2009.

NOTES

[1] Patrick J. Buchanan on The American Conservative website, http://www.amconmag.com/blog/2009/09/10/americas-cultural-crackup/

[2] Charles Francis Potter, Humanism, *A New Religion* (New York: Simon and Schuster, 1930), 128.

[3] William J. Federer, *America's God and Country* (Coppell, TX: Fame Publishing, Inc., 1994), 13.

[4] Ken Ham & Britt Beemer with Todd Hillard, *Already Gone: Why Your Kids Will Quit Church and What You Can Do to Stop It* (Green Forest, AR: Master Books, 2009), 22, 33, 41.

[5] Phil Kerpen, "NY's Tax-Funded Ex-Terrorist," September 9, 2009, *New York Post*.

[6] Tom DeWeese, "Sustainable Development Is the Evil You Face", 8/12/2009 www.worldviewtimes.com/article.php/articleid_5251/Brannon-Howse/Tom-DeWeese.

[7] Ibid.

[8] Carroll Quigley, *Tragedy and Hope: A History of the World in Our Time* (New York: The MacMillan Company, 1966), 1247-48.

[9] Julian Huxley, *UNESCO: Its Purpose and Its Philosophy* (Washington, DC: Public Affairs Press, 1947), 61.

[10] "About the Third Way," posted on the website of the Democratic Leadership Council, June 1, 1998, www.ndol.org/ndol_ci.cfm?kaid=128&subid=187&contentid=895.

[11] Kate Galbraith, "The Three Horsemen of the Third Way," *Slate*, September 29, 1998, http://www.slate.com/id/1001976.

[12] Dana Milbank, "Needed: Catchword for Bush Ideology; 'Communitarianism'," *The Washington Post*, February 1, 2001.

[13] Henry Lamb, "An Unseen Enemy of Freedom," WorldNetdaily.com, September 13, 2008, wnd.com/index.php?pageId=75118.

[14] Ibid.

[15] Melissa Anderson, "Business, Government, Academic Leaders Convene on Sustainable Real Estate Development," September 19, 2008, http://www.news.wisc.edu/15631.

[16] The Commission on Global Goverance, *Our Global Neighborhood* (Oxford: Oxford University Press, 1995), 208.

[17] Ibid.

[18] Maurice Strong, quoted in Daniel Wood, "The Wizard of Baca Grande," *West*, May,1990, 47.

[19] Maurice Strong, quoted in Henry Lamb, "Conspiracy Theories Laid to Rest as U.N. Announces Plan for 'Global Neighborhood'," Hope for the World Update, Fall 1996, 2.

[20] Brannon Howse, *Reclaiming a Nation at Risk: The Battle for Your Faith, Family, and Freedoms* (Bridgestone Multimedia Group, 1995), 190.

[21] See George Gilder, *The Israel Test* (2009) for a complete picture of this very important point. Gilder explains in detail why Jews are hated throughout the world. He also explains why Christians and monotheistic Jews get along so well.

[22] Ibid.

[23] Lynn White, Jr., "The Historical Roots of Our Ecologic Crisis," Garrett de Bell, ed., *The Environmental Handbook: Prepared for the First National Environmental Teach-In* (New York: Ballantine/Friends of the Earth Book, 1970), 21-25.

[24] Naresh Singh and Vangile Titi, *Empowerment for Sustainable Development*, (Zed Books), 27.

[25] Mikhail Gorbachev, *The Search for a New Beginning: Developing a New Civilization* (San Francisco: Harper San Francisco and the Gorbachev Foundation/USA, 1995), 60-62.

[26] Howse, *Reclaiming a Nation at Risk*, 190.

[27] James Redford, "Forrest Mims Did Not Misrepresent Prof. Eric Pianka's Statements," www.geocities.com/tetrahedronomega/pianka-mims.html

[28] David Brower, quoted in Dixie Lee Ray, *Trashing the Planet*, 169.

[29] Paul Ehrlich, *The Population Bomb* (New York: Ballentine, 1968), 135.

[30] Ben Johnson, "Obama's Biggest Radical," *Front Page*, Feb. 27, 2009, www.frontpagemag.com/readArticle.aspx?ARTID=34198.

[31] Ibid.

[32] Ibid.

[33] Ibid.

[34] *Ecoscience*, p. 807 as quoted in Frontpagemag.com "Obama's Biggest Radical" by Ben Johnson, February 27, 2009.

[35] Peter Singer from his book, *Rethinking Life and Death*, as quoted in "Peter Singer: Architect of the Culture of Death" by Donald Demarco posted at www.catholiceducation.org/articles/medical_ethics/me0049.html.

[36] Ibid.

[37] Ibid.

[38] Ibid.

[39] Dr. Erwin Lutzer, *Hitler's Cross: The Revealing Story of How the Cross of Christ Was Used as a Symbol of the Nazi Agenda* (Chicago: Moody Press, 1995), 155.

[40] Ibid. 156.

[41] Alice Bailey, *The Spiritual Hierarchy* (New York: World Goodwill), 4.

[42] ———, *The Unfinished Autobiography* (New York: Lucis Trust, 1951), 137-140.

[43] ——, *The Externalisation of the Hierarchy* (New York: Lucis Trust, 1957), vii. This statement was made by the Tibetan (demon) in August 1934.

[44] Ibid. (September 28, 1938), 61-62.

[45] ——, *Esoteric Psychology II*, 1st ed. (1942), 630-31.

[46] ——, *Externalisation*, 133-135.

[47] Ibid.

[48] Trevor Ravenscroft, *They Speak of Destiny* (New York: Simon & Schuster, 1960), 44, quoted in Erwin Lutzer, *Hitler's Cross* (Chicago: Moody Press, 1995).

[49] Gerald Suster, *Hitler: The Occult Messiah* (New York: St. Martin's, 1981), quoted in Lutzer, *Hitler's Cross*, 77.

[50] David Hunt Peace, *Prosperity and the Coming Holocaust* (Eugene, OR: Harvest House, 1983), quoted in Lutzer, *Hitler's Cross*, 128.

[51] Erwin Lutzer, *Hitler's Cross*, 64.

[52] Alice Bailey, *The Rays and the Initiations*, (1934-1947), 109.

[53] ——, *The Reappearance of the Christ*, 1st ed. (1948), 164-65.

[54] ——, *Education in the New Age*, 1st ed. (1954), 88.

[55] ——, *The Rays and the Initiations*, 1st ed. (1957), 233-34.

[56] ——, *Esoteric Healing*, 1st ed. (1953), 393.

[57] ——, *The Externalisation of the Hierarchy*, 7th printing (New York: Lucis Trust, 1982), 513.

[58] Ibid., 401.

[59] Gary Kah, *The New World Religion* (Noblesville, IN: Hope International Publishing, Inc., 1998), 162.

[60] Ibid., 163.

[61] Ibid., 176.

[62] Robert Muller, speech addressed to the Global Citizenship 2000 Youth Congress, Vancouver, BC, April 5, 1997, transcribed and included in Gary Kah, *The New World Religion*.

[63] Ibid., 163.

[64] Interview with Henry Kissinger on the floor of the New York Stock Exchange with CNBC.

[65] Mikhail Gorbachev, "A New International Agenda," *International Herald Tribune*, January 1, 2009.

[66] Ibid.

[67] Emma Vandore, "Sarkozy, Merkel, Blair Call for New Capitalism," AP/Yahoo News, August 1, 2009.

[68] *The Washington Times*, May 30, 2008. Also see Michael Crichton's *State of Fear* for further information about eco-environmentalism as a religion.

[69] *U.S. District Court Southern District of New York, 2000-07-21*.

[70] David Breese, *Seven Men Who Rule the World from the Grave* (Chicago: Moody Publishers, 1992), 96.

[71] Ibid., 102.

[72] Ibid., 221.

[73] science.jrank.org/pages/7686/Existentialism.html.

[74] Ibid.

[75] "German Men and Women!", *Freiburger Studentenzeitung*, November 10, 1933, quoted in Jeff Collins et al., *Introducing Heidegger* (Cambridge, MA: Icon Books), 96.

[76] Walter Kaufmann, *Existentialism: From Dostoevsky to Sartre* (Cleveland: The World Publishing Company, 1956), 11.

[77] Hubert Dreyfus, *Being-in-the-world: A Commentary on Heidegger's Being and Time*, Division I (Cambridge, MA: MIT Press, 1991), Second Appendix.

[78] David Noebel, *Understanding the Times* (Manitou Springs, CO: Summit Press, second printing, 2006), 26-27.

[79] "Rethinking Whole-Language," *The Executive Educator*, January 1994.

[80] Ibid.

[81] Peter Brimelow and Leslie Spencer, "Comeuppance," *Forbes*, February 13, 1995, 124.

[82] Bob DeWaay, *The Emergent Church: Undefining Christianity* (St. Louis, Park, MN: Bob DeWaay, 2009), 68-69.

[83] Ibid., 69.

[84] Ibid., 13-14.

[85] Lynn Stuter, "Using the Delphi Technique to Achieve Consensus," *Education Reporter*, November 1998.

[86] DeWaay, *The Emergent Church*, 19, 21.

[87] John Perazzo, "Barack Obama's Newest Spiritual Advisor," *Front Page*, March 17, 2009, /readArticle.aspx?ARTID=34385

[88] David Noebel, "Barack Obama's 'Red' Spiritual Advisor," March 28, 2009, at /article.php/articleid-4767/Brannon-Howse/David-Noebel.

[89] Ibid., 23.

[90] DeWaay, *The Emergent Church*, 179-80.

[91] Bonna Johnson, "Meditation Goes Mainstream," *Tennessean*, September 14, 2008.

[92] Andy Crouch, "The Emergent Mystique," *Christianity Today*, November 1, 2004, http://www.ctilibrary.com/ct/2004/november/12.36.html.

[93] http://blogs.echurchnetwork.net/Assets/userBlog/314/052905.mp3.

[94] Andy Crouch quoted in "Hipper-Than-Thou Pastor," *Time*, December 6, 2007.

[95] Troy Dolan, "Velvet Elvis," *Relevant*, http://www.relevantmagazine.com/culture/books/reviews/3176-velvet-elvis.

[96] Leonard Sweet, Brian McLaren, and Jerry Haselmayer, *A Is for Abductive—The Language of the Emerging Church* (Grand Rapids: Zondervan, 2003), 143.

[97] DeWaay, *The Emergent Church*, 196.

[98] Rob Bell, *Velvet Elvis—Repainting the Christian Faith* (Grand Rapids: Zondervan, 2005), 192.

[99] Ibid., 158.

[100] DeWaay, *The Emergent Church*, 196.

[101] Bell, Velvet Elvis, 159.

[102] Frederic W. Baue, *The Spiritual Society: What Lurks Beyond Postmodernism?* (Wheaton, IL: Crossway Books, 2001).

[103] Friedrich Nietzsche, *Beyond Good and Evil*, Walter Kaufman, trans. (New York: Vintage, 1966), section 62.

[104] ——, *The Twilight of the Gods*.

[105] Gerald Suster, *Hitler: The Occult Messiah* (New York: St. Martin's, 1981), 77.

[106] Robert G. Waite, *Adolf Hitler: The Psychopathic God* (New York: Basic Books, 1977), 317.

[107] Nietzsche, *Beyond Good and Evil*, section 225.

[108] Ibid.

[109] Ibid., section 228.

[110] Betsy McCaughey, "Ruin Your Health with the Obama Stimulus Plan," Bloomberg.com, February 9, 2009, http://www.bloomberg.com/apps/news?pid=newsarchive&sid=alzfDxfbwhzs.

[111] ——, "Assault on Seniors," *The Wall Street Journal*, July 23, 2009, http://online.wsj.com/article/SB10001424052970203517304574303903498159292.html.

[112] Ibid.

[113] *Hastings Center Report*, November -December, 96.

[114] Melchior Palyi, *Compulsory Medical Care and the Welfare State* (Chicago: National Institute of Professional Services, 1949), quoted in Brannon Howse, "The Similarities Between America and Nazi Germany," Winter/Spring 2009, *Worldview Weekend Digest*.

[115] Henry T. Edmondson III, *John Dewey and the Decline of American Education: How the Patron Saint of Schools Has Corrupted Teaching and Learning* (Wilmington, DE: ISI Books, 2006), 5.

[116] John Dewey, *The New Republic*, December 5, 1928.

[117] William S. Lind, *Further Readings on the Frankfurt School*, Chapter VI (Free Congress Foundation), http://www.freecongress.org/centers/cc/pcessay6.aspx.

[118] ———, "What Is Political Correctness?", http://freecongress.org

[119] For a complete look at the McCarthy issue, see M. Stanton Evans, *Blacklisted by History* (New York: Crown Forum, 2007).

[120] Alvin Schmidt, *The Menace of Multiculturalism: The Trojan Horse in America* (Westport, CT: Praeger, 1997).

[121] David B. Richardson, "Marxism in the U.S. Classroom," *U.S. News and World Report* (January 25, 1982) 42-45. Cited in Noebel, *Understanding the Times* (1991), 19.

[122] Georgie Anne Geyer, "Marxism Thrives on Campus," *Denver Post* (August 29, 1989), B7. Cited in Noebel, Ibid.

[123] Herbert London, "Marxism Thriving on American Campuses," *The World and I* (January 1987), p. 189. Cited in Noebel, Ibid., 20.

[124] *The Marine Corps Gazette* (December 1994), 37.

[125] Gerald L. Atkinson, "What Is the Frankfurt School?", August 1, 1999.

[126] Ibid.

[127] Benjamin Wicker, *10 Books That Screwed Up the World: And 5 Others That Didn't Help* (Washington, DC: Regnery Publishing, Inc., 2008), 213.

[128] Ibid., 219.

[129] Ibid., 212-213.

[130] Phyllis Schlafly, "Why Women Are Unhappy," *The Schlafly Report*, June 2009.

[131] Phyllis Schlafly, "The Feminists Continue Their War Against Men"

[132] Ibid.

[133] Ibid.

[134] Ibid.

[135] Ibid.

[136] "Understanding Feminists and Their Fantasies," *The Schlafly Report*, December 2002.

[137] "Moms: Is It Easier Being a Single Mom? Many Married Moms Think So," *Deseret News*, July 4, 2009.

[138] Daniel Horowitz, *Betty Friedan and the Making of "The Feminine Mystique": The American Left, the Cold War, and Modern Feminism* (Amherst, MA: University of Massachusetts Press, 1998) for a study of Friedan's leftism and pro-Communist views.

[139] Wikipedia: *The Free Encyclopedia* article on Jedidiah Morse.

[140] Frederic W. H. Myers, Oliver J. Lodge, Walter Leaf and William James, "A Record of Observations of Certain Phenomena of Trance (1889-1890)—Proceedings of the Society for

Psychical Research, 1889-1890," 6, 436-659.

[141] Christopher Chantrill, "War and Its Moral Equivalent," *American Thinker*, June 19, 2008, http://www.americanthinker.com/2008/06/war_and_its_moral_equivalent.html.

[142] David Boaz, "Libertarianism: A Primer in Other Languages," Cato Institute, January 1998.

[143] Doug Bandow, "National Service: The Enduring Panacea," March 22, 1990, Policy Analysis no. 130 quoting Margaret Mead from: "A National Service System as a Solution to a Variety of National Problems," reprinted in *The Military Draft*, ed. Martin Anderson (Stanford, CA: Hoover Institution Press, 1982), 437, 442.

[144] Jane Howard, *Margaret Mead: A Life* (New York: Fawcett Crest, 1984), 253.

[145] Thomas Sowell, "Have We Become a Nation of Sheep?", September 18, 1998.

[146] Theodore Dalrymple, *Life at the Bottom: The Worldview that Makes the Underclass* (Chicago: Ivan R. Dee, 2001), ix.

[147] Ibid., ix.

[148] Ibid., x.

[149] Ibid., xi-xii.

[150] David Noebel, *The Battle for Truth* (Eugene, OR: Harvest House Publishers, 2001), 276.

[151] From Obama-Biden campaign website 2008.

[152] From the website of publicallies.org.

[153] Suzanne Perry, *The Chronicle of Philanthropy*, April 14, 2008, article at www.publicallies.org.

[154] Ibid.

[155] "Michelle's Boot Camp for Radicals," *Investor's Business Daily*, September 4, 2008.

[156] Perry, *The Chronicle of Philanthropy*, April 14, 2008, article at www.publicallies.org.

[157] "Michelle's Boot Camp."

[158] "Fired Up and Ready to Grow: Youth Group's Obama Link Raises Its Profile Nationwide," *The Chronicle of Philanthropy*, April 14, 2008.

[159] Ibid.

[160] Geoffrey Botkin, "The Guiding Hand: The Clinton Influence on Arkansas Education."

[161] Ibid.

[162] Ibid.

[163] Ibid.

[164] Ibid.

[165] Phyllis Schlafly, "Bill Ayer's Plans for Schools," October 24, 2008, eagleforum.org.

[166] *World Core Curriculum Manual* (Arlington, TX: The Robert Muller School, 1985), 2.

[167] Wiker, *10 Books That Screwed Up the World: And 5 Others That Didn't Help*, 198.

[168] "Kinsey and Our Culture," a white-paper by Concerned Women for America, revised by Robert K. Knight, August 2004.

[169] Alfred C. Kinsey, Wardell B. Pomeroy, and Clyde E. Martin, *Sexual Behavior in the Human Male*, (Philadelphia: W. B. Saunders Company, 1948).

[170] Judith Levine, *Harmful to Minors: The Perils of Protecting Children from Sex* (Minneappolis: University of Minnesota Press, 2002), 225.

[171] Sarah Markwood, "Kinsey-Based Sex Education: Putting Children at Risk," article posted at cwfa.org, citing Judith A. Reisman, Ph.D., *Kinsey: Crimes and Consequences* (Arlington, VA: The Institute for Medical Education, Inc., 1998), 178.

[172] Ibid.

[173] ——, "Kinsey-Based Sex Education: Putting Children at Risk" article posted at cwfa.org, citing S. Michael Craven, *Modern Sex Education: The Indoctrination of a Generation*, Cultural Apologetic Series, National Coalition for the Protection of Children and Families, June 21, 2004.

[174] ——, "Kinsey-Based Sex Education: Putting Children at Risk," Concerned Women for America, http://www.cfa.org.

[175] Robert H. Knight, "How Alfred C. Kinsey's Sex Studies Have Harmed Women and Children," citing Linda Jeffry, Ed. D, Col. Ronald D. Ray, *A History of the American Law Institute's Model Penal Code: The Kinsey Reports' Influence on Science-Based Legal Reform 1923-2002* (Crestwood, KY: First Principle Press, 2003).

[176] ——, "How Alfred C. Kinsey's Sex Studies Have Harmed Women and Children," citing testimony, op cit., cited in *Kinsey, Crime & Consequences*, 213, and Kinsey's female volume, 121.

[177] "Kinsey and Our Culture."

[178] Ibid. Knight quoting from *Kinsey, Sex and Fraud*, 20.

[179] "Kinsey and Our Culture."

[180] Janice Shaw Crouse, "Kinsey's Kids," as published on the website of Concerned Women for America, posted on 11/17/2003.

[181] "Kinsey and Our Culture."

[182] "Kinsey and Our Culture," citing Canadian Community Health Survey, Statistics Canada June 15, 2004, results of a comprehensive survey of more than 135,000 Canadians conducted between January and December 2003.

[183] David Noebel, *Understanding the Times: The Collision of Today's Competing Worldviews* (Manitou Springs, CO: Summit Press, 1991), 261.

[184] Bootie Cosgrove-Mather, "50 Years After the Kinsey Report: Indiana U. Celebrates

Groundbreaking Book on Female Sexuality," January 27, 2003, http://www.cbsnews.com/stories/2003/01/27/print/main538117.shtml.

[185] Aldous Huxley, *Brave New World* (New York: HarperCollins, 1932).

[186] Lynne Cheney, "The End of History," *Wall Street Journal*, October 20, 1994.

[187] Governor Roy Romer, while serving as Chairman of the National Governor's Association, said this before an education meeting being covered by C-SPAN.

[188] Brannon Howse, *No Retreats, No Reserves, No Regrets* (St. Paul, MN: Stewart House Press, 2000), 115.

[189] This was from a conversation Brannon Howse had with Mrs. Tucker when they testified before a Senate committee in Kansas on the dangers of school-to-work.

[190] In the February 4, 1998, issue of *Education Week*, Mark Tucker was quoted in an article written by Millicent Lawton.

[191] D. James Kennedy, *Character and Destiny* (Zondervan Publishing House, 1994),

[192] Charlie Butts, "'Licensing' Morality Out of the Law," One News Now, December 12, 2008.

[193] Timothy Leary, *Flashbacks* (Tarcher), 44.

[194] Ibid.

[195] Ron Brandty, "On Outcome-Based Education: A Conversation with Bill Spady," *Educational Leadership*, December 1992/January 1993, 68.

[196] Dr. Dennis Cuddy, *Chronology of Education with Quotable Quotes* (Highland City, FL: Pro Family Fourm, Inc., 1993), 43.

[197] Benjamin Bloom, *Taxonomy of Educational Objectives* (1994), 85.

[198] ——, *All Our Children Learning: A Primer for Parents, Teachers, and Other Educators* (New York: McGraw-Hill Book Company, 1981), 180.

[199] Huxley, *Brave New World*, xvii.

[200] Geoffrey Botkin, "The Guiding Hand: The Clinton Influence on Arkansas Education"

[201] Bloom, 180

[202] Bailey, *The Externalisation of the Hierarchy* (New York: Lucis Trust, 1957), 511.

[203] ——, *The Rays and the Initiations*, 109.

[204] Former President George Bush announcing America 2000, White House, April 18, 1991, *America 2000: An Education Strategy* (Washington: The U.S. Department of Education, 1991), 50, 51, 55.

[205] Lamar Alexander, *Steps Along the Way: A Governor's Scrapbook* (Nashville: Thomas Nelson Publishers, 1986), 85.

[206] René Dubos, *A God Within: A Positive Approach to Man's Future as Part of the Natural World* (New York: Charles Scribner's Sons, 1972), 38, 41.

[207] Norman Cousins, Foreword to Robert Muller, *Most of All, They Taught Me Happiness*, 10-11.

[208] Benjamin Bloom, *Stability and Change in Human Characteristics* (1964).

[209] B. F. Skinner, *Science and Human Behavior* (New York: Macmillan, 1953), 447.

[210] Ibid. 6.

[211] ——, *Beyond Freedom and Dignity*, (New York: Macmillan, 1953), 197.

[212] *New World Encyclopedia*, http://www.newworldencyclopedia.org/entry/B._F._Skinner.

[213] Carol Pomeroy, "Education According to Corporate Fascism," unpublished speech delivered March 3, 1994, at Northwestern College.

[214] www.newworldencyclopedia.org/entry/B._F._Skinner.

[215] Richard Evans, *B. F. Skinner, The Man and His Ideas*.

[216] www.newworldencyclopedia.org/entry/B._F._Skinner

[217] Kenneth Goodman, "The President's Education Program: A Response," *Support for Learning and Teaching of English Newsletter*, March 1978, Volume 3, No. 2.

[218] March/April: A special supplement of *AV Communication Review* is published as "Monograph No. 2 of the Technological Development Project of the NEA." The project is under contract #SAE-9073 with the U.S. Office of Education of HEW, as authorized under title VII, Part B, of the National Defense Education Act of 1958. The contractor is the NEA. I was made aware of this fact by Dr. Dennis Cuddy.

[219] From a keynote address to the Association for Childhood Education International, Denver, Colorado, April 1972, quoted by John Steinbacher and Dr. Dennis Cuddy.

[220] *Certain Failure*, a documentary on H.R. 6 by Geoffrey Botkin.

[221] Cuddy, *Chronology of Education*, 47.

[222] George Grant, *The Family Under Siege*, (Minneapolis: Bethany House Publishers, 1994), 59.

[223] Charles Darwin, *Origin of Species* (New York: Mentor, 1958), 29.

[224] Ibid., Part I, Chapter Five, 177.

[225] Adolf Hitler, *Mein Kampf*, Vol. 1, Chapter 11.

[226] Lutzer, *Hitler's Cross*, 80.

[227] Donald Kagan, "Nihilism rejects any objective basis for society and its morality, the vey concept of objectivity, even the possibility of communication itself," *Academic Questions* 8, no. 2 (spring 1995), 56.

[228] D. James Kennedy, *Lord of All: Developing a Christian World-and-Life View* (Wheaton, IL: Crossway, 2005), 130.

[229] N. L. Geisler and P. K. Hoffman, *Why I Am a Christian: Leading Thinkers Explain Why They Believe* (Grand Rapids, MI: Baker Books, 2001), 93.

[230] D. G. Lindsay, c1990, *Foundations for Creationism* (Dallas: Christ for the Nations, 1998).

[231] D. M. S. Watson, "Adaptation," *Nature*, 124:233, 1929.

[232] Richard Lewontin, "Billions and Billions of Demons," *The New York Review*, January 9, 1997, 31.

[233] Tim LaHaye and David Noebel, *Mind Siege: The Battle for Truth in the New Millennium* (Nashville, TN: Word Publishing, 2000), 140.

[234] Marx and Engels, *Collected Works*, Vol. 3, (New York: International, 1976) cited in Noebel, *Understanding the Times* (2006), 67.

[235] V. I. Lenin, *Collected Works*, 45 vols. (Moscow: Progress Publishers, 1977), 7:409.

[236] Noebel, *Understanding the Times*, 109.

[237] Ibid.

[238] Saul Alinsky, *Rules for Radicals: A Pragmatic Primer for Realistic Radicals* (New York: Random House, 1971), 79.

[239] Ibid., 117.

[240] Bailey, *The Externalisation of the Hierarchy*, 133-35.

[241] "American Capitalism Gone with a Whimper," *Pravda*, April, 27, 2009.

[242] Marx and Engels, *Collected Works*, 182. Cited in Noebel *Understanding the Times*, 66.

[243] Ibid.

[244] Ibid., vol. 3, 175.

[245] W. Cleon Skousen, *The Naked Communist* (1961), 259-62.

[246] Karl Marx, *Das Bleiche Madchen* (*The Pale Maiden*), 55-57.

[247] Richard Wurmbrand, *Marx and Satan* (Bartlesville, OK: Living Sacrifice Book Company, 1986), 18.

[248] Robert Payne, *Marx* (New York: Simon & Schuster, 1968), 317.

[249] Heinrich Marx, letter of March 2, 1837, to Karl Marx quoted in Wurmbrand, *Marx and Satan*, 21.

[250] Wurmbrand, *Marx and Satan*.

[251] Richard Rorty, "Trotsky and Wild Orchids," *Wild Orchids and Trotsky: Messages from American Universities*, ed., Mark Edmundson (New York: Penguin Books, 1993), 47. Cited in Noebel, *Understanding the Times*, 388.

[252] Noebel, *Understanding the Times*, 388.

[253] John Strachey, *Contemporary Capitalism* (New York: Random House, 1956), 310.

[254] John Maynard Keynes, *Economic Consequences of the Peace*, (1920).

[255] Walter Williams, "Counterfeiting Versus Monetary Policy," December 17, 2008.

[256] Zygmund Dobbs, "Sugar Keynes," *The Review of the News*, June 23, 1971.

[257] David Noebel, "How the Socialists Are Destroying America from Within," worldviewtimes. com, March 2009.

[258] James McGregor Burns, *Power to Lead* (Touchtone Publishing), 189.

[259] Mikhail Gorbachev, "A New International Agenda," *International Herald Tribune*, January 1, 2009.

[260] Ibid.

[261] Brannon Howse, "Using the Financial Crisis for Global Governance?", www.worldviewtimes.com, January 12, 2009.

[262] Henry Kissinger, "The Chance for A New World Order," *International Herald Tribune*, January 12, 2009.

[263] Dick Morris, "European Socialism to Run Our Financial System", www.newsmax.com, April 7, 2009.

[264] Gideon Rachman, "And Now for World Government," *Financial Times*, December 9, 2008.

[265] Lyubov Pronina, "Medvedev Shows Off Sample Coin of New 'World Currency' at G-8," July 10, 2009, Bloomberg.com.

[266] Rachel Donadio and Laurie Goodstein, "Pope Urges Forming New World Economic Order to Work for the 'Common Good'," *New York Times*, July 7, 2009.

[267] Robert Muller, *New Genesis: Shaping a Global Spirituality* (Anacortest, WA: World Happiness and Cooperation, 1982), 101.

[268] Cliff Kincaid, "Is Obama's Science Czar a Crackpot?", worldviewtimes.com, July 15, 2009.

[269] Found at website of tonyblairfaithfoundation.org

[270] Ibid.

[271] "When Evangelicals Dine with the Wicked," worldviewtimes.com, August 6, 2009.

[272] Noebel, "How the Socialists Are Destroying America."

[273] George Bernard Shaw, *Intelligent Woman's Guide to Socialism*, 470.

[274] David Noebel quoting *Claremont Review of Books*, Winter 20008/09, 6.

[275] Ibid.

[276] John Stormer, *None Dare Call It Treason* (Florissant, MO: Liberty Bell Press, 1990), 58-59.

[277] John Eidsmoe, *Christianity and the Constitution* (Grand Rapids, MI: Baker Book House, 1987), 391.

[278] Ibid., 394.

[279] Oliver Wendell Holmes, Jr., "The Law in Science-Science in Law," *Collected Legal Papers* (New York: Harcourt, Brace and Company, 1920), 225.

[280] Steve Brown, "Fears Grow over Academic Efforts to Normalize Pedophilia," www.CNSnews.com, July 10, 2003.

[281] "Danger from Foreign Precedent" [editorial], *The Washington Times*, March 25, 2004.

[282] John Dewey, *The Public and Its Problems* (New York: Henry Hold and Company, 1927), 34.

[283] Joseph Story, *Commentaries on the Constitution of the United States*, 3rd ed. (Boston, 1858), 283, 400.

[284] Craig R. Ducat and Harold W. Chase, *Constitutional Interpretation: Powers of Government* (West Publishing Company, 1992), 3; quoting Charles Evans Hughes.

[285] Edwin Meese III, address to American Bar Association, 1985; adapted in "Toward a Jurisprudence of Original Intention," *Benchmark*, vol. 2, no. 1, January - February 1986, 1-10, at 6.

[286] John Leo, "A Way that Seems Right," www.fa-ir.org/ai/casey.htm.

[287] John W. Whitehead, *The Second American Revolution* (Wheaton, IL: Good News Publishers, 1985), 89.

[288] Gary DeMar, *God and Government*, (Powder Springs, GA: American Vision, 1990), 165–66.

[289] Frédéric Bastiat, *The Law* (written in 1859 and now in the public domain).

[290] Ibid.

[291] Ibid.

[292] Ibid.

[293] Samuel Gregg, "Old Europe's New Despotism," www.acton.org/commentary/commentary_267.php).

[294] Alexis de Tocqueville, *Democracy in America*, Vol. II, Book 4, Chapter 6.

[295] Alinsky, *Rules for Radicals*, dedication page.

[296] James Simpson, "Barack Obama and the Strategy of Manufactured Crisis, worldviewtimes.com, March 9, 2009.

[297] Heather Heidelbaugh, "Obama Is Governing as a Community Organizer," Washington Examiner.com, August 21, 2009.

[298] Saul Alinsky, *Rules for Radicals* (New York: Vintage Books, March 1972 edition), 3.

[299] Ibid., 25.

[300] Ibid., 7.

[301] Ibid., 3.

[302] Ibid., 61

[303] Saul Alinsky, *Reveille for Radicals* (New York: Vintage Books, 1989), 21-22. (Original publication was in 1946.)

[304] Ibid., 10.

[305] Ibid., 10-11.

[306] Ibid., 29.

[307] Ibid., 79.

[308] Ibid., 117.

309 Ibid., 150.

310 Trevor Louden, newzeal.blogspot.com/2009/04/obama-file-72-obama-appoints-former.html.

311 Eliza Strickland, "The New Face of Environmentalism," *The East Bay Express*, November 2, 2005.

312 Richard Lawrence Poe, "Hillary, Obama and the Cult of Alinksy," *Free Republic*, November 26, 2007, freerepublic.com/focus/f-news/1930836/posts.

313 *Boston Globe*, August 31, 2008, boston.com/bostonglobe/editorial_opinion/letters/articles/2008/08/31/son_sees_fathers_handiwork_in_convention/?s_campaign=8315

314 Herbert E. Meyer, "A Revolution," May 20, 2009, americanthinker.com.

315 Ibid.

316 Ellis Goodwin "Inhofe Slams Health Reform," *The Express-Star*, August 28, 2009.

317 Peter Gay, *Freud: A Life for Our Times* (New York: W.W. Norton, 1998), 526.

318 Quoted in Ibid., 527.

319 Ibid., 167.

320 Wiker, *10 Books*, 168.

321 Sigmund Freud, *The Future of an Illusion*, James Strachey, trans. (New York: W.W. Norton, 1961), Chapter Two, 13.

322 Wiker, *10 Books*, 169-70.

323 Allan Bloom, *The Closing of the American Mind* (New York, NY: Simon and Schuster, 1988), 173.

324 Norm Geisler and Peter Bocchino, *Unshakable Foundations* (Minneapolis, MN: Bethany Press, 2001), 358.

325 Noebel, *Understanding the Times*, 230.

326 Erich Fromm, *You Shall Be as Gods* (New York: Holt, Rinehart and Winston, 1996), 7.

327 Noebel, op. cit., 228.

328 Ibid., 229.

329 Abraham Maslow, *Toward a Psychology of Being* (New York: Van Nostrand Reinhold, 1968), 169.

330 Noebel, *Understanding the Times*, 230.

331 Wiker, *10 Books*, 169-76.

332 Paul Johnson, *Modern Times* (New York: Harper & Row, 1983), 6.

333 Obama auto team called shareholder lawyer a "terrorist" video posted at hotair.com by Ed Morrissey.

334 Noel Sheppard, "California Assembly Speaker: Conservative Talkers Are Terrorists," newbusters.com, June 27, 2009.

335 James Osborne, "Pentagon Exam Calls Protests 'Low-Level Terrorism,'" Angering Activists," foxnews.com, June 17, 2009.

336 From a keynote address to the Association for Childhood Education International, Denver, Colorado, April 1972, quoted by John Steinbacher and Dr. Dennis Cuddy.

337 Christopher Lasch, "Hillary Clinton, Child Saver: What She Values Will Not Help the Family," *Harper's*, October 1992.

338 "The Real Brophy Issue," *Boston Globe*, November 18, 1985.

339 Brief of Amicus Curia Prepared by Mark A. Rothe for the Family Research Council, October 1996, 4.

340 Hugh Gregory Gallagher, *By Trust Betrayed: Patients, Physicians, and the License to Kill in the Third Reich* (St. Petersburg, FL: Vandamere Press, 1990).

341 Brief of Amicus Curia prepared by Mark A. Rothe for the Family Research Council, October 1996, 13.

342 Ibid. Proctor at 182.

343 Brief of Amicus Curia prepared by Mark A. Rothe and Timothy Quill, October 1996.

344 Ibid., Proctor at 194; Kamisar at 470 n.213. Thereafter, the mercy killing of children became commonplace. Shortening their lives was considered to be a humane measure. 1 Nurem.Mil.Trib. at 834.

345 Ibid., Proctor at 186

346 Ibid., Proctor at 194.

347 Brief of Amicus Curia prepared by Mark A. Rothe for the Family Research Council, October 1996, 27.

348 Betsy McCaughey, "Ruin Your Health with the Obama Stimulus Plan," Bloomberg.com, February 9, 2009.

349 Brief of Amicus Curia prepared by Mark A. Rothe for the Family Research Council, October 1996, 27. Source: See Friedlander at 284; Gallagher at 6-7; G. Sereny, *Into that Darkness: From Mercy Killing to Mass Murder* 34 (1974); 1 Nurem.Mil.Trib. at 794-896. Foreigners and Jews were excluded from euthanasia and screened out of T-4. 1 Nurem.Mil. Trib. at 824, 880.

350 Brief of Amicus Curia Prepared by Mark A. Rothe for the Family Research Council, October 1996, 27, citing: Nurem.Mil.Trib. at 800-04.

351 Simon Wiesenthal, *The Murderers Among Us: The Simon Wiesenthal Memoirs* (New York: McGraw-Hill Book Company, 1967), 309-10.

352 Brief of Amicus Curia prepared by Mark A. Rothe for the Family Research Council, October 1996, 27. Friedlander at 297.

353 Ibid., 1 Nurem. Mil. Trib. At 797.

[354] Ibid., 1 Nurem. Mil. Trib. At 804.

[355] Ibid., Proctor at 212; Gallagher at 14.

[356] Ibid., 1 Nurem.Mil.Trib. at 809.

[357] Ibid., citing: Gallagher, *By Trust Betrayed*, 62.

[358] John Hardwig, "Is There a Duty to Die?" *Hastings Center Report 27*, no. 2 (1997): 34-42.

[359] Tim LaHaye and David Noebel, *Mind Siege: The Battle for Truth in the New Millennium* (Nashville: Word Publishing, 2000), 187.

[360] Grant, *The Family Under Siege*, 145.

[361] Ibid., 145; quoting Peggy Lamson, *Roger Baldwin: Founder of the American Civil Liberties Union: A Portrait* (Boston: Houghton Mifflin, 1976), 138–39.

[362] The D. James Kennedy Center for Christian Statesmanship, Summer 1995.

[363] LaHaye and Noebel, op. cit., 188.

[364] Ibid., quoting *Soviet Russia Today*, September 1934.

[365] Grant, *The Family Under Siege*, 146.

[366] Ibid., 147.

[367] Ibid., 149; quoting William Donohue, *The Politics of the American Civil Liberties Union* (New Brunswick, NJ: Transaction, 1985), 5-6.

[368] Ibid., quoting the *Washington Action Alert*, August 1993.

[369] Ibid., quoting Donohue, *The Politics of the American Civil Liberties Union*, 36.

[370] Ibid., 140.

[371] See R. J. Rummel, *Death by Government* (New Brunswick, NJ: Transaction Publishers, 1994). Also, Stephane Courtois, ed., *The Black Book of Communism* (Cambridge: Harvard Unversity Press, 1999).

[372] Albert Einstein quoted in *Time* magazine, December 23, 1940, 38. Cited at theblackcordelias.wordpress.com/2008/10/12/einstein-on-the-church-in-nazi-germany/

[373] See Paul Johnson, *Intellectuals* (New York: Harper Perennial, 2007) for a look at the strange world of the intelligentsia.

INDEX

ABOUT THE AUTHOR

Brannon Howse is the president & founder of Worldview Weekend, and WVW Broadcast Network that includes WVW-TV & Worldview Radio.

As the author of 17 books, Brannon has been a guest on more than 2,000 radio and television programs and has been featured in such publications as the Washington Times and appeared on such television programs as The O'Reilly Factor with Bill O'Reilly on Fox News & MSNBC among others. For many years, Brannon was the education reporter and frequent guest host of The Michael Reagan Program. Michael Reagan is the eldest son of President Reagan, and Brannon was honored to host Michael's program the week of President Reagan's funeral. Brannon was the literary agent for Michael Reagan's book, Twice Adopted. Due to his area of expertise, Brannon was featured for many years as a frequent guest on the radio program of Oliver North, G. Gordon Liddy, Ken Hamblin, Dr. D. James Kennedy, Phyllis Schlafly, & Beverly LaHaye's Concerned Women For America, among others.

Brannon's understanding of worldviews, trends, and global events has resulted in people attending his two-day training session who work for the Federal Bureau of Investigation, The National Security Agency, an Assistant District attorney of one of the largest cities in America, military officers, police and sheriff officers, doctors, lawyers, teachers, pastors, and successful business owners. Brannon's reputation as a compelling and credible speaker resulted in him being honored as the keynote speaker for the 50th Annual Governor's Prayer Breakfast in Iowa a few years ago.

Brannon is the host of a national radio program that is broadcast nationwide each day from 1-2pm CT on 60 Christian radio stations, the host of The Worldview Weekend Hour, a weekly television program that is viewed in 120 nations around the world.